CHIEF OF MACKAY

Chief of Mackay *is the first part of* The Strathnaver Trilogy *by Ian Grimble. The other two parts are* The World of Rob Donn *and* The Trial of Patrick Sellar.

This is the revised edition of a book that was first published in 1965. It tells the story of a clan which occupied the province of Strathnaver in the extreme north of Scotland, west of Caithness and north of Sutherland, and larger in extent than either of these earldoms. Under successive chiefs, a Gaelic society was maintained here despite the relentless encroachment of the Gordon earls of Sutherland, celebrated in the 18th century by the incomparable poetry of the Mackay bard, Rob Donn. That forms the second volume of the Strathnaver trilogy. The third volume describes the take-over of the Mackay Country by the house of Sutherland and its treatment at the hands of such servants of this family as Patrick Sellar.

CHIEF OF MACKAY

by

IAN GRIMBLE

First published 1965 by Routledge and Kegan Paul
This paperback edition published 1993 by the Saltire Society,
9 Fountain Close, 22 High Street, Edinburgh EH1 1TF

Printed and bound in Great Britain by BPCC Wheatons

A catalogue record for this book is available from the British Library.

ISBN 0-85411-051-8

Front cover: designed using the Stettin print (1631) showing men of Mackay's regiment in the Swedish service during the Thirty Years' War. (Reproduced by permission of the British Museum.)

Contents

Acknowledgements

I would like to acknowledge my debts to the late Kenneth Bell and to Dr Christopher Hill, under whom I studied history at Balliol College. Since then I have received more help than I can acknowledge from the late William Croft Dickinson, from Dr C. V. Wedgwood and Dr Pauline Gregg, Dr John Lorne Campbell and Sir John Neale. I owe a particular debt to Professor Derick Thomson and Mr Walter Humphries, who guided my studies at Aberdeen University for the doctoral thesis of which this study forms a part. In addition, Mr James Dow generously supplied me with the material from the Swedish military archives that I have used in my text, and Mr R. W. Munro has given me valuable help concerning the Munros in this narrative. I have received constant assistance from the staffs of King's College Library, Aberdeen, of the Register House and the National Library in Edinburgh, of the British Museum in London and of Rigsarkivet in Copenhagen. To all of these I owe an apology for the faults that remain in the book in spite of them.

Finally, I would like to express my gratitude to the Saltire Society for its initiative in publishing new editions of this Strathnaver Trilogy.

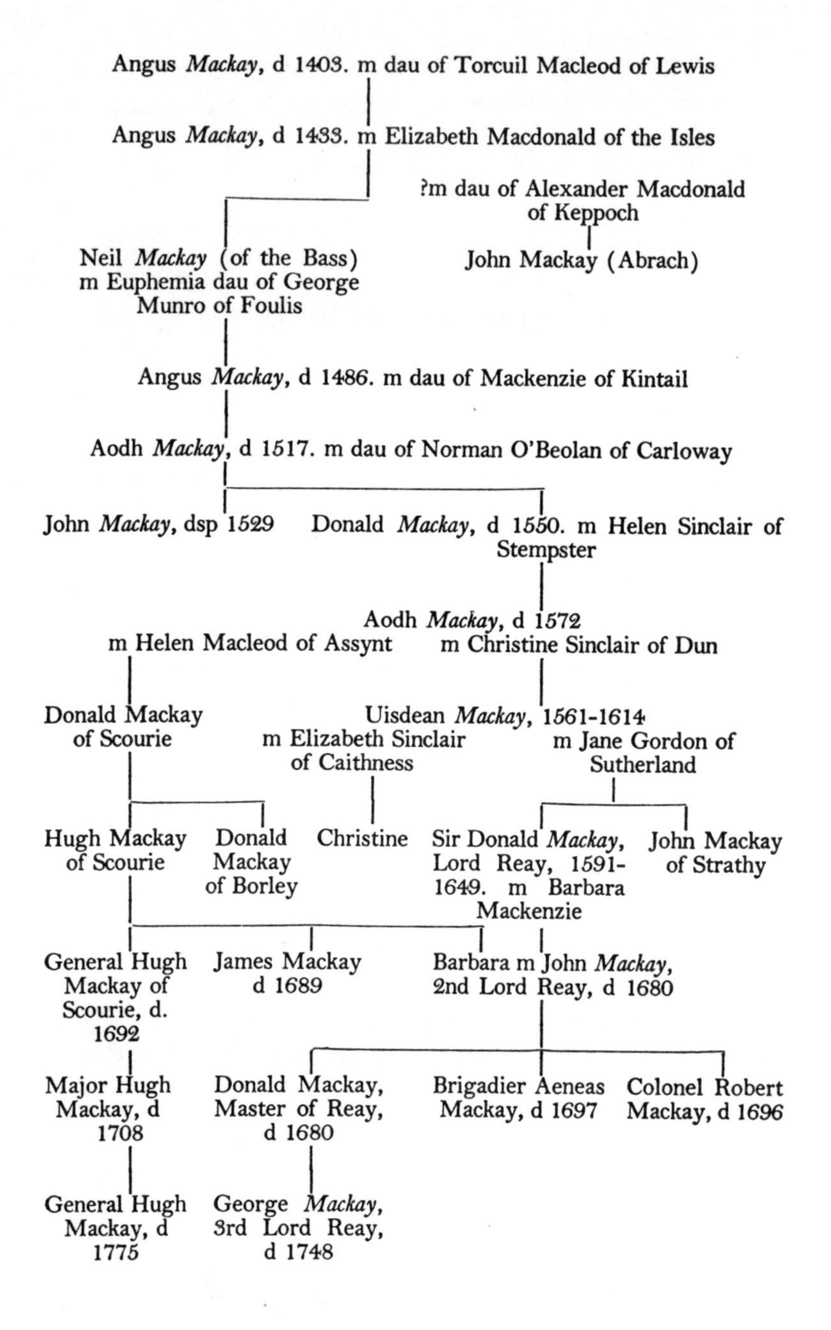
Angus *Mackay*, d 1403. m dau of Torcuil Macleod of Lewis
Angus *Mackay*, d 1433. m Elizabeth Macdonald of the Isles
?m dau of Alexander Macdonald of Keppoch
Neil *Mackay* (of the Bass) m Euphemia dau of George Munro of Foulis
John Mackay (Abrach)
Angus *Mackay*, d 1486. m dau of Mackenzie of Kintail
Aodh *Mackay*, d 1517. m dau of Norman O'Beolan of Carloway
John *Mackay*, dsp 1529
Donald *Mackay*, d 1550. m Helen Sinclair of Stempster
Aodh *Mackay*, d 1572
m Helen Macleod of Assynt
m Christine Sinclair of Dun
Donald Mackay of Scourie
Uisdean *Mackay*, 1561-1614
m Elizabeth Sinclair of Caithness
m Jane Gordon of Sutherland
Hugh Mackay of Scourie
Donald Mackay of Borley
Christine
Sir Donald *Mackay*, Lord Reay, 1591-1649. m Barbara Mackenzie
John Mackay of Strathy
General Hugh Mackay of Scourie, d. 1692
James Mackay d 1689
Barbara m John *Mackay*, 2nd Lord Reay, d 1680
Major Hugh Mackay, d 1708
Donald Mackay, Master of Reay, d 1680
Brigadier Aeneas Mackay, d 1697
Colonel Robert Mackay, d 1696
General Hugh Mackay, d 1775
George *Mackay*, 3rd Lord Reay, d 1748

1

Introduction

In November 1631, the painted chamber of the palace of Westminster was prepared for one of the most mysterious trials in Britain's history.[1] A bench, four feet high, was erected at the upper end of this chamber for the Lord High Constable, the Earl Marshal of England, and the Lords Assistant. Beneath the bench was placed a square table for the Heralds and the Serjeants at Arms. Beyond it stood the pews for the defendant and the appellant. At 8 a.m. on the 28th November, the Earl Marshal, the Earl of Arundel entered the painted chamber, ushered in by nine Heralds and three Serjeants at Arms. He moved through the crowded chamber brandishing his Marshal's truncheon of gold tipped with black, and retired into the upper House of Parliament. He returned with the Lord High Constable of England, and after all the Lords had taken their places, the two men welcomed the arrival of Garter King of Arms. Garter brought a message from Charles I, King of England, Scotland, Ireland and (allegedly) France, which authorised the business of the court. Garter King of Arms delivered to the Lord High Constable his silver staff headed with a crown of gold, whereupon the Earl Marshal delivered a key to a Herald as a signal that he should introduce the appellant with his sureties. Charles I had revived the cumbrous and archaic ritual of a Court of Chivalry, unheard-of within living memory by the citizens of London.

[1] Rushworth 1659, II: 112-28. *State Trials*, III: 486-519. B. M. Egerton 7083. Sloane 1435, ff. 156-93. *P.RO.* Vol. 217.

(Note that footnotes are documented under References, page 185.)

But a sight even more bizarre was to be witnessed when the appellant stepped before these surviving office-holders out of England's mediaeval past. For he was a Celtic tribal Chief from the far north of Scotland, so far that it was impossible to say where, and the recording clerk could only surmise that it must be 'rather more northward of the isles of Orkney.'[1]

It was known in the south of England, however, that these Celtic peoples of the Scottish Highlands were the Scots of the aboriginal stock from Ireland, in contrast to the Lowland Scots who spoke the English tongue. 'The language of the Highlanders is a kind of Irish,' noted Richard James the antiquarian at this time, 'and they report and praise themselves for the old inhabitants of the land, calling the other landlopers and usurpers. Their garments are a blue friese slashed jerkin, and plaidens and truses, and black and green and blue bonnets. The most part of them are black haired and eyed and of whitish countenance.'[2] Even if many of the Gaelic communities of Scotland had lost the physical traces of their Indo-European origins by this time, the Chief who entered the painted chamber at Westminster as appellant on the 28th November 1631, seems to have answered the antiquarian's description perfectly. An observer noted that he was 'of a swarthy complexion, having very black hair, head and beard.' His bearing was impressive, being 'comely, firm and very portlike.'[3] He did not wear the Highland dress that Richard James described, but a suit and cloak of black velvet. His doublet was slashed in the fashion of the day, and hung with silver buttons and loops of silver and black silk. He carried his sword in an embroidered silver belt and round his neck hung the jewel of his order of knight baronet of Scotland by a tawny ribbon. He was accompanied, not by his clansmen, but by five knights.

He was the forty-year-old Chief of Mackay; so that those who understood the correct usage addressed him simply as Mackay, although James VI had bestowed a knighthood on him, and Charles I had created him Lord Reay. One Englishman, unused to the social grading of a Celtic Chiefship, compromised by addressing him as Lord Mackay, while others took refuge in the social distinctions they understood, and referred to him as the Lord Reay. But when that gifted traveller and courtier

[1] *State Trials*, III: 488. [2] James 1953. [3] B. M. Egerton 7083.

Sir Thomas Roe wrote to the Winter Queen at the Hague about the Court of Chivalry, he gave Mackay his correct title; and so did that punctilious arbiter of etiquette, Charles I, when he wrote a letter to his cousin about these proceedings.

After Mackay had entered the painted chamber of the palace of Westminster, a herald introduced the defendant. A man with a great bush of red hair entered, dressed in scarlet heavily overlaid with silver, his cloak lined with plush of sky-blue. Here stood a representative of the Germanic peoples of south-east Scotland, as true to type, as it chanced, as the swarthy Celtic Chief. He was a gentleman adventurer from Fife called David Ramsay, or Ramsay Redhead, and the appeal that Mackay had brought against him was one of treason. 'Ramsay denied all,' recorded a clerk, 'and said Reay was a liar, a barbarous villain; and threw down his glove, protesting to gar him die for it.' His intemperate conduct contrasted with that of his accuser. 'Reay was temperate, without any passion, but smiling replied, "Mr Ramsay, we will not contend here. Answer to my bill." '[1] In the bitter personal hostility of these two men, the privileged spectators of the Court of Chivalry were introduced to the conflict of races which is such a recurrent theme in Scotland's history.

The storm of Mackay's treason charge had burst over the court of Charles I in March 1631. Mackay had been commissioned by the King to raise and command a regiment of his own clansmen in the Thirty Years War that had originated in the expulsion of the King's sister, the Winter Queen, and her husband from the throne of Bohemia. The Protestant champion, Gustav Adolf of Sweden, had commissioned the Marquess of Hamilton to raise further forces in Britain, and Hamilton sounded Mackay, who had five years' successful experience of recruitment, to discover the price of his assistance. Hamilton's agent was David Ramsay.

Had Mary, Queen of Scots, died without giving birth to James VI, the father of Charles I, the heir to the throne of Scotland would have been Hamilton. The discontents in Scotland were already audible that were to lead to the great rebellion. In that emergency, Charles I gave great powers to his cousin Hamilton, and was betrayed by him. But Mackay received the

[1] *State Trials*, III: 485.

impression in 1631, rightly or wrongly, that Hamilton was already planning to raise an army, ostensibly for use in the European war, but actually for use in Scotland. He did not speculate that Hamilton might be raising such an army with the King's connivance, to enforce his episcopal policy in Scotland. He assumed that it would be used against the King, and when he returned from Europe to London in March, he told Lord Ochiltree of his fears, who informed the Lord Treasurer in a form that involved half the nobility of Scotland: and the Lord Treasurer informed the King.

'The court is presently in an uproar. The matter is related by the Lord Ochiltree to his Majesty in most ample form, with many circumstances more than the Lord Reay reported, reflecting upon a number of noblemen in Scotland who should have been upon this plot with the Marquess of Hamilton. The Lord Reay is sent for by the King. He is examined by some of the Lords of the Privy Council, the King being present. He confesseth all to the King, as is before related in his accusation against Ramsay, with many other circumstances. . . . Reay and Ochiltree are committed to their lodgings. The Marquess humbly desireth his Majesty that he may be committed to the Tower of London until he were tried. . . . David Ramsay is sent for out of Holland. He cometh over into England in all haste. He is confronted with the Lord Reay; Ramsay denieth all.'[1] Amid all this commotion Charles I remained completely unmoved, never wavering in his confidence in Hamilton's loyalty. 'His Majesty kept his thoughts private to himself,' wrote Rushworth, 'and having a great affection to Hamilton, as soon as he came into his presence, embraced him with great kindness and discovered to him what he was accused of: but said, "I do not believe it. And that the world may know I have confidence in your loyalty, you shall lie in my bed-chamber this night." '[2] The King had given his verdict before any trial had taken place.

It could be proved that Mackay had not lied in his statements, even if the conclusions he had drawn were false, and even if Lord Ochiltree had embroidered them. Mackay had made a detailed written statement in London on the 18th May 1631, and he was examined upon this twice by the Privy Council on the 21st June. There were thus three consistent versions of

[1] Gordon 1813: 456. [2] *State Trials*, III: 494.

Mackay's allegations, denied in their entirety by Ramsay. But a charge as grave as treason, involving the King's cousin, depended upon Mackay's uncorroborated testimony. So the Court of Chivalry was decreed by Charles I in which, if Mackay's appeal were allowed, the issue would be decided by personal combat between the Highlander and the Lowlander.

'Your Majesty commanded me to write you some relation,' Sir Thomas Roe told the Winter Queen, 'of the business that so much perplexed us of Mackay and Ramsay: but the matter was so tender . . . that I durst not enter into a forbidden secret until now that it hath had an open hearing in a court held by the Lord High Constable . . . All I can say is that I wish your Majesty to suspend your opinion of Mackay and the cause. For though it is clear the Marquess is innocent, yet the rhodomontades and discontents of Ramsay may have given some occasion. I excuse none. Your Majesty's name was used in court in his defence by Ramsay, in my opinion, not to purpose, and he was reprehended. He is not a man on whose discretion to rely.'[1] He was nevertheless Hamilton's confidential agent.

It was not only for his allusions to the King's sister that David Ramsay was reprehended. He had denied every sentence of Mackay's statement while his protector Hamilton was in London, and he repeated this denial in the Court of Chivalry. But by this time, Hamilton had left the capital for Europe, and David Ramsay faced the law. When he was admonished by the Earl Marshal that he must answer the charges, he lost some of his truculence, and 'in general acknowledged all the particular circumstances of time and place alleged by Reay, and the discourse to that effect: but concluded that no treason was intended or uttered, and craved counsel to answer, which was granted.' When the court convened again on the 5th December, Ramsay had changed his dress to black, and his written statement of defence merely softened the incriminating passages of Mackay's own statement. No one witnessing the trial could any longer doubt which of the two men was a liar, as Sir Thomas Roe, that experienced diplomat, so adroitly informed the Winter Queen.

But the machinery of a Court of Chivalry was too intricate to be brought to an abrupt halt. There must be replications and

[1] *C.S.P.D.* 1625-9 Add.: 420-1.

protestations, exceptions and points of honour: flights of erudition by Doctor Duck and Doctor Eden and Doctor Reeves, disquisitions on blue blood and moral worth by the Earl Marshal. The case continued into 1632 before the Court decided that Ramsay could not be absolved, neither was there sufficient evidence to convict, therefore the issue should be decided by a public duel. The Earl Marshal said 'that the Lord Reay had governed himself in the whole process of the cause with much prudence and moderation, and wished that Ramsay had used the like moderation in his defence.'[1] Then the Lord High Constable rose, holding the glove and appeal of Mackay in one hand and the glove and answer of Ramsay in the other, pronounced that the two men should meet in Tuthill Fields, Westminster, on the 12th April, and there fight from sunrise until sundown, if need be, in the presence of the King. The Court then turned its attention to the choice of weapons, the provision of surgeons, refreshment and the reconnoitring of the ground, as though it were planning a military campaign. Mackay and David Ramsay made their last appearance before the Court on the 10th April 1632, to learn that after all their anxiety the King had decided to postpone their combat until the 17th May.

The fight with 'a spear, a long sword, a short sword and a dagger, each of them with a point,' was the talk of the town as the trial had been.[2] Sir Thomas Edmondes wrote to Sir Harry Vane delightedly, 'the cause between Lord Mackay and David Ramsay will be brought to a resolution in a few days . . . The court has granted a battle.' Sir William Calley told his cousin Edward Nicholas how his son had ridden to London to witness it, only to discover that it had been postponed until May. Calley did not think that his son would remain until it took place: which was just as well, because it never took place.[3] On the 8th May Charles I again changed his mercurial mind, revoking the letters patent that had set such antique machinery in motion. On the same day he wrote a letter to the Marquess of Hamilton himself, explaining the reasons for his latest decision.

'James. Since you went I have not written to you of Mackay's business, because I neither desire to prophecy nor write half

[1] *State Trials*, III: 505. [2] *State Trials*, III: 509.
[3] *C.S.P.D.* 1631-3: 270, 311.

news. But now seeing (by the grace of God) what shall be the end of it, I have thought fit to be the first advertiser of it to you. I doubt not but you have heard that (after long seeking of proofs for clearing the business as much as could be, and formalities that could not be eschewed) the combat was awarded, the day set, weapons appointed. But having seen and considered all that can be said on either side, as likewise the carriage of both the men, upon mature deliberation I have resolved not to suffer them to fight. Because, first, for Mackay, he hath failed so much in his circumstantial probations, especially concerning Muschamp, upon whom he built as a chief witness, that nobody now is any way satisfied with his accusations.

'Then, for David Ramsay, though we cannot condemn him for that that is not, yet he hath so much and so often offended by his violent tongue that we can no ways think him innocent, though not that way guilty whereof he is accused. Wherefore I have commanded the court shall be dismissed and combat discharged, with a declaration to this purpose that, though upon want of good proof the combat was necessarily awarded, yet upon the whole matter I am fully satisfied that there was no such treason as Mackay had fancied.' Charles had already assured Hamilton of this before he set up the Court of Chivalry. 'And for David Ramsay, though we must clear him of that treason in particular, yet not so far in the general but that he might give occasion by his tongue of great accusation, if it had been rightly placed, as by his foolish presumptious carriage did appear.

'This is the substance, and so short that it is rather a direction how to believe others than a narration in itself: one of my chief ends being that you may know David Ramsay, that you may not have to do with such a pest as he is, suspecting he may seek to insinuate himself to you upon this occasion. Wherefore I must desire you, as you love me, to have nothing to do with him. To conclude now, I dare say that you shall have no dishonour in this business. And for myself, I am not ashamed that herein I have shewn myself to be your faithful friend and loving cousin, Charles R.'[1]

What is to be made of this extraordinary letter, with its worried warning from an absolute monarch to a marquess

[1] *State Trials*, III: 513–4.

against a mere mercenary soldier from the provinces? Faced with an accusation that might have brought him to a slow and painful death, David Ramsay had behaved with a contemptuous truculence, as though he were in possession of some secret that assured him of the most powerful protection. But Ramsay's odd behaviour and the King's letter to Hamilton were not the strangest incidents in this affair.

Lord Ochiltree, who had first reported Mackay's suspicions to the Lord Treasurer, with considerable enlargements, was committed to Edinburgh for trial by Charles I, in the same month of November 1631 in which the Court of Chivalry was set up at Westminster. But Ochiltree's trial was first postponed, then dispensed with altogether, and he was committed a close prisoner to Blackness Castle by order of a most mysterious letter from the King. He did not emerge from his captivity until after Charles I's execution, seventeen years later.[1]

Mackay had mortgaged his property to raise a regiment in the King's service, and had been reduced to penury by the King's failure to meet a liability that he had formally recognised. Nevertheless it is clear that Mackay was motivated solely by loyalty to the King in his accusations, whether or not they were without foundation. His ruin was completed by the expense of the trial, and his life was endangered by the combat. Yet Charles never hinted that he had stopped the combat in order to preserve the life of a faithful servant, and he ignored Mackay's petitions for payment of the money so long his due. Between the date of the trial and of the combat, Mackay wrote in desperation to Lord Carlisle: 'I am brought to so low an ebb of means and moneys that I know not what way to subsist until the day of my trial, neither know I what way to furnish myself with any kind of equippage fit for my birth or quality.' He begged Carlisle to use his influence that the King might 'be so graciously pleased as to cause to be given me part of the moneys which is due unto me. I caused a petition to be presented to his Majesty but had no answer thereof.'[2]

Whether Carlisle was the best choice of advocate seems doubtful; but perhaps Mackay had little choice. In June 1632 a correspondent wrote to Hamilton from London concerning some secret. 'None here knows of it but the Treasurer and

[1] *R.P.C.* (NS) IV: 369, 630. V: xliv. [2] B. M. Egerton MS. 2597, f. 62.

Carlisle, to which two you are more obliged than to all the court besides. If the ambassador and you carry it handsomely it will never be suspected, and I shall be glad to see you here before anybody know it. You will do yourself much right to provide some place for David Ramsay with the King of Sweden, for he hath disobliged so many great men here, and the King himself is so displeased with his behaviour, that he is utterly lost in this place. He is to be set at liberty, giving in security (whereof I am one) not to meddle with Mackay, neither at home nor abroad: and I believe he must depart this country, which I desire may be before your arrival. The King will give him some money towards his journey . . .'[1] Carlisle, to whom Mackay made his desperate appeal, was deep in Hamilton's confidence. Ramsay the dangerous pest was to receive a remittance from the King himself to hasten him from the country, while Mackay's acknowledged debts remained unpaid. Hamilton, despite the King's explicit instructions, advanced Ramsay, when he could, to a colonelcy. Ochiltree remained in close confinement for life, without trial. If Mackay's allegations were merely an invention, they nevertheless led to some unaccountable consequences.

It is unlikely now that the mystery behind either will ever be solved. Nor is it of more than slight historical interest to establish the earliest date when Charles I thought of using troops raised ostensibly for the European war for service against his own subjects, or the date on which Hamilton first contemplated the betrayal of his King. It is a curiosity of history that both Charles and Hamilton followed such courses later, and that a Celtic Chief ruined his career by bringing allegations that appear to have anticipated their thoughts, and their actions, by many years.

But it is possible to unravel a more important mystery; how the most remote Celtic Chief in the British Isles ever obtained access to the English court in London. His forbears had rarely travelled south to a royal court at Inverness, except on a summons that they dared not ignore. They had scarcely attended at Edinburgh, except as prisoners. None of Mackay's forbears had ever borne any title except that of their immemorial Chiefship. There is not even any evidence that the father of Sir

[1] *H.M.C.* Hamilton: 26.

Donald Mackay, first Lord Reay could write a letter in English.

His appearance, therefore, in an influential position among the rulers of England and Scotland, early in the seventeenth century, is a curiosity: as such it is noted among the marginalia of Anglo-Scottish history. But in the dark corners of the kingdom where dwelt the Celtic victims of the success story of the English-speakers his career marked a watershed in the fortunes of his people.

This watershed embraces the whole of Celtic Scotland during the seventeenth century to an extent that varied from one area to another. One of its features was the transformation that took place of the patriarchs of a patriarchal society. Since any change in the status or outlook of the tribal father was bound, sooner or later, to have a profound effect upon his clan, or children, this transformation is worth examining as part of the background to the upheavals in the Highlands in later centuries.

The Chiefship of Mackay may not offer the most suitable vantage point from which to study the evolution of the Celtic tribal father in Scotland, from mediaeval into modern times. But perhaps there is no perfect example. There are, however, advantages as well as limitations in following a single family of Celtic Chiefs, however faint the features of some of them may be. The story of the Mackay Chiefs is that of the tribal patriarchs most distant from Edinburgh in the whole of the Scottish mainland, and most distant from London in the whole mainland of Britain.

2

The Northern Outpost of Gaeldom

THE province of Strathnaver lay in the extreme north-west of the Scottish mainland, an oblong whose western side faced towards the Hebrides, its longer northern side towards the north Atlantic. Its other two sides were unprotected by the sea: to the east lay the earldom of Caithness, to the south the earldom of Sutherland.

The long horned cairns at Rhinnivie near the mouth of the Naver river commemorate the stone-using folk who lived here several millennia before Christ. Later metal-using people have left their mementoes and while the Romans do not appear to have landed when they sailed around these coasts, whole networks of brochs attest that their inhabitants kept a wary eye on the sea approaches. Long after the Romans left Britain, Pictish Christians planted a monolith in what is now the cemetery behind Farr Bay, on which an intricately carved cross is sculptured.

It has been dated to about the year 800, when the Norsemen were arriving, to raid and to settle. It may be these who built Castle Bharraich on its promontory in the Kyle of Tongue, guarding a coast peppered with Norse place-names. Strathnaver was already populated by the descendants of many different races before the first Mackays arrived, bringing with them the Gaelic language. The very name of the province, rendered into Gaelic as *Srath an Fhamhair*, Valley of Giants, almost certainly derives from some lost pre-historic language, like so many river names. By the time the Mackays received their first royal charters of ownership from the Scottish Crown in the Middle Ages, the river Naver which flows down the centre of their territory had given its name to the entire region. To this day it is also known as *Duthaich 'Ic Aoidh.* the Mackay Country.

The patronymic Aodh, anciently spelt Aedh or Aed, was that of the last High King to be enthroned at Tara; but it does not appear to derive from Ireland in the case of the Mackays of Strathnaver. That most distinguished genealogist Iain Moncreiffe proposed that their progenitor was the eldest son of King Malcolm Canmore by his second wife Margaret, who chose for him the Saxon name Aethelred. This became Gaelicised to the royal name Aodh or Aedh. When he was invested as the last Abbot of Dunkeld, an office previously held by his great-grandfather Crinan, he was thereby debarred from the throne.

But he was not prevented from making a marriage with the heiress of the kingdom of Moray, and this was to prove fateful for his descendants. For whatever his forfeited rights as the eldest of Queen Margaret's sons, the succession of any of them involved at least a double usurpation. The senior dynast of the Scottish royal house had been Queen Gruoch (*alias* Lady Macbeth), whose grand-daughter Aodh had married. There were also the descendants of Malcolm Canmore's son by his first marriage with a member of the Scottish royal house. The sons of the Saxon Queen did succeed, one after another, but not without repeated attempts to restore the true heirs.

When her youngest son David succeeded in 1124 Angus son of Aodh, King of Moray, tried to assert his rights. David had been the senior baron of England, and he brought with him a whole entourage of Anglo-Normans to help him rule his new kingdom. The Mackay back-lash was a Gaelic attempt to recover the authority of the Crown from all these foreigners, and it failed. But it was not until about 1163 that the Clan Mackay were expelled from Moray itself 'extra montanes Scociae'—beyond the mountains of Scotland. Thus this evicted aristocracy arrived in the remotest corner of the Scottish mainland.

They took care to preserve symbols of their status and their rights. One is the oldest clan banner in existence. On it is sewn the lion rampant within a royal tressure flory-counter flory. Above this is depicted the hand which attests true descent. As late as 1503 the chiefs of Clan Mackay were still using for their heraldry, without challenge, the three stars of the royal house of Moray.

By then an event had occurred which was of the highest consequence within Gaelic Scotland. The MacDonalds of the Isles had acquired royal Stewart blood by marriage with a daughter of Robert II and Donald, the son of this union, became heir to the great earldom of Ross *jure uxoris* when he married Lady Margaret Leslie. An island dynasty which was now wholly Gaelic in culture but half Norse by descent had suddenly acquired extensive rights and possessions throughout the mainland of the Highlands. When he stepped ashore to claim them, he found himself opposed by the two great clans of Mackenzie and Mackay.

The MacDonalds descended in the male line from King Somerled, who had wrested the southern Hebrides and much of the old mainland kingdom of Dalriada from the Norsemen. But they also descended from the Norse Kings of Man, and it was only as recently as 1266 that their islands had passed to the Scottish Crown. These were still known as *Innse Ghall*—the Foreigner Isles. Donald of Islay did indeed possess Mackay subjects. In 1408 he had bestowed upon them a charter written in Gaelic for lands in that island. But these did not descend from the kings of Moray; more probably from the kings of Ireland.

Donald of the Isles marched his host into Aberdeenshire, where he met the opponents to his claim to the earldom of Ross on the field of Harlaw in 1411. After this bloody but inconclusive engagement he took steps which must have gone far to reconcile him to the two powerful clans of the northern mainland. Angus the Mackay Chief had succeeded his father in 1403. Donald bestowed on him his sister Elizabeth of the Isles in marriage, and with her hand came a charter in 1415 which stated in Latin: 'We, Donald of Islay, Lord of the Isles, have given, conceded and confirmed by this our charter to the noble Angus Aodh of Strathnaver . . .' The great-grandson of Angus and Elizabeth secured registration of this charter by the Lords of the Scottish Privy Council in 1506: who ordained that it should retain its validity 'in all times to come.'[1]

The Chief who obtained this registration succeeded his father in 1486. His personal name was Aodh, and since this possessed no recognised equivalent either in Latin or in English, it was apt to assume bizarre forms in both languages. When Aodh received his confirmation in a precept from James IV dated 1496, he was described as 'nobilis vir Odo M'Ky de Straithnauer.' The instru-

[1] Mackay 1906: 375-6.

ment which followed on this precept in 1497 designated him in English 'our lowit squyar Y Mcky of Straithnauer.'[1]

During the 16th century the first maps were made which defined this province. The one that Gerard Mercator published in Germany in 1595 shows a region which extends far into modern Caithness in the east, and as far as Assynt down the coast to the west. It is likely that Timothy Pont had drawn his map earlier than this, although it was not published by Bleau until the mid-17th century. It is on a larger scale, and does not include the west coast from Cape Wrath to the Assynt border.

As for the other Gaelic clan which had attempted to bar the passage of the Lord of the Isles when he reached the mainland, Donald took the unprecedented step of appointing Dominic Mackenzie to be Abbot of Iona in 1421. He remained in this office until his death over forty years later, despite the opposition of the Mackinnons, who had established something of a prescriptive right to its emoluments. It proved to be an inspired appointment, for Abbot Dominic carried out essential repairs to the abbey's structure after years of neglect.

The earliest administrative link between Strathnaver and the territories adjacent to it, of which historical evidence survives, was provided by religion. The Mackay country and the earldoms of Caithness and Sutherland constituted the diocese of Caithness, in the new religious organisation established by Queen Margaret and consolidated by her sons.[2] Andrew, first historical Bishop of Caithness, was recruited from Dunfermline during the reign of her son David I, but it is uncertain whether he found it expedient, or even possible, to reside in his diocese. John, the second Bishop, was blinded and had his tongue torn out within his diocese: the third was roasted on his own fire. Both incidents have been described as protests against the new taxations of the church, and they may be interpreted less as anti-Christian acts than as incidents in the Gaelic opposition to the Normanising policies of Queen Margaret's sons.[3] There is no evidence that the Bishops of Caithness maintained any ministry in Strathnaver before the sixteenth century.

Evidence is also lacking to date the disappearance of the Celtic church from Strathnaver.[4] The early sculptured cross at

[1] Mackay 1906: 376-7. [2] Barrow 1960 ii: 22-38.
[3] Bentinck 1926: 51-6. Barrow 1956: 1-27. [4] Beaton 1909: 68-88.

Dalness in the Naver valley and the late Celtic cross in the cemetery of Farr are alone sufficient to give several centuries to the span of this church's activities in the Mackay country. Future excavation on Eilean Naoimh and at other early Christian sites will throw light on the first arrival of the céli Dé in Strathnaver, and on the date of their disappearance. Queen Margaret's biographer, the prior of Durham who received the Bishopric of St Andrews, referred to the many Celtic holy-men of his time who lived in the world but not of the world, practising their austerities in their cells, 'angels on earth.'[1] He could scarcely have been referring to religious life in the diocese of Caithness, yet the céli Dé perhaps continued in Strathnaver for long after they had disappeared from the parts of Scotland with which he was familiar.[2]

The fourth Bishop of Caithness was established behind the bulwark of the new feudal earldom of Sutherland, erected by William the Lion.[3] At Dornoch in the extreme south-east, Bishop Gilbert's cathedral was built, and he planned the planting of a ministry. That he could write of an 'ecclesia' already in existence at Farr suggests that the Celtic church was still maintained there.[4] The earliest surviving evidence of supervision by a Bishop of Caithness of a parish in Strathnaver belongs to the year 1549, and Farr was then still the sole parish in the whole province. In the year 1549 the Bishop admonished the Earl of Caithness: 'the said Reverend Father desires the pollution of the church and sanctuary of Farr to be amended, for that the said Earl not only gart take away all insicht and gear put therein in keeping, but also took out of the same aged and decrepit men and bairns.' In addition to secular goods, the Bishop ordered the Earl 'to cause restore the spuilzie of the chalice and christening stock, eucharist and ornaments of the altar of the said church of Farr, since the sacrament cannot be administered for want thereof.'[5] There is no evidence that any other parish was erected in Strathnaver before the Reformation.

The earliest reference to the size of Strathnaver's population is that of Fordun's continuator, who estimated that Angus, husband of Elizabeth of the Isles, was the leader of 4,000 men:

[1] *Vita* 1867: 247. [2] Barrow 1960: 8-9. [3] Barrow 1956:20.
[4] Johnston 1928: 15-6, 20.
[5] *H.M.C.* 2nd Report: 177-8.

'quatuor millium de Strathnarvern'.[1] This figure suggests that the province was far from sparsely populated in the early fifteenth century, and proves that the Chief of Mackay was then known in metropolitan Scotland to be a man with a formidable reserve of military power.

Every known marriage of a Chief of Mackay was exogamous until the seventeenth century, and until the sixteenth century the Chiefs invariably chose their wives from the principal houses of Scottish Gaelic society. Of the six Chiefs who ruled during the fifteenth century, the first married a daughter of Torcuil Macleod of Lewis; his son, Elizabeth of the Isles; his grandson, a daughter of Munro of Foulis; his great-grandson, a daughter of Mackenzie of Kintail; his great-great-grandson, a daughter of O'Beolan of Carloway.[2] O'Beolan's daughter was of the oldest Irish stock, since her family had arrived in the Scottish Highlands as Celtic church leaders.[3] The O'Beolans had held the earldom of Ross, but they did not retain any political importance into the fifteenth century. Of the other alliances, it is interesting that the Chiefs of Mackay married into the houses of Lewis and the Isles while they were still at the height of their power, and into the advancing mainland families of Kintail and Foulis as the balance of power tilted towards the century's close. It was not until the sixteenth century that a Chief of Mackay married a Sinclair of Caithness or a Gordon of Sutherland.

Even exogamy could not protect the Chiefs of Mackay, living in a world of limited choice at the extreme northern outpost of Gaelic society, from marriage within the uncanonical degrees that required a church dispensation. Nor could a marriage of the most solemn dynastic kind necessarily be celebrated with sufficient formality in the eyes of a church that maintained no ministry in the province.[4] Since the succession of legitimate heirs to the chiefship was at stake, the Chiefs of Mackay sometimes took extraordinary steps to remedy this situation. Aodh, Chief of Mackay, who secured recognition from James IV of his title to Strathnaver in 1496, and registration of the Lord of the Isles' charter in 1506, also obtained formal legitimation of his two sons under the Privy Seal in 1511.[5]

This unprecedented attempt by Aodh to ensure the safety of

[1] Scotichronicon 1759: II. 489. [2] Mackay 1906.
[3] Mackenzie 1903: 92-3. [4] Anton 1958: 89-102. [5] *R.P.S.* I: no. 2286.

Duthaich 'Ic Aoidh by means of legal documents is explained by some of the events that occurred between his succession in 1486, and his death in 1517.

The greatest military power in the north with which the Celtic peoples had formerly had to contend was the Orkney-Caithness earldom. But its Sutherland had been detached from it in 1201 by William the Lion to form an outpost of southern feudal power. In the middle of the fourteenth century, Orkney and the remainder of Caithness bad been split into separate earldoms, to be united briefly in the person of William Sinclair in 1455. When the northern isles were annexed to the Scottish crown in 1472, Sinclair resigned his rights in Orkney in return for lands in Fife, and the two earldoms remained separate for ever after. The kingdom of Earl Thorfinn the Mighty had been divided permanently into three units, and what had once been merely its southern pendicle was now the most strategically significant of the three.

On the other side of Strathnaver, the Lord of the Isles was forfeited for treason in 1475, and lost the great earldom of Ross to the Scottish crown. In 1493 the lordship itself was abolished for ever, and John of the Isles lived a pensioner at the court of James IV. To east and west, the Chief of Mackay witnessed the crumbling of ancient power: but the power of the earldom of Sutherland increased, and it was the fate of that earldom during his chiefship that provided him with the most salutory lesson of all.

James IV, who succeeded to the Scottish crown in 1488, gave powers to the earls of Argyll and Huntly as his Lieutenants of which they made effective use. Huntly used them to obtain the earldom of Sutherland for his second son, Adam Gordon, in the following manner. In 1494 he obtained a 'brieve of idiocy' from James IV against Earl John, who had maintained himself in the earldom of Sutherland in troubled times for nearly forty years. The 'idiot' Earl John had been married first to a daughter of the Lord of the Isles, by whom he had as his heir a son, John. By his second marriage, the Earl had a son named Alexander. He also possessed a daughter, Elizabeth, whom Adam Gordon married in about 1500. The 'idiot' Earl John appears to have been living at least until 1508, and his second wife was drawing widow's terce as a Countess as late as 1512. His heir, John does not appear to have obtained infeftment of the earldom until 1512, and then he was barred, pending a brieve of idiocy against him also. The earldom was administered in the interval by Andrew, Bishop of Caithness, an illegitimate royal Stewart.

At Flodden in 1513 were killed James IV and his Lieutenant the Earl of Argyll. The third Earl of Huntly and his brother Adam Gordon fled the field, to obtain the second brieve of idiocy against Earl John the younger, declare his brother a bastard despite the status of his mother as a widowed Countess, and take possession of the earldom of Sutherland in the name of Adam Gordon's wife. Between the first brieve of idiocy in 1494 and the second in 1514, the Chief of Mackay obtained his title to Strathnaver from James IV, registered his charter from the Lord of the Isles, and secured the formal legitimation of both his sons. If the legal activities of Strathnaver and Sutherland during these twenty years had any connection with one another, then the Chief of Mackay anticipated that Adam Gordon might become his neighbour, some years before Flodden removed whatever difficulties may have remained in his path. The last surviving precaution of Aodh, Chief of Mackay, was to secure confirmation from the new Earl to the Mackay titles within the earldom itself. In 1517 he entered into a bond of friendship with Adam Gordon: and on his death, John Mackay his son reaffirmed the same bond, as the new Chief, in 1518. 'It is agreed and fully accorded betwixt an noble and mighty lord, Adam Gordon, Earl of Sutherland, on the one part, and an honourable man called John Mackay of Strathnaver on the other part.' The first Gordon Earl of Sutherland had formally recognised both John's legitimate succession to Aodh his father, and also his title to Strathnaver.[1]

It seems unlikely that Aodh would have obtained the first royal grants of title to the Mackay country from James IV, if he had not given active support to that King's Highland policy. After the deposition of the Lord of the Isles, his grandson Donald Dubh fled to Lewis. Mackay took part with the Lieutenant of the King, the Earl of Huntly, in his expeditions to Lewis in 1503, 1505 and 1506. A lost correspondence between Mackay

[1] Mackay 1906: 384-7.

and James IV is noted in the Lord Treasurer's accounts, which record payment in May 1502 'to an man that brought writings to the King from Aodh Mackay, by the King's command.' An identical payment was made at the end of 1506 to another bearer of 'writings from Mackay to the King', while the movements of a messenger in January 1507 prove that Mackay was then still in Lewis.[1]

The Chief of Mackay was present with a contingent from Strathnaver on the field of Flodden.[2] The following winter the Lords of Council drew up a memorandum of the 'head men that shall take the rule of the Northland upon them, and to answer to the King's grace and Lords of Council therefore.' It is noteworthy that while three men were named for Caithness, Mackay alone was named as ruler of Strathnaver: 'for the lands of Caithness, the Earl of Caithness, the Laird of Inverugie and the Laird of Berriedale; for the lands of Strathnaver, Mackay; for the rule of Sutherland, my lord Bishop of Caithness.'[3]

The two sons who succeeded, one after the other, as Chiefs of Mackay between 1517 and 1550 had been provided by Aodh their father with unassailable titles. The need for this is apparent. In 1504, Ross and Caithness were erected into sheriffdoms, while the territories of Sutherland and Strathnaver which lay between continued to lack this organ of administration and justice throughout the sixteenth century. The only secular authority was thus that of the King's Lieutenant, the Earl of Huntly, brother of the *de facto* Earl of Sutherland, and a member of the Council of Regency during the minority of James V. The spiritual authority continued to be exercised by members of the Stewart family, most of whom were connected with the royal house, though not all of them were either legitimate or consecrated. The Bishopric of Caithness was not, however, peculiar in this respect.[4]

After James V had attained his majority, he was troubled by consequences of his father's harsh treatment of the rulers of the Western Isles, and of the power given to the Lieutenants of the King. In 1539 Donald Gorm of Sleat, Chief of the Skye Macdonalds, rose in alliance with the Macleods of Lewis:

[1] *A.L.H.T.*, II: 147. III: 354, 361. Mackenzie 1903: 118-22.
[2] Mackay 1906: 76.
[3] *A.L.C.P.A.*: 7-8. [4] Bentinck 1926: 98-9. Donaldson 1960: 38-9.

though his death in Kintail soon brought this rebellion to an end.[1] James V thereupon entertained the Scottish islands to a display of the Crown's power, sailing with a strong fleet from the Forth to Orkney, and thence through the Hebrides to Dunbarton, during the early summer of 1540.

Pitscottie wrote that Mackay was among the Gaelic Chiefs whom James V brought back with him to his court. 'Some of them he put in ward, and some of them bade at court, and other some of them were kept as pledges for keeping good order . . . wherethrough he was greatly rejoiced when he saw all his north country in subjection, and at peace and rest.'[2]

But in fact the Chief of Mackay had scored the tactical advantage of attendance at court before the daunting of the Isles took place, and had obtained a charter to his lands from James V under the great seal at Stirling in December 1539.[3] In it, the Chief of Mackay was enjoined to attend three courts annually at Inverness, while his titles in Strathnaver were enlarged by a free barony of Farr. The name was chosen presumably because Mackay's castle called Borve stood on a jutting promontory of Farr headland, while the only known church in Strathnaver probably stood in the neighbourhood of the ancient burial-ground behind Farr Bay. The instrument of seisin upon this charter, issued in February 1540, stated (in Latin) that there had been no additional grant of land by the King, but merely a confirmation of title to property 'held by our deceased illustrious predecessors.'[4] If anything, the title of the Chief of Mackay was somewhat diminished by this charter and instrument of seisin, inasmuch as both referred to 'Donald Mackay in Strathnaver' rather than to Mackay of Strathnaver.

But it was confirmed in respect of lands in Orkney, Caithness, and Sutherland, in addition to Strathnaver. In July 1540 the Chief received a charter from the Bishop of Caithness at Dornoch, concerning the barony of Durness and the fishings of Farr, in which he was designated Donald Mackay of Strathnaver. A last communication from James V in November 1542 addressed him as Donald Mackay of Farr.[5] The battle of Solway Moss, at which Mackay's heir had been taken prisoner by the English, had been fought a few days earlier. In the following

[1] Nicholson 1930: 53, 55-6. [2] Pitscottie 1814: 357-8. [3] Mackay 1906: 388-90. [4] Mackay 1906: 392. [5] Mackay 1906: 396.

month James V died, leaving his one-week-old daughter as Queen of Scots. When James V had succeeded to the throne at the age of one year, the King's Lieutenant in the north had added the earldom of Sutherland to the possessions of the Gordons: these now attempted to add Strathnaver also, using the same methods.

Solway Moss brought to an end the security that the Chiefs of Mackay had won for their country by means of feudal charters, earned by feudal services to the Kings of Scots. It also evoked the first surviving statement by a native of the diocese of Caithness of the nature of Gaelic society in northern Scotland, and of the manner in which it was imperilled. For the fullest possible understanding of some of the descriptions and attitudes contained in this remarkable document, it is necessary to examine its literary antecedents in Scottish Gaeldom.

These extend back to the Duan Albanach, a poem composed during the reign of Malcolm III in the eleventh century in Gaelic.[1] It praises the succession of kings, Duncan, Macbeth, Lulach and Malcolm III with complete impartiality. There is an interval of over two centuries before the Scottish Gaelic voice is heard in verse again, in the poem composed by Blind Arthur in 1310. By this time, the crown of the Scots had long been worn by French-speaking Normans, and the bard's theme was the Gaelic opposition to the Norman nominees whom they had planted in Scottish Gaeldom. 'Tryst of a fleet against Castle Sween, welcome is the adventure in Inis Fáil; horsemen travelling the billows, brown barks are being cleansed for them. Tall men are arraying the fleet, which swiftly holds its course on the sea's bare surface: no hand lacks a trim warspear, in battle of targes, polished and comely.'

This elegant and confident poem depicts MacSween of Knapdale's expedition to recover his possessions from Robert I's supporter, Menteith. 'Of quilted hauberks is arrayed the bark's forefront in form of jewels, of warriors with brown-faced girdles: Norsemen and nobles are they.' Expecting success, they carried their womenfolk with them. 'There are highplaced beds for stately damsels; speckled cushions are arranged for them, couches for the ladies where each may lie alone. Speckled

[1] Jackson 1957: 125-37.

cushions of satin and sendal, these are the strewings of the ships.' Irishmen as well as Norsemen manned the fleet. 'When was heard the warrior's muster, the trumpets' cry summoning them to ply their art, they had with them the golden heroes from Ireland, to form the slim-fingered, bright, ruddy-cheeked band.'[1]

A century later the theme remained the same, but the confidence had largely evaporated. 'I am displeased with the wind from the south,' sang a bard of the Western Isles, 'for it keeps John from land, now that it has borne him forth.' John Macleod of Harris and Dunvegan, was in the army of Donald, Lord of the Isles, which marched to Harlaw in defence of his title to the earldom of Ross in 1411. 'Janet's son, white his sails, did he wish to come over sea, it is not a wind from the south that would stay John, son of William, of swift steeds.' But in the event, the MacLeod Chief returned safely from Harlaw. 'Son of William, who dispensed mead, son of Janet of royal lineage; were I to hear of his coming from the north, my gloom would have left me.'[2] Angus, Chief of Mackay, perhaps contributed to the defeat of the Lord of the Isles, for he tried (though without success) to bar his passage at Dingwall, with the force of four thousand men from Strathnaver that Fordun's continuator noted. Donald of the Isles restored amity by giving the Chief of Mackay his sister Elizabeth in marriage, and formalised the new relationship in the charter of 1415.

Although Elizabeth of the Isles may have found the amenities of Castle Borve and the north coast of Scotland simpler and more restricted than those of the Lordship, they probably did not differ in kind. From Cape Wrath to County Kerry it was a society in which the harp sounded. 'In the hero's stronghold is concert of harps in hands of minstrels; his household go from games of back-gammon to walk in shaded garden.' In the fifteenth century it was still possible to describe the household of a Chief of Macgregor in such terms. 'A harp in special grant me at my request, thou King, thou whose countenance is as the ripe bloom of an orchard, for it is a matter that thou hast by thee.' In this instance a Scottish poet was addressing one whom the *Annals of Ulster* described as 'the general protector of the learned companies of Ireland.' He was able to acknowledge that his patron,

[1] Dean 1937: 257-9. [2] Dean 1937: 22-5, 261.

'not paltry of vow, has given me his food and bragget, a harp besides to reward my song.'[1]

The songs of the fifteenth-century bards already showed that devoted attention to nature which especially distinguishes Gaelic poetry: to 'all that they found of wonders beneath the banks of each swift stream.' They looked beyond the anxieties of the day to where 'each ear of corn carries its full burden. Cows yield sweet milk in milking folds; the fallow land is most rich in grass; throughout its smooth demesne and mountain it is a lovely land under its weighty crops.'[2] The biographer of James IV has written: 'the fifteenth-century poet lived too close to nature to love it. He turned with a shudder from illimitable moorlands and lochs fading into the sunset.'[3] The attempt to generalise about Scotland from a study of its English-speaking peoples alone has frequently produced such judgements as this.

As remarkable as the contrast between the attitudes to nature of the English and Gaelic poets in fifteenth-century Scotland, is the contrast of subject-matter in the popular balladry of the two language-groups. The Gaelic ballads contained persons and plots, many of which were already over a thousand years old: while these were also incorporated into more recent occurrences, such as the invasions of Magnus Barefoot of Norway (1093–1103). The collections of these ballads that were made in Strathnaver in the eighteenth century are rich in examples.[4] The Lowland ballads were concerned with such current affairs as the fate of the Maid of Norway in 1290, the mediaeval wars of Percy and Douglas, the execution of Johnnie Armstrong in 1530. In place of the Ossianic heroes of the Highlanders, who are related to people and events of the third century, the mediaeval English hero Robin Hood had conquered the imaginations of the English speakers in Scotland as far north as Aberdeen by the end of the fifteenth century.[5] The Lowland poets of the fifteenth century as well as of the sixteenth stated explicitly that the language they used was English, and philology confirms it. The fashion for defining the language of the makars as 'Scots' is an altogether more modern one.[6]

The earliest surviving Gaelic prose in Scotland, approx-

[1] Dean 1937: 31, 43, 263. [2] Dean 1937:28-9, 36-7. [3] Mackie 1958: 3.
[4] Campbell 1872: 218-23. Sage 1892: 371-99.
[5] Mackie 1958: 149. [6] Donaldson 1961: 289-91.

imately contemporary with the Duan Albanach, consists of the entries in the Book of Deer. By the fifteenth century the language was being used for charters, medical treatises, annals and genealogies.[1] The wholesale destruction of muniments, particularly those of the Lordship of the Isles and of the Macleods of Lewis, has made it difficult to assess the full range of the language's use, but it does not appear that Gaelic was ever widely adopted for purposes of correspondence in Scotland, after the habit of letter-writing had arisen in the country. A Scottish Gaelic letter earlier than the eighteenth century is a rarity, to be associated less with literature than with cryptography.[2] The fact that the first surviving letter from a native of the diocese of Caithness was written in English is partly explained by the fact that it was addressed to Henry VIII. But it would be misleading to suggest that it might otherwise have been written in Gaelic.

The author of the letter was at pains to explain to Henry VIII that he was one of the Gaels, generally known in the sixteenth century as Irish, to distinguish them from the Lowland Scots. He also identified himself by the dress which the Gaels wore, as a 'redshank', and accounted for his ability to write English by mentioning that he had received education in a Scottish university. He signed himself 'John Eldar, Clerk, a Redshank.' It is possible that the first name was assumed like the other two; in about 1543, when he wrote this letter, he might have passed, in other contexts, as a Sinclair in Caithness, a Sutherland in the new Gordon earldom, or a Mackay in *Duthaich 'Ic Aoidh*. Now that feudal vassalage extended over these areas, surnames must have been used, if at all, in a feudal context. It is sufficient evidence of this that the first Sinclair was not created Earl of Caithness until 1455, yet his name is the commonest in Caithness to this day.

What is important in John Eldar's signature is that he had distinguished himself as one of the natives of the diocese of Caithness who was of Irish, or Gaelic extraction despite his ability, as a clerk, to write in English.[3] He assured Henry VIII 'what true faithful hearts the most part of the commons of

[1] Mackay 1906: 372-4. Campbell 1963: passim. Mackinnon 1912: 106-28, 298-301.
[2] Matheson 1958: 211-2. [3] Eldar: 23-32.

Scotland (if they durst speak), beyond the waters of Forth, have to your Highness.' He used here the term for the ancient boundary between the Lothians and Scotland proper which had been applied as late as the fourteenth century in the kingdom itself.[1] He went on to explain that the general affection of the common people was given its lead in the 'love and favour the valiant Irish lords of Scotland, otherwise called the redshanks . . . bears unto your said Majesty.' The enemy against which they sought Henry's support was the same that the MacSweens of Knapdale had fought in 1310, and against which the last Lord of the Isles had made his disastrous treaty with England. It was the Norman feudal order that controlled Scotland in the name of yet another child sovereign; the same order as the Tudors had destroyed in England in 1485. There is some expression of the current political and religious controversy in John Eldar's words, but several passages make plain that to a redshank the issue remained fundamentally a racial one. 'The Babylonical bishops and the great courtiers of Scotland repute the foresaid Irish lords as wild, rude, and barbarous people, brought up (as they say) without learning and nurture; yet they pass them a great deal in faith, honesty, in policy and wit, in good order and civility.'

John Eldar told Henry VIII that the inhabitants of the old Scotland north of the Forth looked to him to rescue them from the Anglo-Norman feudal domination 'because they understand and hear how mercifully and how liberally (as I have said) your Highness hath ordered the lords of Ireland.' It was John Eldar's thesis that many Gaels thought they would fare better under Tudor rule than under the shifting factions that contended for power in Edinburgh. In making bishops his principal targets, John Eldar brought his case as near as he was able to the contemporary issue, without disguising his own attitude. With the bishops he grouped 'their adherants', 'their partakers', 'the great courtiers.' In 1541 another royal Stewart became Bishop of Caithness at the age of nineteen, who never took holy orders; while a pension was reserved from the bishopric for an illegitimate grandson of James IV.[2]

The redshank gave Henry an illuminating glimpse of Irish society in the northern Highlands in the mid-sixteenth century.

[1] Dickinson 1961: 39. [2] Donaldson 1960: 38-9.

'Please it your Majesty to understand that we of all people can tolerate, suffer and away best with cold, for both summer and winter (except when the frost is most vehement), going always bare-legged and bare-footed. Our delight and pleasure is not only in hunting of red deer, wolves, foxes and grouse, whereof we abound and have great plenty, but also in running, leaping, swimming, shooting, and throwing of darts: therefore, in so much as we use and delight so to go always, the tender delicate gentlemen of Scotland call us Redshanks. And again in winter, when the frost is most vehement (as I have said), which we cannot suffer bare-footed so well as snow, which can never hurt us when it comes to our girdles, we go a-hunting; and after that we have slain red deer, we flay off the skin by and by, and setting of our bare foot on the inside thereof, for need of cunning shoe-makers, by your Grace's pardon we play the souters; compassing and measuring so much thereof as shall reach up to our ankles, pricking the upper part thereof also with holes, that the water may repass when it enters; and stretched up with a strong thong of the same, meeting above our side ankles. So, and please your noble Grace, we make our shoes.'

Here was a picture of the kind of society over which Henry VIII's forbears had presided when they were Welsh princes not unlike the Lords of the Isles or the Chiefs of Mackay. 'And although a great sort of us Redshanks go after this manner in our country, yet nevertheless, and please your Grace, when we come to the court . . . waiting on our lords and masters, who also for velvets and silks be right well arrayed, we have as good garments as some of our fellows which give attendance in the court every day.' Much redshank ignominy underlay that phrase: 'waiting on our lords and masters.' But the author brought up on the nineteenth-century Scottish histories did not see in John Eldar the exponent of opinions long held and deeply felt; only 'this rascally turncoat.'[1]

If the Chiefs of Mackay had hitherto shared the opinions of John Eldar, they had not found it politic to base their actions on them. They had opposed the Lord of the Isles in 1411 and helped to destroy Macleod of Lewis in 1506. They had fought for the King of Scots against English armies at Flodden in 1513 and at Solway Moss in 1542. Perhaps they regretted having

[1] Skene 1902: 408.

helped to destroy the bastions of Gaeldom in return for feudal charters when these proved to be valueless. Be that as it may, they moved, after Solway Moss, towards a standpoint apparently identical to that of John Eldar, by steps that must now be examined.

The political factors in Scotland after Solway Moss were these. The heir presumptive to the baby Queen of Scots was Hamilton of Arran, provided his parents' marriage was not pronounced invalid by the Church. If it were invalid, the heir was Stewart of Lennox. Behind these rival principals stood the French Queen Mother, Mary of Lorraine, anxious to safeguard the inheritance of her daughter as a Catholic sovereign. In opposition to her aims and methods, a new social order consisting chiefly of English-speaking burgesses, lairds and religious reformers gradually reached a position of power in Scottish politics. It was their object to substitute alliance with protestant Tudor England for the former Stewart policy of alliance with Catholic France. Hamilton of Arran won the struggle for the regency and chose, after some indecision, to throw in his lot with the Catholic party. His rival Stewart of Lennox thereupon committed himself to Henry VIII in England, and to the growing party of the Reformers in Scotland. The brother of Lennox, Robert, Bishop of Caithness, an unconsecrated youth, thus became involved dynastically in the Reformation movement. The Bishop protected himself against the opposite dangers of a Catholic victory or a complete Reformation. He married his sister Helen, a widow who had also contributed one of the illegitimate sons to her cousin James V, to the Earl of Sutherland: and to these he conveyed the greater part of his episcopal properties for safe keeping.[1] The other Gordon Earl, on the other hand, espoused the Catholic faction and became in 1546 Chancellor of Scotland.

While the Chief of Mackay had escaped from Solway Moss, and received a fresh favour from James V within a few weeks of the King's death, his son had been carried a prisoner to England. The Bishop of Caithness left his episcopal properties in the care of the Earl of Caithness and of the Chief of Mackay during 1543, while he made a visit to Henry VIII, to negotiate

[1] *S.B.*, I: 107-8. III: 86.

for his support in substituting his brother Lennox for Arran, as Regent of Scotland. Henry VIII required that the Bishop should secure the surrender to him of the castle of Dunbarton, where Robert Stewart had been Provost of the Collegiate Church before his elevation.[1] Bishop Robert returned to Scotland to arrange this, but without success. Meanwhile, the Chief of Mackay's son returned from England with other repatriated prisoners from Solway Moss, influenced either by bribery or by conviction to promote the cause of the Protestant Anglophiles in Scotland. He took part in 1544 in an unsuccessful attack on the Regent Arran at Glasgow.[2]

The first step taken by the Queen's Lieutenant in the north, the Earl of Huntly,[3] in the face of these treasons was to advance his brother Alexander Gordon to the bishopric left vacant, as he apparently assumed, by Bishop Robert Stewart's rebellion. But Huntly had overreached himself. Bishop Robert returned to his diocese; his arraignment by Parliament was blocked by Cardinal Beaton; he continued to enjoy his emoluments without receiving a pardon.[4] The Lieutenant's brother next aspired to the bishopric of Glasgow, took the title of Archbishop of Athens, and was ultimately accommodated in the see of Galloway.[5]

In 1547 the Earl of Sutherland was created Lieutenant of Scotland north of the Spey, following Huntly's appointment as Chancellor in the previous year.[6] The Chief of Mackay's son added to his earlier treasons in 1548 by taking part with the English forces in the capture of Haddington that resulted in the baby Queen's removal to France.[7] In 1549 Huntly was created Earl of Moray.

In the same year the Earl of Caithness attempted to heal the growing antagonisms in the north. He invited the Stewart Bishop of Caithness, the Gordon Earl of Sutherland, and the Mackay Chief of Strathnaver to a meeting of reconciliation in his castle of Girnigo near Wick. Caithness and the Bishop were young men in their early twenties: Mackay was in the last year of his life. Girnigo castle could not have been unfamiliar to him, for he had married a grand-daughter of an Earl of Caithness. But this was the first Sinclair marriage among the chiefs of

[1] Bentinck 1926: 110. [2] *R.P.S.* IV: no. 2939. [3] *S.C.M.* 1849: 142-4.
[4] *S.B.* I: 107-8. [5] Donaldson 1960: 58. [6] Gordon 1813: 128.
[7] *R.P.S.* V: no. 1116. Mackay 1906: 398-9.

Mackay, and it was perhaps insufficient to make the elderly Chief feel comfortable among the important young men who all spoke a different language from his. It was believed, indeed, that expressions of amity were exchanged between the four men. But whatever conversation passed between them, it was irrelevant to the plans that the Gordons were about to execute with respect to Strathnaver.[1]

The Chief of Mackay died in 1550, and was succeeded by his son Aodh. The new Chief had lived at the court of Henry VIII in London after his capture at Solway Moss. Whether or not he subscribed to the views of John Eldar, the new Chief had fought openly for alliance with England, as opposed to alliance with France. But Henry VIII had brutally overplayed his part, and perhaps hastened the very outcome that he feared, when Mary, Queen of Scots was sent to France instead of being espoused to his own son. By the time when Aodh succeeded as Chief of Mackay, peace was restored at last between Scotland and England: the French party headed by Queen Mary of Lorraine was triumphant. The new Chief could expect to receive the penalties of treason.

So secure was Queen Mary in her triumph that she was able to leave Scotland altogether for over a year, while she paid her last visit to her mother, her daughter, the son of her first marriage, and all the beloved people and places she had put behind her in order to make her daughter's throne secure through the French alliance. Queen Mary took with her to France the Earls of Sutherland and Huntly-Moray, upon whom her power in Scotland so largely depended, and it need not be doubted that the Earls used this opportunity to impress upon Queen Mary the propriety of destroying Mackay.[2] Nor was there the slightest reason why Queen Mary should reject their advice. She had devoted her life, through eight years of peril since her husband's death, to defeating Tudor policy with French aid. There could be no grounds in her eyes for condoning Mackay's treason.

While the Queen and the two Earls were in France, the son of the bastardised and murdered heir to the Sutherland earldom was murdered as his father had been. The young Chief of

[1] Mackay 1906: 91-2. *S.B.*: III, 109-10.
[2] cf. Mary of Lorraine 1927: 372.

Mackay was the first cousin of John Sutherland, the latest victim in the legitimate succession to the earldom. Whether he took the offensive against such an immensely powerful faction as the Stewart-Gordons in revenge for his cousin's fate, or whether he did so because he had nothing to lose so long as this faction remained in power, is beyond speculation. A short time before 1630, the Gordon chronicler interpreted events thus: 'Aodh Mackay, the son of Donald Mackay, taking the occasion and opportunity of Earl John's absence, assembled the inhabitants of Strathnaver and entered into Sutherland with all hostility. But Alexander Gordon, convening together some of his countrymen, opposed himself against Aodh Mackay and chased him into Strathnaver. Alexander, not contented therewith, presently went into Strathnaver which he invaded and spoiled, carrying from thence a great booty of goods and cattle the year of God 1551.'[1]

Evidently, the Chief of Mackay could have expected to lose his titles to *Duthaich 'Ic Aoidh* as soon as the northern Lieutenant and the Chancellor of Scotland returned from France. He could have expected this on the grounds of treason or of local lawlessness: and be could have expected that the charges would be preferred against him by Gordons exercising their official powers. In fact, they were anticipated by the Bishop of Orkney, using the legal device that had served to obtain the earldom of Sutherland for Adam Gordon. In October 1551, the Bishop registered a precept, showing that Aodh's grandparents had not been properly married, that Aodh's father was consequently illegitimate, and that Aodh was therefore incapable of inheriting from him. Recognitions of title by sovereigns, Earls of Sutherland, and Bishops of Caithness, formal legitimations under the Privy Seal of Scotland, all of these counted for nothing.[2]

The character of Robert Reid, Bishop of Orkney, is as hard to read as his motives in this transaction. Knox described him as greedy and avaricious, and the agreement which the Chief of Mackay was compelled to make with him in September 1551 might appear to support such a judgment. This agreement between Bishop Robert Reid and Aodh, son of Donald Mackay of Farr, stated that the late Chief's lands were now in the hands of the Queen whom the Gordons had just visited in France,

[1] Gordon 1813: 128, 133. [2] *R.P.S.* IV: nos. 1371-5.

because 'he died bastard without lawful heirs, and as the Governor has consented that Aodh should have the lands for composition of 4000 merks Scots—a sum he cannot pay—the barony of Farr and other lands, holden of the crown or other overlords, are to be the Bishop's heritably. But when 1000 merks are paid, the barony of Ardurness shall be resigned to the Bishop or elect of Caithness, or to the Governor, for a new presentation to Mackay: and similarly Strathnaver, holden of the bishopric of Moray, shall be resigned on receipt of the second 1000 merks, Farr and other lands, when the remaining 2000 merks are paid: provided always that Mackay cause the Bishop to have the revenues until the 4000 merks are paid, his obligations being reduced as the instalments.' This may be the earliest example of the use of the term 'Strathnaver' for a barony similar to Ardurness or Farr, within a province which is left unnamed.[1]

Catholic Lesley and Calvinist Buchanan left judgments of Robert Reid totally at variance with that of John Knox: Buchanan considered him to be 'a good man and of consummate wisdom.' He had been Abbot of Kinloss, where he installed a fireproof library, and of Beauly where he built the nave whose ruins commemorate him still. He became Bishop of Orkney in 1542 where he busied himself with the problems of reform.[2] This Bishop obtained the overlordship of Strathnaver province in 1553, and at once bestowed the heritable use upon the Chief of Mackay.[3] It should not be assumed that it was Robert Reid who waited until Donald, Chief of Mackay died in 1550, and then showed him to have been a bastard, incapable of owning or of transmitting his properties to his posterity. All that is certain is that Robert Reid moved fast enough, after such proceedings had been instituted, to secure the superiority of Strathnaver for himself, and its dominium utile for Mackay. That the Gordons had been outwitted for the present is disclosed by their subsequent acts, and by the comment of the Earl of Sutherland's grandson. 'Bishop Reid was a great favourer of Mackay's house and family. He obtained from the Queen a gift of Mackay's lands in Strathnaver, fallen into her Majesty's hands by reason of the bastardy of Donald Mackay, the father of Aodh Mackay;

[1] *A.L.C.P.A.*: no. 611.
[2] Donaldson 1960: 32, 34. [3] *R.P.S.* IV: no. 1901.

which gift Bishop Robert Reid took in his own name, but to Mackay's use.'[1]

In 1553, the year in which the Bishop of Orkney obtained the superiority of *Duthaich 'Ic Aoidh*, the Bishop of Caithness entered into the first of that series of transactions with his brother-in-law the Earl of Sutherland, by which the church properties of the diocese of Caithness were alienated by degrees to the Gordons. Indeed, the enterprise may have begun earlier, for one of the agreements has its date torn away.[2] Thus the Earl was enabled not only to enlarge his possessions in Sutherland, but also to gain footholds in Strathnaver and Caithness. The charter of 1553 gave to Earl John and Helen Stewart his wife the properties of Skaill and Ardurness in Strathnaver, Scrabster and its lands in Caithness, the castle of Skibo and the palace and city of Dornoch in Sutherland. 'Because the said castles of Scrabster and Skibo and the palace of Dornoch are built in an Irish region, among fierce and unsubdued Scots, so that neither he nor his predecessors have been able to enjoy them without very great expenses, he, with the consent of his dean and chapter, appoints the Earl and Countess and their said heirs hereditary constables of the castle of Scrabster and palace of Dornoch for ever . . .'[3] Skibo later went to Gray of Swordale, being ruinous 'and destitute of plenishing', and, of course, in 'an barbarous and savage realm.'[4]

In 1554 the Queen Mother assumed the regency. She had with difficulty ousted Hamilton of Arran, the heir to her daughter's throne, and she was faced by the growing menace of the Reformation party. The succession of the Catholic Mary Tudor to the English throne eased this problem, but the Queen Mother Regent required all the support she could win, and as the Gordons provided the backbone of this support, it was sound policy on her part to increase their power in the land by any means which they might suggest. That power lay in the chain of earldoms extending from Huntly, through Moray to Sutherland; fortified by the offices of the Queen's Lieutenants; but weakened by the 'unsubdued Scots' in the surrounding hills. Almost immediately after she had assumed the Regency, the

[1] Gordon 1813: 137.
[2] *S.B.*, I: 112-3. III: 97-100, 116-24.
[3] *R.G.S.*, IV: no. 1669. [4] *R.G.S.*, V: no. 561.

Queen Mother travelled to Inverness where she held a circuit court and summoned Mackay to appear before it.'[1]

Centuries of experience lay behind the reactions of a Celtic Chief to such a summons. If he presented himself, he might be imprisoned or even executed. If he went into hiding instead, a King might be murdered in metropolitan Scotland, or a faction of nobles might lose power, and the danger would be past. But neither could occur fast enough to save Mackay when he ignored his summons, because the Earl of Sutherland was poised to spring, as his grandson recorded. 'Aodh Mackay of Farr being summoned at this time to compere before the Queen at Inverness (for that he had spoiled and molested the country of Sutherland during Earl John's absence in France), did contemn the summons and precept of warning: whereupon the Queen granted a commission to John Earl of Sutherland against Aodh Mackay and his country.'[2] Complaints had been lodged with the Privy Council in 1553 concerning fresh 'enormities, slaughters . . . and oppression,' alleged to have been committed by the Chief of Mackay.[3] But it appears to have been decided that acts committed in 1551 and amply punished at the time (according to the Gordon chronicler) should be used in evidence in preference to these. The most serious blow the Gordons had suffered between then and 1554 was that they had lost the title of Strathnaver to the Bishop of Orkney.

'So Earl John, assembling all his forces, entered into Strathnaver, sacking and spoiling before him in all hostile manner, and possessed all the places of doubt . . . But when Earl John perceived that Aodh Mackay would not abide and fight him, he besieged the strong castle and fort called Borve, the principal strength of that country, not two miles distant from Farr. After a short siege he took it by force and hanged Ruairidh Mac Iain Mhóir, captain thereof. This fort was demolished by Earl John.' It remains as he left it, to this day.[4]

Aodh attempted a standard ruse of guerilla warfare. 'In the meantime that Earl John was at the siege of the castle of Borve, Aodh Mackay came secretly with a company of men into Sutherland where he burnt the church of Loth.'[5] But in the end

[1] *S.B.*, I: 111. [2] Gordon 1813: 134.
[3] *R.P.C.*, I: 147. [4] Gordon 1813: 135. Balfour 1825 I: 306.
[5] Gordon 1813: 134–5.

he was forced to submit, and carried south a prisoner. It is not uncharacteristic of the Queen Regent that she formally dissociated herself from the Gordon vendetta against him. On the 15th March 1555, he received a remission under the Privy Seal (for what it was worth) for his part in the Glasgow affair ten years earlier.[1]

It appears, indeed, that the Gordons began to feel disobliged to the Queen Regent, especially when the Bishop of Orkney died in 1558, and the superiority of Strathnaver was not immediately bestowed either upon the Earl of Sutherland, or the Earl of Moray-Huntly. But the succession of Elizabeth Tudor to the English throne perhaps contributed also to their belief that the Protestant faction in Scotland was more likely to be victorious. Both Earls joined the Lords of the Congregation in 1559, just when the Regent had most need of the support of her Catholic subjects. Sutherland celebrated his change of religious allegiance in new transactions with his Bishop.[2] In 1560 the Queen Regent died defeated in Edinburgh castle, and in the following year the great Earl of Moray and Huntly was once again High Chancellor of Scotland, under the new dispensation, to welcome the Queen of Scots to her kingdom.

He received a shock. The young Queen gave his earldom of Moray to her illegitimate brother James Stewart. She made a progress to Inverness in 1562, and hanged the Gordon captain of the castle when he refused her admission. At Corrichie in October the Earl of Huntly was defeated by his successor in the earldom of Moray, and died of apoplexy on the field, being 'gross, corpulent and short of breath.' His body was brought to Edinburgh, and there propped up in its coffin to be convicted of treason. His son was also convicted of treason, and was imprisoned, while all their estates were forfeited. On the 28th May 1563 Earl John of Sutherland was likewise condemned to death, 'his dignity, name and memory to be extinct and deleted, and all his lands, offices and goods to be confiscated.' Earl John fled abroad, while Mary bestowed his earldom on another of her illegitimate half-brothers, Robert Stewart, who had previously been supported by the church.[3]

The motives of the Queen of Scots in pursuing such a rigorous

[1] *R.P.S.*: IV: no. 2939. [2] *S.B.* I: 112-3.
[3] G.E.C. *A.P.S.* II: 579-80. *S.B.*, I: 121.

policy against the Gordons can only be surmised. It would be pleasant to suppose that this intelligent young woman considered the eradication of such survivors of a byegone feudal age as the Earls of Sutherland and Huntly to be in the best interests of her kingdom. But the pattern of the Queen's acts during the brief period of her life that she spent in Scotland does not easily support such an interpretation. It is more probable that she was revenging the betrayal of her mother. How well-informed she was on this subject is proved by her truly surprising knowledge of details that lay outside the politics of metropolitan Scotland. She apparently knew, for instance, how her mother had lent her presence and authority to the Gordon plan to destroy the Chief of Mackay, and to acquire Strathnaver. She apparently understood how her mother had finally disappointed Gordon hopes in this respect. No sooner had the Queen of Scots reached Aberdeen after the victory of Corrichie than she granted Aodh, Chief of Mackay, a remission for his treasons at Haddington during her minority.[1] She summoned him to accompany her to England on her proposed visit to Queen Elizabeth: it is unlikely that she was ignorant of Mackay's visit to the court of Queen Elizabeth's father twenty years earlier, after the battle of Solway Moss.

The events of the twenty years between Solway Moss in 1542 and Corrichie in 1562, in so far as they concerned the title to *Duthaich 'Ic Aoidh*, are instructive. It is evident that the loss of this title by the Chief of Mackay was not really due to the nature of his grandfather's marriage, the illegitimacy of his father, or even to his own part in the discords either between Sutherland and Strathnaver or between Scotland and England. *Duthaich 'Ic Aoidh* was one of the fields of expansionist enterprise, like the earldom of Sutherland and the bishopric of Caithness, of the senior members of the Stewart and Gordon families who controlled the organs of Scottish government. Disagreement between them provided Mackay with a respite, not his own skill or good behaviour.

The family affairs of the Stewarts and Gordons as easily completed his ruin. The first step towards it, quite beyond his control, was the decision of Queen Mary to relieve her cousin Helen Stewart, Countess of Sutherland of the consequences of

[1] *R.P.S.*, V: no. 1116. Mackay 1906: 398-9.

her husband's forfeiture: 'knowing her to be an honourable personage, descended of good and noble lineage.'[1] The Countess was granted a liferent of the forfeited lands, including those conveyed to her husband by her brother the Bishop. In the same year 1563, Queen Mary compensated her son and heir Alexander Gordon with lands in Aboyne; while the Bishop issued a new charter confirmed under the Great Seal, which granted his nephew church properties that had previously been granted to his father.[2] The awful ritual of attainder, the ringing parliamentary phrases: 'his dignity, name and memory to be extinct and deleted, and all his lands, offices and goods to be confiscated'; these words were seen within a year to signify that the Stewarts and Gordons were merely redistributing their property among themselves. James Stewart, the new Earl of Moray, did attempt to enforce the sentence of execution against Huntly's heir; a wise precaution in the author of his father's death. But the Gordon chronicler related how 'the captain delayed to perform until he had first spoken the Queen; who, hearing thereof, refused and disclaimed the warrant. And thereupon she commanded the captain not to proceed against him till he had a warrant from her own mouth to that effect.'[3]

Queen Mary married her first cousin Henry Stewart, Lord Darnley; and consequently quarrelled with her half-brother James Stewart, Earl of Moray. As none had greater cause to hate Moray than Gordon of Huntly, she gave him a remission for his part at Corrichie in February 1566,[4] restored him to his father's earldom, and appointed him Chancellor. She rehabilitated John, Earl of Sutherland by letters under the Great Seal. Bishop Robert Stewart's latest charter of 1563 received royal confirmation.[5] While Mackay was still without security of title to his lands, the men who had received capital sentences two years earlier were already once again in possession of all the property they had then forfeited.

Queen Mary gave birth to a male heir to the thrones of both England and Scotland, although her husband Darnley denied paternity. In December 1566, the Queen restored to the Archbishop of St Andrews a part of his lost jurisdiction, especially

[1] *S.B.*, I: 120-1. [2] *R.G.S.*, IV: no. 1669.
[3] Gordon 1813: 143. [4] *S.C.M.* 1849: 154-6. [5] *R.G.S.*, IV: no. 1669.

in the sphere of marriage and divorce: the Reformers were warmed by an increased allowance. On the 21st December, Mary granted to the Earl of Huntly the superiority of Strathnaver, as it had been held by Bishop Robert Reid of Orkney.[1] Darnley was found dead on the 10th February 1567: Bothwell was brought to trial for his murder and acquitted on the 12th April. On the 24th, Bothwell intercepted the Queen and conducted her to Dunbar, where he opened divorce proceedings against his wife, the sister of the Earl of Huntly, in the court which Queen Mary had restored the previous December. Huntly conducted his sister home to Strathbogie without complaint, while Bothwell married Queen Mary.

It is to be observed that Mary was not ignorant of the long resistance of the Chiefs of Mackay to the attempts of the Gordons to subjugate them. It is clear, furthermore, that she did not place *Duthaich 'Ic Aoidh* in subjection to Huntly because of any fresh misdemeanour on the part of Mackay, or of any further discoveries of bastardy among his ancestors. She did so as a convenience in the family relations of the Stewarts and the Gordons. As such, it proved to be but of little use. Within a month of her marriage with Bothwell, Queen Mary was defeated and imprisoned by a faction of Confederate Lords, while Bothwell fled. She abdicated in favour of her son, escaped in the following year, and sought asylum in England, where she spent the remaining nineteen years of her life. While these kaleidoscopic changes were taking place in metropolitan Scotland, events no less portentous to Mackay were occurring in the neighbouring earldoms. In 1567 John, Earl of Sutherland was poisoned by a member of his own family in Helmsdale castle. The Earl of Atholl, one of the Guardians of the baby James VI, obtained the guardianship of his heir, and bestowed it upon the Earl of Caithness. The Gordons had been as suddenly unfortunate as the Queen who had so recently awarded them the prize of Strathnaver.[2]

Huntly met the predicament with the organs of government, so far as they would serve him. He used the last Parliament of Mary, Queen of Scots, to endorse her gift to him. On the 19th April 1567 it was recorded that the Queen 'granted and gave

[1] *R.P.S.*, V: no. 3141. *R.P.C.*, I: 670.
[2] Buchanan 1958: 149. Gordon 1813: 150.

heritably to her trusty cousin and Councillor George, Earl of Huntly, Lord Gordon and Badenoch, her Highness' Chancellor, all and sundry the lands and baronies . . . which pertained heritably of before to umquhile Donald Mackay of Farr, and pertaining to our said Sovereign . . . by reason the said umquhile Donald was born and deceased bastard without lawful heirs of his body gotten or lawful disposition made by him of his lands and goods during his lifetime . . .'[1] It is revealing to examine the series of falsehoods which the High Chancellor of Scotland was able to place upon the Scottish statute book concerning a Chief of Mackay who had done outstanding service to a King of Scots. Thus, even if Donald Mackay had been born illegitimate, he did not die so, since he was formally legitimised. Neither had it ever before been asserted that the present Chief, his son, was illegitimate. But such was the improvement made by the Queen's last Parliament upon her gift to Huntly. In the first Parliament of her infant son James VI, during the December of the same year, a lofty concern for the means by which 'all Scotland may be brought to universal obedience' resolved itself into a private vendetta against two Gaelic Chiefs: 'how may John Moidart and Mackay be dauntoned.'[2] Such was the government against which John Eldar, Clerk and Redshank, had appealed to Henry VIII for rescue.

But the machinery of government would not serve to remove the young Earl of Sutherland from his legal guardian the Earl of Caithness. The Bishop of Caithness even proved unhelpful: he may have been inspired with caution by the fates of his nephew Darnley, his brother-in-law the Earl of Sutherland, and his cousin the Queen, for he possessed a notable taste for survival. Caithness found his fifteen-year-old ward in the episcopal castle of Skibo, the 'fortalice' which its owners described as 'ruinous in walls, thek, rowis, doors, windows, timberwork and ironwork', besides being 'environed with clans and broken men', the natives of 'an barbarous and savage realm.'[3] It was delivered to Caithness by order of the Bishop. The young Earl was taken to Girnigo and there married to his guardian's thirty-two-year-old daughter, a common outcome of such a situation among the Anglo-Norman barons, whose traditional practices had outlived

[1] *A.P.S.*, II: 558.
[2] *A.P.S.*, III: 44. [3] *R.G.S.*, V: no. 561.

the Middle Ages in this corner of Europe. The whole family then took up residence in Dunrobin castle.[1]

Huntly remedied this in 1569 by a raid in which the ward was abducted from Dunrobin during the absence of his guardian in Edinburgh, and conducted to the safety of Strathbogie. For this act of lawlessness no charge was ever preferred against him. In June 1569 the Chief of Mackay travelled to Elgin, where he made his submission to Huntly as his vassal, according to the ex-Queen's gift, and received a charter from him for the Mackay lands.[2] No doubt Mackay added to the grandeur of his superior's entourage when he accompanied him to Aberdeen and there, in July 1570, signed himself 'leal, true and faithful man and servant' to Huntly in the presence of the Earl of Sutherland; as men had done in England before the battle of Bosworth in 1485.[3]

It is possible that Mackay hastened to accept Huntly as his superior while Sutherland was still a minor, unable to transact business. It was illegal to transfer a superiority under Scottish law, without the vassal's consent. The subsequent embarrassment which this caused is revealed characteristically in the sophistries of Sir Robert Gordon's account of the matter. 'Mackay, upon his submission to the Earls of Huntly and Sutherland, and upon his faithful promise to assist Earl Alexander' (that is, Sutherland, the writer's father) 'against the Earl of Caithness in time coming, obtained from the Earl of Huntly the heritable right and title of the lands of Strathnaver for the sum of 3000 pounds Scots money. Yet Huntly still retained the superiority of Strathnaver to himself.' Even a Celtic Chief could not be made a vassal of two superiors at once under Scottish law. It is an interesting disclosure that the Gordons, having obtained the earldom of Sutherland, substantial property from the diocese of Caithness, and the overlordship of Strathnaver (though they had lost Moray), were already planning to use the military strength of Clan Mackay to assault the Caithness earldom.[4]

Apparently the Earl of Caithness anticipated them, by summoning Mackay as soon as be returned to Strathnaver: this he

[1] Gordon 1813: 151. *S.B.*, I: 132-3.
[2] *R.P.C.*, I: 670. Mackay 1906: 399-411.
[3] *S.C.M.* 1849: 228-9. Reay MSS. 1/2B, 1/3B, 1/4B, 1/5B.
[4] *S.B.*, I: 134. Gordon 1813: 163.

was empowered to do both as legal guardian of the abducted Earl, and as Justiciar of the north. There are two accounts of what followed, one by Sir Robert Gordon, the other by an anonymous chronicler of uncertain, perhaps earlier, date.[1] These are in substantial agreement with one another, but it has not been established which account is based on the other. They state that in 1570 the Master of Caithness, Mackay and Sutherland of Duffus descended on Dornoch. The Bishop's castle and the tower of the cathedral held out for a week in defiance of the guardian's authority. Before these were captured, the cathedral of St Gilbert was destroyed in this last legitimate assault on the stronghold of the Gordon Earls and Stewart Bishops.

It is possible that the object was to rescue the daughter of the Earl of Caithness, who was the wife of the young Earl of Sutherland. She had not been carried with her husband to Strathbogie, for some reason that cannot now be determined; and her life was a grave obstacle to the Gordon interest. It need not be doubted that she returned north with Mackay, though Huntly's divorce proceedings against her in Edinburgh, on the grounds of her adultery with Mackay, raise the question why he did not obtain any formal evidence of this from Mackay when he had the Chief so entirely at his mercy in Elgin. The Gordon chronicler later back-dated the adultery with Mackay even further, to the time of the marriage in Caithness: 'an unfit match indeed, a youth of 15 married to a woman of 32 years, but a match fit enough to cover her incontinence and evil life which she led with Aodh Mackay, for the which she was afterwards divorced from Earl Alexander.'[2] Either the Gordons possessed astonishing knowledge of the domestic secrets of Girnigo castle, or this is a falsehood similar to those emblazoned on the Scottish statute books, or the charge relates to the last months of Mackay's life, since he died in 1572. Meanwhile the young Earl of Sutherland was presented by his relatives with a second wife scarcely less bizarre than the first to whom his guardian had married him. Before he returned to Dunrobin on attaining his majority in 1573, he was married to Jane Gordon, the discarded wife of the Earl of Bothwell.[3]

[1] Gordon 1813: 156-7. *Conflicts* 1780.
[2] Gordon 1813: 151. [3] *S.B.*, I: 141.

A new chief of Mackay, who had lost the independence of his predecessors, confronted a new Earl of Sutherland who was not his overlord, and who could not legally acquire the overlordship without Mackay's consent.

3

Celtic Chiefs as Feudal Vassals

THE forty-two years of Uisdean Mackay's chiefship are instructive. He succeeded at the age of eleven, as the Earls of Caithness and Sutherland prepared to fight for the carcase of Strathnaver. He was the first Chief who succeeded as the vassal of a feudal overlord, and who consequently lacked the authority over his clan that his ancestors had enjoyed. *Duthaich 'Ic Aoidh* was still defined as Strathnaver, a province equivalent to the sheriffdom of Ross or the earldom of Sutherland in the eyes of officials ignorant of the latest juggling with terms in official documents.[1] But the child-Chief inherited a parcel of circumscribed and subordinate titles within it.

To all these handicaps was added the fact that Uisdean was merely the third son of his father. His two older brothers were sons of his father's first marriage to his first cousin, the daughter of Macleod of Assynt. Mary Queen of Scots did not so much as wait for the Papal dispensation to arrive before she married her own first cousin Darnley: yet she had alienated property from a family that had obtained formal legitimation in respect of the heirs of an irregular marriage. The clear lesson was that nothing could protect the titles of the two sons of Mackay's first marriage, if either attempted to succeed to the Chiefship.[2]

Uisdean was the offspring of his father's second marriage to a Sinclair of Caithness, and on his succession he was brought up in the safety of Girnigo castle by the Earl of Caithness as his guardian. Both Uisdean's mother and his grandmother had been Sinclairs, and when he reached competent age, he married

[1] *R.P.C.*, I: 610. [2] Mackay 1906: 105-6.

one of the Earl of Caithness's daughters. Sir Robert Gordon did not assert that Uisdean's was a usurpation, promoted by the Earl of Caithness in the Sinclair interest: he referred to Uisdean's elder brothers as 'bastards'.[1] But he accused Caithness of having abducted Uisdean Mackay with the intention of murdering him, just as he had murdered the late Earl of Sutherland, added the chronicler with his usual extravagance.[2] He wrote this after Uisdean had escaped alive from Girnigo castle, with the Earl's daughter as his wife, and after he had shewn himself consistently grateful to the Earl after attaining his majority, until the Earl's death.

It is unfortunate that a work of such malice and mendacity cannot be checked in its facts for the decades of violence that lay ahead. The only other near-contemporary source, the anonymous *Conflicts of the Clans,* cannot be proved to be an independent one. Nevertheless, the broad outlines of what occurred can probably be salvaged with fair accuracy from these two accounts, and there are certain details which raise no suspicion of doubt.

For instance, Gordon related that John Mór Mackay, whose son had defended castle Borve and been hanged after its capture, took upon himself the government of Strathnaver. It cannot be determined whether he was the senior living member of the Chief's family, but this appears probable. Gordon stated that he was lured to Girnigo, and there put to death. Uisdean's elder brother John Beg Mackay thereupon took over the rule of his clan, and was murdered at Durness in 1579. The responsibility of the Earl of Caithness is all the harder to fathom because Uisdean, who was at this time eighteen years old, now left Girnigo without hindrance, to take up the government himself.[3]

Whatever the real relations had been between Uisdean and his murdered elder brother John Beg, the young Chief made an enduring settlement of land upon his other brother Donald, son of Helen Macleod of Assynt. The property lay down the west coast of Strathnaver, as far removed as was possible from the territories of the Gordons and Sinclairs, but adjacent to Assynt. It was called Scourie after one of its townships, a name to be made famous by Donald's varied and distinguished descendants.[4]

[1] Gordon 1813: 173. [2] Gordon 1813: 179. [3] Gordon 1813: 173-4.
[4] Reay MS. 144, f. 86.

Castle Borve was not rebuilt after its destruction in the time of the late Chief, and it is likely that Uisdean moved from Girnigo to a house in Tongue that his father had already built there.

He granted no charter, however, alienating land to the tribal head of that branch of his clan which lived in the area of Strathnaver most exposed to the Earls of Sutherland. This branch was known as that of the Abrach Mackays, after a son of the Chief who was married to Elizabeth of the Isles. This son's mother was a daughter of Macdonald of Keppoch, and since she came from Lochaber, her son was known as Iain Abrach, or John of Lochaber. It is also told that the Abrach Mackay lands were first bestowed on his branch as a reward for his defence of Strathnaver, when the son of Elizabeth of the Isles was taken south by James I, and kept a hostage for good behaviour on the Bass Rock.[1] There is no documentary evidence to support the legend which accounts for the name Neil Bhass, by which John Abrach's half-brother was known. They were sons of a remarkable father, and sufficiently remarkable in their own lives to have attracted to themselves legends that may also be truth.[2]

John Abrach's victory over an invading force of Sutherland men at Druim na Cùb near the Kyle of Tongue in 1433 was noted by Fordun's continuator, by Lesley, and by Sir James Balfour, in addition to Sir Robert Gordon. And Strathnaver folk who could understand neither Latin nor English still remembered the victory in Durness in 1841, in the dark days of the evictions, when women fought the officials from Dornoch.

> 'N tràth chunnaic na gaisgich na h-armagan rùisgte,
> An clobha, 's an corran, an cabar, 's an t-sùist,
> Chlisg iad le feagal, is thubhairt cuid dhiù,
> " 'S miosa so do na Cataich no cath Dhruim na cùb."

(When the heroes saw the weapons unsheathed, the tongs and the sickle, the stake and the flail, they leapt with fear and some of them said, "this is worse for the Sutherland men than the fight of Druim na Cùb".)

The lands of John Abrach's descendants extended along the southern frontier of Strathnaver, from where the Mudale valley rises into the great western deer forest beside Assynt, east-

[1] Mackay 1906: 61-5. [2] Gordon 1813: 303-4.

wards past Loch Naver and Badenloch to that most inflammable area where the Kildonan valley runs from Sutherland into Strathnaver, and Caithness is near, and the ill-endowed Gunns clung to their innacessible acres among the hills between these three provinces. The principal townships in the centre of the Abrach country were Rossal and Achness in the heights of the Naver valley, and Gnub Mór and Gnub Beg on the north shore of Loch Naver. As will be demonstrated, the head of the Abrachs used any of these townships for his designation, and none of them acquired the status of Scourie as a title, in the neighbouring barony to the west.

So bitter was the hostility of the Abrach Mackays for the unfortunate Gunns that it can be seriously questioned whether they could have been of the same race. Sir Robert Gordon, indeed, offered them a Norse pedigree: 'they are called Clan Gunn from one called Gunn, whom they allege to have been the King of Denmark's son, and came many days ago from Denmark and settled himself in Caithness.'[1] Others have believed that 'they were a species of Swiss.'[2] The legend of their progenitor, a Danish princess wrecked on the rocks of Caithness, has interesting overtones of the historical fate of the Maid of Norway. It may yet be possible to throw further light on the possibility that the Gunns are a remnant of the Picts, forced beyond the Scarabens, and into the barren hinterlands of Ben Griam.

The first grave issue of Uisdean's chiefship exploited the mutual antipathy of the Abrach Mackays and the Gunns, fanned by their insecurity of title within their immemorial homeland, exposed between the territories of the rival Earls. Caithness possessed the advantage that his family were Justiciars of the diocese of Caithness. But Sutherland had gained an advantage in 1576, when the Earl of Huntly had died, and his fourteen-year-old son had gone through the form of transferring the ward and nonentry of Strathnaver to the Earl of Sutherland.[3] This was followed by a second illegality in May 1583, when the superiority of the lands and barony of Farr was transferred also.[4] But the efficacy of these transactions was not dependent upon whether they infringed the statute of 1401, which forbade

[1] Gordon 1813: 92-3. [2] Sinclair 1899: 24. [3] *S.B.*, I: 141.
[4] *R.G.S.*, V: no. 580. no. 1546.

the imposition of a new superior on a vassal without that vassal's consent. It sufficed for them to be enforced on the spot and ratified in Edinburgh.

It appears between the lines of Gordon's chronicle that the conspiracy to liquidate the Clan Gunn originated in about 1582, that the Gunns were supported by the Earl of Caithness and Mackay, and that five years of bungling and brutality achieved little. In 1585 the Earl of Sutherland took over the protection of the Abrach Mackays, leaving Uisdean, a rebellious vassal without a charter to his lands, the Chief of a fragmented clan. By then the Earl of Caithness had died, and was succeeded by a grandson not yet twenty years old. He was invited to Dunrobin, where he agreed to an alliance of Earls against the Gaelic peoples in their neighbourhood, in 1586. Uisdean could bring the Gunns no relief, and when they scattered before the Earls they were set upon by the Abrach Mackays.[1]

Mackay resisted until 1588, when the alliance of the two Earls was turned against himself. Then he made feudal submission to the Earl of Sutherland, the first Chief of Mackay ever to have done so. Sir Robert Gordon, who was eight years old at this time, recorded that 'a meeting was appointed between Earl Alexander and Mackay at Inverness. So having met there and conferred together, they appointed a second tryst at Elgin, where they passed a contract between them and made a perfect and final reconciliation in the month of November 1588.'[2] The dues for Strathnaver, which Uisdean had held for sixteen years without a charter since his father's death, were computed at £50,000 Scots. Earl Alexander released him from this debt. The Earl also offered Uisdean the hand of his daughter Jane in marriage, who must have been as much younger than Uisdean as his present wife was older than he; 'she being then fifteen years of age.'[3] Uisdean was made free to contract the first Gordon marriage in the family of the Chiefs of Mackay in December 1589, by means that are clothed in a discreet silence by her brother the chronicler.

It is noteworthy that while the most respectable alliances of Highland Chiefs could hardly escape generating families of bastards, incapable of inheriting their fathers' property, the

[1] Mackay 1906: 110-2. Gordon 1813: 182-4. *S.B.*, I: 149.
[2] Gordon 1813: 195. [3] Gordon 1813: 200.

Lowland nobility were unrestricted by the most conventional marriage ties, and yet remained legitimate. Thus, Jane Gordon had been formally married to the Earl of Bothwell, after a dispensation had been received from the Pope. The grounds for anulment were therefore invalid, while a second dispensation for her marriage with the Earl of Sutherland her cousin could have no greater validity than her first. If her daughter Jane could nevertheless be described as legitimate, it is questionable whether she could be Uisdean's lawful wife, or whether her children could take precedence over the issue of Uisdean's first marriage. But even this occurred.

The Earl of Sutherland had not sacrificed his daughter nor £50,000 Scots for nothing. Already, by February 1589, his new vassal Mackay was before Girnigo castle with his clansmen and a remnant of revengeful Gunns in his following. When they failed to capture this most impregnable stronghold, they sacked the town of Wick. The brother of the Earl of Caithness attempted a counter-raid during the summer and Uisdean descended on him from the heights of Brora. 'Uisdean Mackay being then at Dunrobin, was sent by Earl Alexander to make head against them, until he himself should come with greater forces. So Mackay, assembling speedily some five or six hundred of the inhabitants of Sutherland, with these he made haste towards the enemy, whom he followed with all possible diligence. And having used extraordinary celerity in his march, he overtook them, contrary to all expectation.'[1] Gordon's account of the military prowess of the Mackays turns suddenly from blame to praise, and sheds light on the antiquity of the tactics that Montrose used later in the Highlands with such effect. A new order of Gordon objectives becomes discernible. The private army of Gaels that they now possessed for the first time might be used to expropriate the Sinclair earldom of Caithness, before the Mackays were themselves destroyed, and Strathnaver integrated into Sutherland.

In the autumn of 1590 the Earl of Caithness himself attempted an invasion of the fertile strip of eastern Sutherland, and this time Uisdean was not at Dunrobin to oppose him, but in Strathnaver. So he marched east along the coast 'even to the gates of Thurso, and brought home a great booty without let

[1] Gordon 1813: 198.

or impediment.'[1] Beside the modern road that runs along the coast from Sutherland into Caithness stands a great rock, cleft in two. It marks the ancient boundary between Caithness and Strathnaver, and near to it is a hollow in the hills where the marauding Mackays were said to conceal their stolen cattle. It may have been at this time that they earned their bye-name *Clann Mhic Aoidh nan Creach* (Mackays of the Raids).

While Uisdean raided with impunity as Sutherland's vassal, the Earl of Caithness attempted to repair his past errors of judgment by making his separate peace with the Gordons, at Strathbogie in 1591.[1] He claimed that his aunt Elizabeth Sinclair was still Mackay's lawful wife, and that their child was his heir. But Uisdean's second wife had just given birth to a son. The hosts of the Earl of Caithness in Strathbogie gave him the macabre advice that he should seek his remedy on behalf of his aunt in a legal manner: this was written into the decreet-arbitral, and preserves the last surviving information about Elizabeth Sinclair.[2]

A further problem remained, resulting from the death of Robert Stewart, Bishop of Caithness and uncle of the Earl of Sutherland. He had survived every vicissitude of the Reformation and of his family's fortunes. He had conveyed the most commodious properties of the diocese to relatives who held them for his convenience. What they did not require themselves, they bartered profitably, as when Sutherland gave Caithness some of the church property in Caithness, in return for some of the Sinclair Earl's property in Sutherland.[3] The Bishop had succeeded in acquiring and preserving for life the priory and revenues of St Andrews, where he made his permanent home. But spiritual affairs had not monopolised his attention. He had also married a daughter of the Earl of Atholl who divorced him on grounds of impotence: although he was known to have begotten at least one illegitimate offspring. He inherited the earldom of Lennox after the murder of his brother the Regent; but he passed this to his nephew when James VI (who was his great-nephew) compensated him with the earldom of March.

In 1580 the General Assembly of the Church of Scotland had declared the office of diocesan bishop 'unlawful and without warrant in the Word of God', and had called on all who held it

[1] Gordon 1813: 204. [2] *S.B.*, I: 156. [3] Gordon 1813: 205.

to resign. The Earl of Sutherland visited his uncle the Bishop at St Andrews at this time, and received a fresh grant as a precaution.[1] It appears that the first presbyteries were erected at Inverness and Dingwall in 1581, but this example was not followed in the diocese of Caithness. Lord Burghley in England received a report at this time on the state of religious belief in Scotland. It contained the information that the majority in Sutherland were still Catholic.[1] The Countess Jane remained a Catholic until her death in 1628.[2]

In 1586 Bishop Robert Stewart died at St Andrews, among the friends described by Melville, 'who colluded with the revellers of the town to hold the ministry vacant, and in the meantime took up the stipend and spent the same at the golf, archery, good cheer.'[3] Bishop Robert was described by the editor of the Privy Council Register as 'nominal Bishop of Caithness since 1542', and it would be a hazardous undertaking to expound the content of the word 'nominal' in this context.[4]

Bishop Robert Stewart had enjoyed his prosperity through good sense joined to royal blood, and his nephew Earl Alexander of Sutherland lost the benefit of this royal connection with the Bishop's death. In 1594 Earl Alexander died also, and the restoration of the royal connection was left to his son.

This son, the offspring of Jane Gordon of Huntly and her cousin Alexander Gordon of Sutherland, was also the second cousin of James VI, through the King's Lennox grandfather whose sister was the Earl's grandmother. The young Earl of Sutherland was also the King's cousin through the Huntly stock: these baronial families were intensively inter-bred over a period of centuries. But neither Gordons nor Stewarts possessed the blood royal of Scotland, save by descent from the Norman baronial family of Bruce, after it had been consecrated in the veins of Robert I. This was the royal connection that it was necessary for the Earl of Sutherland to claim with James VI, and it was a fabrication.

A daughter of Robert I married William Sutherland, sometimes distinguished as fifth Earl of Sutherland, who died in about 1371. On her marriage, her brother David II bestowed a charter

[1] Hume Brown 1902, II: 206. [2] *S.B.*, II: 151. [3] Bentinck 1926: 149.
[4] *R.P.C.*, IV: 60n.

of regality upon the Earl and Countess, limited to the heirs of their bodies. But there was no such heir, and the daughter of the 'idiot' Earl whom Adam Gordon married descended from the second marriage of the fifth Earl, to Joanna of Menteith. The regality of Sutherland had lapsed, and James VI was hoaxed by the Gordons when he revived it in their favour. He was particularly partial to any claim of kinship through the Bruces, as his English cousins of that stock were to discover in 1603.[1] Yet policy, as well as sentiment, underlay his strengthening of Gordon power. He created Huntly a Marquess and pardoned his repeated treasons. He bestowed a charter of regality upon Sutherland, not confined to the possessions of the fourteenth-century earldom, but embracing the diocesan properties and 'the heritable sheriffship of Sutherland and Strathnaver which his father had gotten before from Huntly'; another of Gordon's inventions. But he did not exaggerate in recording 'the uniting of Strathnaver, Edderachillis and Durness to the earldom of Sutherland as a portion and part thereof.'[2]

James VI maintained the power of the Gordons, whom he knew to be concealed Catholics, as a counterweight to the power of the Calvinist party in Scotland. He also designed to employ them in their historical role as the scourge of the Gaels, whom it was the intention of James VI to destroy. The evidence for both of these statements of the King's motives will be given in sequence, and would sufficiently explain the new charter of regality to Sutherland. But according to the Gordon chronicler, who was the Earl of Sutherland's brother, James VI was also the victim of a hoax, through his weakness for cousins of Bruce descent, and through the help of Lord Elphinstone the Treasurer, whose daughter the Earl of Sutherland married. 'Alexander Elphinstone being then Treasurer of Scotland, John, Earl of Sutherland by his means took a new infeftment of the whole earldom of Sutherland, by resignation thereof into his Majesty's hands in the month of April 1601 years: not only confirming the old regality of the earldom of Sutherland granted by King David Bruce to William, the third of that name . . . but also containing divers other privileges.'[3]

One of these privileges was of an unexampled nature. The

[1] Grimble 1957: 161. [2] Gordon 1813: 243. *R.G.S.*, VI: no. 1170.
[3] Gordon 1813: 243.

Earl of Sutherland and his two younger brothers Sir Robert Gordon and Alexander had as yet no heirs. But their elder sister, married to Mackay, had already borne a son. It was therefore possible that a Celtic Chief might succeed to the new regality, just as a Gordon had acquired the earldom a century earlier. There was indeed this difference, that half of the regality's territorial area now consisted of lands that had formerly been the independent possessions of these Celtic Chiefs. It is sufficient evidence of the racial nature of the King's prejudices that he consented to bar the Celtic branch of the family from the succession. The earldom of Sutherland was never henceforth to be alienated from the surname of Gordon. Failing male heirs of the Earl and of his brothers Robert and Alexander, it was to pass to a collatoral branch of the Sutherland Gordons. If these should fail, the earldom was to pass to the house of Huntly that had never hitherto possessed it, a form of succession without descent which is perhaps unique in the annals of the European peerage.[1]

The enlargement of Sutherland's jurisdiction in the north was a fresh danger to the Earl of Caithness, who gave vent to his emotion in a hunting expedition through the Gunn country into western Strathnaver. Such an exercise was a martial display that could operate as the call-up of vassals for a rebellion in the Highlands, as late as the eighteenth century.[2] So it was interpreted in Strathnaver in 1601. The Earl of Caithness found his considerable host blocked at Kinbrace by Mackays from the north, Macleods of Assynt from the west, and Earl John with Munros from the south. By the slopes of Ben Griam which descend in a long parabola to Badenloch, the forces met where earlier and weaker victims, the Gunns, had suffered destruction after the Earl of Caithness had betrayed them. Mackay, whom the Earl had betrayed also, taunted him to fight. But his followers had tired of the notion of hunting and 'went away at break of day in a fearful confusion, fleeing and hurling together in such headlong haste that everyone increased the fear of his fellow companion.' The victors of the unfought battle amused themselves by erecting a heap of stones on the shoulder of Ben Griam which they called *Càrn Teichidh*, the Cairn of Flight.[3]

Mackay was next summoned, in January 1602, with his

[1] Gordon 1813: 243. [2] Ramsay 1888, II: 404-5. [3] Gordon 1813: 240-3.

superior the Earl of Sutherland to send a hundred men to assist Elizabeth of England in her Irish war.[1] At this time Hugh O'Neill held the last stronghold of Irish Gaeldom in Ulster, which fell early in 1602 at the decisive defeat of Kinsale. The Irish law was abolished, the schools were suppressed, the race reduced to serfdom. 'Fuar lem in oidhche seo d' Aodh' (Cold I reckon this night for Hugh), lamented a bard of the exquisite literature of lamentation that alone remained of Ulster.[2] Another bard accused the Scots of having supported the English assault on Ulster, but Mackay was not among them.

The following summer, Uisdean enjoyed another amenity of his altered status in the northern world. In August 1602 he took ship from Cromarty with the Earl of Sutherland, Sir Robert Gordon and Macleod of Assynt, to pay a social visit to the Earl of Orkney in Kirkwall.[3] The earldom had been bestowed by Queen Mary on an illegitimate half-brother whom Randolph had described to the English Queen as vain, worthless and full of evil. The Englishman's judgment was confirmed by the experience of the Orcadians whose ancient Norse society he had destroyed, and whose fertile islands he had reduced to poverty. This latest extension of Stewart tyranny had extended less heavily to Shetland, and it was in Orkney that Patrick Stewart, the second Earl, now resided.[4] He had built himself splendid palaces at Birsay and Kirkwall, in each of which Mackay and his neighbours from Assynt and Sutherland spent eight days.

The Chief of Mackay had witnessed the fate of Ulster from the vantage point of one who had received an invitation to attend. He saw something of the fate of Orkney as the guest of Earl Patrick himself. He was given his next opportunity to witness the process of genocide as it was being attempted in Lewis. Here James VI had drawn up his first scheme of expropriation in 1598 with the twelve men who became known as the Fife Adventurers; and had given Bishop Robert's nephew, Stewart of Lennox, a special commission of Lieutenancy over the north of Scotland with powers to help the Adventurers.[5] But this attempt failed because the Lewis islanders had not been prepared like the inhabitants of Ulster for colonisation: that is, they had not been defeated in battle, and the five or six

[1] *R.P.C.*, VI: 343. [2] Blacam 1929: 142, 147. [3] Gordon 1813: 248.
[4] Donaldson 1958: 10-2. [5] *R.P.C.*, V: 467-8, 480.

hundred hired troops of the Adventurers failed to defeat them.[1] After the Adventurers evacuated Lewis in 1602, James VI gave a fresh commission of Lieutenancy to Lennox, and another to Huntly, and divided their responsibilities carefully. He harangued a Parliament reluctant to co-operate, with a tirade about the racial inferiority of Hebrideans. He caused the Privy Council to command all Chiefs of Highland clans to appear before it and to find caution for keeping the peace.[2] At a time when the Adventurers themselves lacked enthusiasm, Mackenzie of Kintail gave James VI support for his project, and was rewarded by membership of the Privy Council. Here the matter rested when, in 1603, James VI inherited the throne of the Tudors.

In 1605, James VI and I was able to give his attention to the matter once more. Tormod Macleod of Lewis had travelled to London in a desperate attempt to dissuade the King, but the Adventurers poisoned the mind of James VI against Macleod: he was imprisoned in Edinburgh without trial for ten years.[3] When the next assault on Lewis also failed, the King's anger found noteworthy expression. He chose Huntly to be the instrument of his vengeance. Huntly was called upon to equip an expedition at his own expence, taking as his reward 'the whole North Isles except Skye and the Lewis in feu.' Huntly's response was that 'his Lordship offers to take in hand the service of settling the North Isles . . . and to put an end to that service by extirpation of the barbarous people of the Isles within a year.'[4] The Lords of the Privy Council were moved to record: 'anent the Lieutenancy, they think it likewise unreasonable that the King's power should be put in the hands of a subject to conquer lands to himself.'[5] In interpreting the motive behind this submission, it must be remembered that the royal power had not been exercised in Gaeldom by either of the Lieutenants for any other purpose for a century.

James VI responded by reminding his Lieutenant that his task was one of extermination. He wrote in May 1607 that Huntly's commission was 'the extirpating of the barbarous people in those bounds . . . and also that the said Marquess, before the expiring of the year, shall plant those Isles with

[1] Grant 1959: 188-200. [2] Mackenzie 1903: 210-2. [3] Grant 1959: 203.
[4] *R.P.C.*, VII: 361. [5] *R.P.C.*, VII: 342.

civil people.' That, added the King, did not include Gaels from the mainland, either 'Badenoch or Lochaber men.'[1] The mainland Chiefs, nevertheless, were called upon by the Privy Council to provide armed men and ammunition, and Uisdean was ordered with the Earl of Caithness, Macleod of Assynt, Ross of Balnagown and Munro of Foulis to attend at Trotternish in August 1608.[2] The following February, Uisdean and the other mainland Gaels were charged not to receive any fugitive islanders within their bounds.[3]

Whatever Uisdean's motive may have been for doing so, he defaulted, was denounced by the Privy Council for failing in his duty, and declared a rebel. It was a grave decision on Uisdean's part. He had enjoyed ample evidence of the advantages of supporting Edinburgh's policies, to which the career of his neighbour Mackenzie of Kintail provided corroboration. His family history told him emphatically of the dangers of any other course.[4]

Salvation of a sort came to the islanders, not through the belated sympathy of such as Mackay, certainly not through any spark of humanity in James VI: but through the greed of the Marquess of Huntly. The King had offered him lands in feu, and Huntly tried to bargain over the size of the feu-duties.[5] James VI revealed the nature of the leash by which he controlled the Gordons: he attacked Huntly for his Catholic convictions. The Fife Adventurers selected this impasse to cut their losses, selling their interest in Lewis to Mackenzie of Kintail. Mackenzie, in a Privy Council packed with Lowlanders bitterly hostile to the Irish Redshanks, had no difficulty in preventing the release of Macleod of Lewis from his prison.

But James VI modified his policy of extermination in 1609, as appears in a letter he wrote to the Privy Council in Scotland. His Gaelic policy had just achieved such a spectacular success in the southern Hebrides that he was able to relax his severity.[6] The King had launched an armament in the south at the same time as he had despatched Huntly in the north, composed of Lowland levies drawn from the garrisons of Ireland. It was commanded by Stewart of Ochiltree, accompanied by Andrew Knox, Bishop of the Isles, who summoned the Chiefs of the

[1] *R.P.C.*, VII: 525. [2] *R.P.C.*, VIII: 740. [3] *R.P.C.*, VIII: 746.
[4] *R.P.C.*, VIII: 749-51. [5] *R.P.C.*, VII: 523. [6] *R.P.C.*, VIII: lviii.

Isles to meet the King's commissioner on the island of Mull. It was the suggestion of the Bishop himself that the Chiefs should be inveigled aboard a ship on the pretext that they were to hear a sermon from himself. Once aboard, they were carried to the mainland and imprisoned. In August 1609 they purchased their freedom by signing the statutes of Iona. These provided that masterless vagabonds were to be expelled from the islands, beggars to be treated as thieves. The greater number of Gaels could be fitted *ad hoc* into either category. Bards were to be first placed in the stocks and then driven from the country; a measure that struck at the popular culture of the Gaels, even if it was not aimed to destroy Gaelic literature and learning. Every gentleman was to send his eldest son to school in the Lowlands; a measure designed to create a separate class of alien landowners over the Gaelic peasantry of the Highlands.[1]

The provision of the statutes for the planting of churches and ministers raises the question of peoples' beliefs in those areas still untouched by the ministry fifty years after the abolition of the Catholic religion. Huntly was a hardly concealed Catholic: his aunt, the dowager Countess of Sutherland, made no secret of her religion. Earl John was later placed in confinement on suspicion of being a Catholic, while his brother Alexander never wavered from the Catholic faith. Only Sir Robert Gordon seems to have treated religion as a hazardous but rewarding department of politics, as his uncle Bishop Robert Stewart had once taught. In April 1581 the General Assembly proposed the erection of Presbyteries in the far north, but they did not reach beyond Ross-shire.[2] In 1597 the General Assembly appointed a deputation to visit the northern Highlands,[3] but nothing appears to have come of it: which may not have surprised this body, since it was also examining the Earl of Sutherland's hospitality to Popish emissaries, one of whom was Huntly's uncle James Gordon, whom it charged Sutherland to deliver up on pain of rebellion.[4]

Throughout the second half of the sixteenth century there are fugitive references to a John, Farquhar and Donald Reid, as exhorters, readers and ministers in the Mackay country. A George and William Mernis were reported to be serving in

[1] *R.P.C.*, IX: 24. [2] *Presbytery Records of Inverness* 1896: vi.
[3] Mackenzie 1886: 417. [4] *S.B.*, I: 138.

Durness, one of whom was still styled minister there five years after his death. But these provide evidence that an effort was being made to replace the Catholic ministry and even to carry the Christian message to areas which had received no ministry since the days of the Celtic church.[1] The zeal which finally crowned their efforts with success was that of the Munros from Ross-shire. A Provost of Tain wrote in 1605: 'the greatest number of the said ministry are Munroes.'[2] Robert Munro was already Minister of Durness in 1603, and he was to remain in that extreme north-west corner of Britain for nearly thirty years.

James VI was at least as concerned to restore bishops as to plant ministers, and in 1604 he appointed Alexander Forbes from Aberdeenshire to be Bishop of Caithness.[3] In 1610 the General Assembly itself restored episcopacy, and in the following year Bishop Forbes was appointed to the Scottish Privy Council so that he could give advice on 'the incivil and barbarous behaviour of the most part of our subjects of Caithness, Sutherland and Strathnaver.'[4] One report declared that 'the chief cause of the frequent . . . murders and slaughters committed within the bounds of Caithness, Sutherland, Strathnaver and Ross is reset given to the authors of the said crimes by the noblemen, barons and gentlemen within the said bounds.'[5]

Whatever the personal relations between Uisdean and the new Bishop, he made formal acknowledgement at this time of the ancient friendship between the Chiefs of Mackay and of Forbes, overshadowed by the Gordons of Huntly in Aberdeenshire. Whereas Mackay had designated himself by this name alone in the treaty which he signed with the Earl of Sutherland in 1588, he arranged to be designated 'Mackay-Forbes' in the royal charter which he obtained for his lands in 1608. He also adopted the coat-of-arms of Forbes with a heraldic difference.[6]

He was designated in the language of his country *Uisdean Dubh na Tuaigh*, Dark Uisdean of the Battle Axe. But soon after he reached the age of fifty he laid aside his weapons, and left his son to fulfil the vassal's task of baiting the Earl of Caithness on the instructions of his superior of Sutherland. Uisdean himself kept open house at Tongue. 'He bred and brought up the young men still in his own company, that by daily conversing

[1] *Fasti*, VII: 106. [2] Crawford MS. [3] Bentinck: 1926: 165.
[4] *R.P.C.*, IX: 237. [5] *R.P.C.*, VIII: 480. [6] *S.B.*, I: 170. Mackay 1906: 412.

together familiarly, they might accustom themselves mutually to love one another.' So wrote Sir Robert Gordon in his surprising encomium on the Chief of Mackay.[1] This company was joined by a remarkable guest.

There is no record of a piper in the household of a Chief of Mackay earlier than the reference to 'Donaldo McCruimien lie pyper' in that of Uisdean in May 1612.[2] The sudden distinction of Mackays in the art of pibroch in the seventeenth century requires a particular explanation, just as the disappearance of Donald Mór MacCrimmon from Skye was a mystery in need of solution. This brief, fortunate reference to Uisdean's piper, confirms the circumstantial evidence, and was the first of a chain of fortunate events that culminated in preservation of the MacCrimmon art itself by Mackay musicians of a later century.[3]

The art for which the Mackays were to become so famous reached them in the seventeenth century, and did not originate with their race. The bagpipes were indigenous among the peoples of Britain and of many other parts of Europe. Barbour's account of Bannockburn did not mention the bagpipe among the musical instruments heard at that battle, whereas it was heard at Harlaw in 1411, nearly a century later. Perhaps a piece of fifteenth-century pipe music of the Munros called *Blar bealach nam brog* can be called the earliest surviving embryo of 'pibroch', the new art form of theme and variations given to the instrument by the Gaels. The masterpiece of pibroch is appropriately a salute to the music it superseded, *The Lament for the Harp Tree*. The first great composer and exponent of pibroch was Donald Mór MacCrimmon, who became piper to Mackay. He had raised this form of composition to new heights of invention with the salute to Macleod, *Faillte nan Leodach*, which he performed at Dunvegan in 1601.[4] He also composed *Cille Chriosd*, when it is said that a party of enemies were burned to death in a church while this music was played outside. This is said also to have been the cause why Donald Mór was forced to flee from Skye and to seek asylum in Strathnaver.

Meanwhile Mackay's son Donald became involved in an intricate and bizarre plot to ruin the Earl of Caithness, by proving his complicity with Arthur Smith, a false coiner. This

[1] Gordon 1813: 302. [2] Mackay 1906: 414. [3] Maclean 1953: 283.
[4] Nicholson 1930: 201.

man had previously been apprehended in Edinburgh and convicted. But 'during the time of his imprisonment . . . he made a lock of such exquisite invention and ingenious device that the like could not be found again. This was presented to the King's Majesty as a rare and curious piece of work', and James VI could not bring himself to let such an artist perish.[1] Arthur Smith thereupon escaped, and by 1612 the Privy Council learned of the trickle of false coins that were being found 'in the north parts of the kingdom.'[2] The Earl of Sutherland was in France at the time, while his brother Sir Robert Gordon guided his Scottish affairs, and Sir Robert lost no time in tracing the responsibility to the Earl of Caithness. Arthur Smith was indeed in Thurso (not in Wick or in Girnigo, as might be expected, had he been employed by the Earl of Caithness), and Sir Robert despatched Donald Mackay to arrest him there, with a junior Gordon in attendance. In May 1612 these rode into Thurso where they apprehended Smith: and Sir Robert took care to leave it on record that it was Strathnaver men who murdered him, while the Gordon attendant was not present. 'During this tumult, Arthur Smith was slain by the Strathnaver men, who had him in their hands at the town's end, when they first heard the noise, being loth that he should have been retaken.' A nephew of the Earl of Caithness was also killed in the skirmish, and Sir Robert placed in the mouth of this other dead witness words that proved his uncle's guilt.[3] But there is no corroborative evidence to support the accusation.

Sir Robert waited in Edinburgh to take the appropriate steps against the Earl of Caithness as soon as he heard the results of Donald Mackay's exploit. The Earl, vexed by the death of his nephew, and 'that such a disgraceful contempt, as he thought, should have been offered unto him in the heart of his own country', brought a summons against Gordon and Donald Mackay, and 'sent a gentleman in all haste to court, to inform his Majesty against his adversaries, and to excuse himself; which, when Sir Robert Gordon understood, he posted into England, lest the King should be sinistrously informed against him or his friends. Sir Robert arrived before the other at court.'[4] This outstanding energy was one of the secrets of Sir Robert

[1] Gordon 1813: 279. [2] *R.P.C.*, IX: 352. [3] Gordon 1813: 282-3.
[4] Gordon 1813: 284-5.

Gordon's success: he was not only 'before the other' on horse-back on numerous occasions, but he also took the trouble to commit voluminous (if not always convincing) evidence to paper in defence of his actions. As his writings are a magpie's nest of unacknowledged quotations from other writers, it is evident that he even found time for extensive reading also.

Sir Robert Gordon did not succeed in ruining the Earl of Caithness through the Arthur Smith case, though this was not due to any serious error of judgment on his part, while the attempt provided invaluable experience for the next venture. One reason for failure was the King's decision that the dispute between the Earl and the Gordons should be tried in Edinburgh, not by law, but among friends.[1] Caithness insisted that the Earl of Sutherland and the Chief of Mackay should be summoned to the arbitration: he scorned to deal with a younger brother and a son. This was refused on the grounds that the Earl of Sutherland had been abroad during the foray in Thurso, while Mackay was no longer fit to travel. The Earl of Caithness betrayed a *folie de grandeur* which was to serve him ill in his approaching contest with Sir Robert Gordon. 'It galled him to the heart to be thus overmatched, as he said, by seconds and children; for so it pleased him to call his adversaries.'[2]

The negotiations in Edinburgh petered out.[3] It was one of those incidents that support a view that jurisdiction in Edinburgh was a test of the power of the two parties in dispute: where these were too evenly matched, there could be no result. In December 1613, Sir Robert strengthened his own hand by obtaining a pardon from the King for Donald Mackay and the Gordons involved in the Thurso murders. But the Earl of Caithness secured a rival success by laying information before the Archbishop of St Andrews that Sutherland was a Catholic, and thus securing his removal to Edinburgh under a cloud.[4]

In 1614 Caithness was provided with the opportunity to make his triumph complete. The illegitimate Stewart dynasty that had been planted by Queen Mary in Orkney raised a rebellion, and Caithness received a royal commission to apprehend Earl Patrick and his natural son Robert, and bring them to Edinburgh. By the 25th August he was reporting from Kirkwall: 'this day we

[1] Gordon 1813: 285. [2] Gordon 1813: 285. [3] *R.P.C.*, IX: 413-4.
[4] Gordon 1813: 298.

are busy about landing of the great piece of ordnance, that we may batter both the castle and the other houses which annoy us and our men in the town, and thus make our service the shorter.'[1] The Earl appears to have delighted in letter-writing in an age when not all of the Scottish nobility were literate. Most of his papers were destroyed, in circumstances that will be examined, but the few letters that have escaped show him to have possessed the fluency of habitual letter-writers, and an elegance of hand, striking in any age.[2]

After Caithness had taken Earl Patrick's palace in Kirkwall, he wrote in wonder: 'I assure your lordship it is one of the greatest houses in Britain, for I will bring with me to your lordship cannon balls both broken like golf balls upon the castle, and cloven in two halves'.[3] The Earl's comment, the earliest extant upon Earl Patrick's palace, is amplified by the modern verdict that it is 'possibly the most mature and accomplished piece of Rennaissance architecture left in Scotland.'[4] It may have inspired the Earl of Caithness in the extensions to Castle Girnigo, which he already called Castle Sinclair: and these in turn may have contributed to his fatal insolvency. For the present, he was readmitted to the Privy Council with lengthy encomiums, reimbursements and pardons.[5]

Perhaps, in his hour of triumph, the somewhat guileless Earl overlooked the omens of what occurred in September 1614. Dark Uisdean of the Battleaxe died, leaving as his successor the first Chief of Mackay who was half Gordon in blood, and more than half Gordon in upbringing.

[1] Sinclair 1899: 116. [2] Gordonstoun MS. 68. [3] Sinclair 1899: 119.
[4] Marwick 1952: 36. [5] *R.P.C.*, X: 278, 289-91.

4

An Imp of That Same Stock

DONALD, the new Chief of Mackay, lost his father before he was twenty-four years old, and had never known his grandfather Aodh. Of his Gordon relatives, his uncle Sir Robert outlived him, while his grandmother the Countess Jane was still vigorously alive until Donald was thirty-eight years old. Their influence upon him is attested by his correspondence with both: his first surviving letter to Sir Robert Gordon is dated 1612, when Donald was twenty-one years old. No correspondence survives with his own father, neither is there any evidence that Uisdean was able to compose a letter.[1]

In his youth Donald was made a party to the military policies of the Gordons in Caithness and in Lochaber, and was initiated into the mysteries of their legal processes in Edinburgh. He was made a brother at law with Lord Mackenzie of Kintail, a year after Mackenzie had been raised to the peerage. These two officially dependable Gaels were appointed justices of the peace for Inverness and Cromarty under James VI's plan to extend the English system of local government to the Highlands.[2] In February 1611 Lord Mackenzie died, but not before Donald Mackay had married his eldest daughter, Barbara. The new Chief of Mackay succeeded in circumstances apparently more favoured than any of his predecessors and conducted himself in awareness of the cause, as a junior relative of the Gordons of Sutherland.

That first winter of Donald's chiefship, the winter of triumph for the Earl of Caithness, was one of anxiety to the house of

[1] Gordonstoun MS. 9. [2] *R.P.C.*, IX: 79.

Sutherland. Earl John was in ward in Edinburgh, charged with being a Catholic, a faith that his mother in Sutherland proclaimed openly. Sir Robert attended his wife's confinement at her father's home in Salisbury, waiting to intercede with James VI for his mother and brother, poised to intercept any approach to the King by the Earl of Caithness. That winter, he recorded ominously, 'there fell out great abundance of snow (more than ordinary) throughout all Scotland, which storms continued all the spring, even until the month of May next ensuing, whereby the most part of all the horses, nolt and sheep of the kingdom did perish; but chiefly in the north.'[1] Sir Robert's child was born and died: his sister Lady Jane Mackay died, scarcely six months after her husband Uisdean: the Earl of Caithness arrived in England to see the King.

From Edinburgh the Earl of Sutherland wrote in great distress to his brother in England on the 23rd February 1615. 'I may not with reason urge you to come to court again, but if it please God your lady recover health and your own leisure could serve to take an start to London, albeit your stay were but for two days only, to try what Caithness have done, for so far we heard his reward will not be so great as he looked for . . .' It was sufficient, in that he had undermined the unsavoury reputation attributed to him, by presenting himself for personal inspection: always an important factor in the favour of James VI.[2] Sir Robert rushed to court 'to prevent the Earl of Caithness's aims and machinations', but he was too late. The Earl received a royal pardon for any offence he might have given in the recent quarrel, just as Mackay and his Gordon accomplice had already done.[3]

Donald Mackay reached Edinburgh on the same day that Earl John received this ill news of the Earl of Caithness out of England. Mackay brought his uncle a report on the affairs of Sutherland and Strathnaver, so that the Earl wrote to Sir Robert in England, 'I remit the particulars of these countries to Mackay's letter.' The only outstanding issue was the 'settling of the marches betwixt Mackay and me', and Earl John mentioned this without perturbation. Indeed, he was anxious that some honour should be bestowed on his Mackay kinsmen, and

[1] Gordon 1813: 309-11. [2] *S.B.*, II: 113.
[3] Gordon 1813: 321.

he suggested that Mackay's brother John might be knighted by the King on his return home from abroad. 'My own opinion is that you use your means to see if you can get John Mackay made a knight before his homecoming. I remit the particulars anent him to his brother Mackay's own letter, not doubting but you will have an care of him and haste him home, seeing all his friends in the north think that he is dead.'[1]

The Chief's younger brother was an indifferent correspondent, it appears, though he possessed the neatest hand of any of his family: nor was he in any hurry to curtail his travels. In January 1616 he was writing to Sir Robert Gordon from Saumur, asking for money because everything was so expensive.[2] He wrote again from Edinburgh in September, but by then his elder brother had received the knighthood.[3] This was a part of the Chief's reward for his adherence to the house of Sutherland in the fresh emergency that had occurred.

Earl John's advice to Sir Robert to haste John Mackay home was a reflection of his own nostalgia for Dunrobin, perched between the hills of his earldom and the Moray Firth, for Dornoch whose church 'had been well repaired ere now, and many good turns done that never will be done in my absence.' He begged Sir Robert 'to show the King's Majesty of my dutiful behaviour in all things the ministry hath put to my charge' and how 'I daily haunt the preachings and have subscribed sundry articles at the ministers' desires.' Earl John could not, it appears, pretend to his brother that he had been converted. But he longed for home, and for one brief spring he was granted his desire. It was the spring following that winter of snow-storms, and Earl John wrote from Dunrobin in May 1615: 'such an year was never seen with us. Many will perish in these countries through famine.' There was no need for Sir Robert to return north. 'The marches betwixt Mackay and me is continued while summer next, in respect of this evil and stormy summer that men may not stay in the hills for storm.' Mackay had also returned from Edinburgh, to continue his attendance on the Earl. 'Mackay and I dwelleth this winter in Dornoch if I get leave to stay at home. The whole gentlemen of the country will dwell there also, so by time we think to make the town better.' Earl John concluded by asking his brother to send north the

[1] *S.B.*, II: 115-7. [2] Gordonstoun MS. 25. [3] Gordonstoun MS. 26.

finest virginals he could buy, 'seeing my bairns are learning to play and sing.'[1]

But in September 1615 the Earl of Sutherland 'sickened at Dunrobin from whence he was transported to Dornoch, where he died and was buried with his ancestors, leaving his eldest son John (a child of six years and six months) to undergo the miseries of of nonage.' Sir Robert Gordon wrote that his dead brother 'was exceedingly beloved by the inhabitants of his country, especially by the common people, unto whom he had been a loving father and a careful master.'[2] It is possible to understand why Earl John should have been remembered locally with affection, by reading his letters: it is equally understandable that his reputation should have been enhanced in retrospect by contrast with that of Sir Robert Gordon, who now arrived to rule as Tutor of Sutherland.

According to the Tutor, the late Earl had died 'overburdened with debt',[2] and the Earl's last letters made frequent mention of this. His religious persecution had contributed to this, but so also had the fraudulent transactions of his forbears. Earl John had recognised this in his last letter to Sir Robert: 'the difficulty that is found in this action is the gift of bastardy which is the ground of our gift of nonentry. It [is] naught worth, seeing that bastardy was disponed in the Queen's minority, and was revoked by Act of Parliament in her majority. So you must be careful to find remedy hereof, viz. you must obtain of the King's Majesty an gift of the said bastardy, or else an ratification of his Highness's mother's deed.'[3] Not even the charter of regality had been able to still the fear of the Gordons that their title to Strathnaver might one day be exploded, and the means by which they had gained possession of it exposed. The fact that the Tutor was worried by this problem at the time of his brother's death, may explain his treatment of Mackay on his return to Sutherland.

Earl John had mentioned Mackay's intention of wintering at Dornoch, and his wish that the gentry might be encouraged to follow this example. The Earl had also mentioned the family debts. It required no sinister motive for Mackay to have bought a house in Dornoch, to have paid in cash for the estate and jointure of the widowed Countess, or to have invested in other

[1] *S.B.*, II: 118-21. [2] Gordon 1813: 313. [3] *S.B.*, II: 119.

property within the earldom. But it seemed otherwise to the new Tutor when he arrived there in December 1615, to shatter the amity between Gordon and Mackay. Sir Robert told Mackay that he would hinder 'any man to purchase lands in Sutherland, except the natural inhabitants of the country.'[1] This ignored the fact that Mackay's forbears had owned land within the Sutherland earldom long before the first Gordon set foot in it. Sir Robert told his nephew and vassal: 'they should join their forces together against their common enemy the Earl of Caithness, that so they might be the more able to resist him in this alteration of affairs, and get such conditions from him, both together and jointly, as he would grant to neither of them severally.' He also reminded Mackay that he was half-Gordon himself and 'that the greatest honour Mackay had was to be descended of that house and to be a branch thereof.' The young Chief 'not only gave over all the possessions he had in Sutherland, but also promised to join with him in all things which concerned the good estate of the house of Sutherland.'[1] Mackay had not apprehended that if ever the Earl of Caithness were to be ruined by the Gordons, it would be his turn next.

Armed with this undertaking from the Chief whose clan was necessary to carry out any act of violence which the Gordons might plan, the Tutor made researches for a pretext to replace the Arthur Smith incident. He chose an episode that had occurred in November 1615 at Dounreay near the Strathnaver-Caithness border, where some corn had been fired. The property upon which this arson had occurred belonged originally to Sinclairs of Dounreay and Dunbeath, and had passed to Lord Forbes through his wife, the sister of the last Sinclair laird of Dounreay. This Lord Forbes was described by Spalding as a Chief much decayed, 'an naked life-renter of an small part and portion of his old estates and living of Forbes.'[2] This may account for his residence upon his wife's property. The Tutor wrote that 'the Earl of Caithness took in evil part that another than himself should obtain the inheritance of a Sinclair in Caithness': thus defining his own emotions, when Mackay had made a purchase in Sutherland. When the cornyard of Sandside on the Dounreay estate went up in flames, Caithness suggested that tenants of

[1] Gordon 1813: 326. [2] Spalding 1850: 167.

Mackay might be guilty, but Sir Robert Gordon rapidly secured evidence that incriminated the Earl of Caithness himself.'[1] All seem to have agreed that the fire was caused by Gunns, of the dispossessed clan with particular grounds for wishing to be revenged on the house of Caithness. Corn belonging to Lord Forbes was burnt without doubt, whoever was to blame: and Gordon stated that Forbes could never have prosecuted his action without Gordon support. 'Without them, the Lord Forbes could do little herein.'[2]

He related that the evidence, connecting the Earl of Caithness with an arson committed by Gunns, was found in the following manner. A Gunn came to the estate of his younger brother Sir Alexander Gordon of Navidale, the oasis beneath the great cliffs of the Ord that marked the boundary between the two earldoms. This man said the Gunns had committed their arson on the Earl's instructions, and asked for protection in return for giving evidence. Such protection was difficult to give to a witness who confessed that he was an accessory: but Sir Robert states that he gave it. He then rode to Edinburgh with Mackay and Lord Forbes, where he was in time to prevent the King's earlier pardon to the Earl of Caithness from passing the seals 'until this matter were tried.'[2] Mackay and Forbes brought the action against Caithness before the Privy Council.[3]

Perhaps Mackay had already made his bargain with Forbes by which the estate of Dounreay passed into his hands. His reward from the Tutor of Sutherland followed immediately. Sir Robert took Mackay with him to London and 'made his nephew known to the King and Prince, by whom he was graciously used and knighted by the King at Theobalds, who withal desired him to do his duty to the house of Sutherland, seeing that by them he had the honour to appertain to his Majesty.'[4] If this was another reference to the supposed Bruce connection, as is most probable, it was the reverse of the truth. While the house of Sutherland did not descend from the sister of David II, the Chiefs of Mackay did descend from Robert II through their forbear Elizabeth, daughter of the Lord of the Isles.

James VI had created hundreds of knights since he came to

[1] Gordon 1813: 330. [2] Gordon 1813: 334. [3] *R.P.C.*, X: 490-2, 771, 773.
[4] Gordon 1813: 335.

England, more than Elizabeth Tudor in the whole of her long reign. There is not even an official record of all of his creations, including that of Sir Donald Mackay. But this young Celtic Chief, 'of a swarthy complexion, having very black hair, head and beard'[1] may have given him especial satisfaction. Here was a Gael, weaned by his Gordon cousins from 'the Irish barbarity' to 'the English civility,' an embodiment of the success of the Celtic policy of James VI especially pleasing to his eye because he 'was comely, firm and very portlike.'[1] Perhaps the King put his arm round his neck or pinched his cheek as he used to do at this time to test the responses of the attractive young men whom his courtiers paraded so purposefully before him.[2] It is even possible that the twenty-five-year-old Chief of Mackay was the Gordon candidate in this most competitive field, though it is perhaps unlikely that the worldly-wise Sir Robert Gordon could have made so unsuitable a choice. For Mackay's emotional responses, though extremely positive, lay in more conventional directions, as he demonstrated as soon as he had returned to Edinburgh.

Here the newly dubbed knight fell into the company of Mary Lindsay, daughter of the 11th Earl of Crawford, 'a sad spendthrift.' Dissipation had, in fact, become the family occupation: the 12th Earl earned the reputation of the 'prodigal' Earl and was succeeded by an Earl described as 'wild, prodigal and tyrannical.' Of their womenfolk, the only daughter of the 12th Earl ran away with a common jockey at the age of twelve, while her aunt Mary Lindsay was in 1610 'ravished and away took' by a servant of the household.[3] In August 1616 Sir Donald, Chief of Mackay, a married man, sailed out of Leith with Mary Lindsay in Thomas Anderson's barque.

Mackay's wife had just borne him another son when he reached Strathnaver with Mary Lindsay, and she was living in Durness. Mackay insisted that the child was not his own, and treated Lady Barbara Mackay with the severity of an injured husband. She sent this account of what followed to the Privy Council, or it was sent in her name. 'There is many that, although they abuse their bodies in that filthy and detestable vice of whoredom, yet they entertain their wives with all shows of love and kindness. Nevertheless he has so far given over

[1] B.M. Add MS. 7083. [2] *Nugae Antiquae*, I: 382. [3] *G.E.C.*, III, 516-7.

himself to the pleasures of his filthy lust and to the following of his own humours in that point, that he has entered in most violent, inhuman and detestable courses against the said complainer his lawful spouse . . . In the month of August last, the said complainer being then lying bedfast in her house of Durness . . . and being but . . . days delivered of a bairn unto him, he without pity or compassion . . . caused lift the said complainer out of the bed where she lay, transported her out of the chamber where she lay to another house without a roof, where he has made her a close prisoner.'[1]

Even if this was overstated, a great deal of it was true by Mackay's own admission. Treating the affair casually in his first letter to the Tutor after his return, from Durness in September, Mackay discussed the unreliability of mails and the business of the Earl of Caithness before remarking: 'the Clan Kenzie and I is likely not to sort well anent my wife.' He added that she had been brought 'to bed of an boy which by all reason and likelihood I have nothing ado with.' Then he turned to discuss the current question of the bishopric of Caithness.[2] It is significant that the estrangement between Mackay and his wife did not date from the arrival of Mary Lindsay in Strathnaver, as Sir Robert heard confirmed by a correspondent in Easter Ross. 'I doubt not but ye have heard of the misfortunate trouble renewed and fallen forth again betweixt Mackay and his wife, who was delivered of an son, the which Mackay refuses to be his own.' But even if his wife were guilty, this could not render the presence of Mary Lindsay innocent. 'Our whole friends regrets this unhappy enterprise that Mackay has taken on him in bringing with him to Strathnaver the Earl of Crawford's sister; in doing whereof he has lost many friends, and in special, the Kirk of Scotland cries out terrible on him.'[3]

So did his grandmother, the aged Countess of Sutherland. 'One thing I write with grief of heart,' she confided to her son the Tutor, 'your sister's son Mackay's home-bringing an sister of the Earl of Crawford to his great disgrace, loss of the Chancellor and his alliance, and (that which is worst) hurt of conscience. If he might have proven any cause of partesing against his wife (as I am in doubt of it) this beastly course has taken that away, and I hear her friends think to intend partesing

[1] *R.P.C.*, XI: 2. [2] Gordonstoun MS. 23. [3] *S.B.*, II: 122.

against him, and so cause her to break her liferent. He has not come to this country since his coming from England, neither received your brother nor I any advertisement from him except at his first landing, that he was come home. I pray God send him an better advisement nor I hear he is of.'[1] But the man whom the Countess described as 'your brother', that is, Sir Alexander Gordon of Navidale, seems to have remained loyal to Mackay.

Alexander Gordon was a Catholic, which may largely account for his remaining quietly in Navidale. While Sir Robert wrote to him of kings and courtiers, Sir Alexander would reply in such vein as this. 'There is an universal fever in these parts, wheron great death follows. We have lost two good fellows in that sickness, Alexander Mac William Mac Ian Mac Kenneth, and Ivor Mac Connichie, whereof I am sorry, yet the will of God must be done.' This he mentioned in November 1616, before passing to a local dispute in which he had used the judicial offices of Mackay. 'I convened the gentlemen of the country before Mackay (who was here for the time)'. Evidently the two men lived in close amity, which appears also in Sir Alexander's concern for Mackay's reputation. 'I doubt not but ye have heard ere now how Mackay took away with him an sister of the Earl of Crawford's. I am sorry he should have lost so good an fame as he had for so wild an cause. Advertise me how he is thought of there for it, or if his Majesty has heard of it. He thinks to put her away shortly.' This has the appearance of an inspired leak, especially as Sir Alexander, alone of any of these correspondents, knew the whereabouts of Mary Lindsay. 'She is great with child and remains as yet in the isle of Loch ?Loyal. He repairs noways to his married wife, nor thinks not to do. My Lord of Kintail and his friends thinks hard of the misusage of his sister. Mackay thinks to get divorcement, and they think to pay him with recompensation. They are under trysting after Andrewsmas.'[2]

Mackay informed his uncle the Tutor that it was in July 1616, while he was in Edinburgh, that he had received 'advertisment' of his wife's infidelity, 'whereof I thought very ill.' He confessed that 'in the meantime I fell in fantasy with an sister of the Earl of Crawford called Mistress Mary . . . so that the

[1] *S.B.*, II: 124. [2] *S.B.*, II: 126-8.

gentlewoman became with child.'[1] While Mary cowered in Strathnaver, awaiting a child whose paternity Mackay claimed, and Barbara lived confined in Durness on 'some little bere bread and water', with a child whose paternity Mackay disowned, the Privy Council added its verdict to those that had been given already.

James VI, Mackay was reminded, had been 'graciously pleased to confer unto him some degrees of honour whereof none of his predecessors were ever capable, and of which he himself has proven most ingrate and unworthy.' The Lords of the Privy Council found that Mackay 'in the month of August last brought with him to his bounds and country the said Mary Lindsay, placed her in the house of John Mac Angus Ruadh his kinsman, where he kept her the space of twenty days, and that thereafter he brought her to his own house of Durness,' from which he evicted his own wife. They ordered Mackay to the Tolbooth, there to remain at his own expense during their pleasure. To this charge there was added the sum of 2000 merks, the price of Sir Donald's remission for his adultery.[2] Mackay had received timely warning that 'the English civility' was a hazardous and expensive way of life.

A letter to the Tutor from Edinburgh shows him to have been briefly subdued by self-pity and pious thoughts.[3] But he was soon freed. He reconciled himself to his wife, who continued to bear children of unquestioned paternity until she was the mother of six. Mary Lindsay, having borne a son to Mackay, was heard of no more. He arranged to sell some lands on the west coast to pay his debts, and gave Sir Robert notice of his intentions in April 1618. 'I have gathered all my debts to one, and . . . I am resolved to sell the lands of Edderachillis by-west Laxford, with this year's salmon, which will pay all my debts. The Tutor of Kintail and I is in speaking for the lands, so that I have given promise to him, ere Whitsunday either to sell the lands to him by your advice, or else to cause your worship to relieve him of his cautionary. Therefore I will request your worship to provide the ten thousand pounds against Whitsunday, and to buy the land yourself . . . Otherwise I will be forced to sell that land to the Tutor.' Pounds Scots were

[1] Gordonstoun MS. 43. [2] *R.P.C.*, XI: 2-3. XII: 293.
[3] Gordonstoun MS. 42.

presumably meant, when Sterling was not mentioned.[1]

Sir Donald, the first Chief to obtain a title other than that of Mackay, the first to write letters in English and to possess Gordon blood, was also the first on record as having treated *Duthaich 'Ic Aoidh* as a disposable asset, to be sold in lots in order to pay personal debts incurred far beyond its borders.

An expence that Mackay incurred at the end of 1618 was of a more traditional nature, occasioned by the marriage of his sister Mary to Sir Hector, brother of Munro of Foulis.[2] It had already been reported to Dunrobin that 'Mackay and the Laird of Foulis are fallen in exceeding great.'[3] The wedding was celebrated at the New Year in Tongue, and immediately it was concluded, Mackay departed south to Rossal in the Abrach country, 'almost healthless', as he confessed, from drinking healths. 'Please you that my sister Mary is married to Hector Munro of Clynes,' he wrote to Sir Robert from there on the 4th January 1619. But he had more serious news to broach: he had arranged for his other sister to marry a Sinclair, a kinsman of the Earl of Caithness. 'Anna is shortly to be contracted with Brimms,' he stated in the blunt manner characteristic of him, 'which you shall show my lady your mother. I will seek her ladyship's help to pay the dowry; as for your own I doubt not of.' He concluded by attributing his healthless condition to 'drinking your health oft.'[4]

This news aggravated a situation already tense. Sir Robert Gordon had once again set the stage for the downfall of the Earl of Caithness. A charge of arson had been laid against him in Edinburgh, while Gunn witnesses rehearsed their evidence at Dunrobin. The lively prejudices of James VI had been nursed, and his pardon stopped at the seals. Mackay's disgraceful behaviour with Mary Lindsay had not been exploited, except perhaps in a way that encouraged him to put some of his lands on the market. For if the King should grant a commission of fire and sword against Caithness, it would have to be executed, and only clan Mackay could execute it unless Sir Robert called in outside assistance.

But even before Sir Robert received the jocular news of Anna Mackay's proposed marriage to Sinclair of Brimms, he was suspicious as to Mackay's loyalty. It appears that Sir Robert

[1] *S.B.*, II: 136. [2] Reay MS. 8/1. [3] *S.B.*, II: 123. [4] Gordonstoun MS. 89.

made a practice of intercepting letters, and did not hesitate to complain to his mother of what he found in them. This must be concluded from the fact that the Countess wrote to Mackay, demanding an explanation for the disloyalty of which he was accused. 'The world shall know the contrary,' he replied to his grandmother sharply, 'in testimony whereof, I am most willing that all alleged particulars be settled by the friends and oversman already chosen by Sir Robert and me.' Mackay was becoming fretful of the honour of being half-Gordon. 'I pray your ladyship to remember what travail, troubles and crosses your ladyship had to bring my house to the obligation of duty and blood that the Earl of Sutherland, your ladyship's grandchild, has me at this day. Likewise your ladyship should be as careful to see the same continue as your ladyship was then to bind us in friendship . . . We have all the honour as to be descended of your ladyship, therefore none should be so careful to see the same settled as your ladyship. But the wrong way it is to settle by bosting me. For the world knows that I am an imp of that same stock that himself is of.' He loosed one final barb: 'if I had untercepted letters of my uncle's, it had been thought evil manners.'[1]

Sir Robert Gordon received conflicting information. Lord Forbes thought that, so far from Mackay's having conspired with Caithness, the Earl 'is not well minded to Mackay, your sister's son, therefore write to him to be circumspect of himself.'[2] On the other hand, Lord Elphinstone wrote: 'as to your sister's son, Sir Donald, what shall I write to you of him? But since both you and I do know him, and have seen what we have seen of him, I beseech you to be the more ware and circumspect with him; and keep yourself the more wisely, and know and know not, but be ever upon your own guard with him. For of truth I fear him more nor I do any man living, that he shall be the greatest enemy that the house of Sutherland shall have.'[3] These words were written exactly four weeks after Mackay had sent his letter to Sir Robert from Rossal at the New Year, telling him of the purpose of marriage between his sister Anna and Sinclair of Brimms.

The Tutor of Sutherland made a careful examination of what had occurred in the north during 1618. During January and

[1] *S.B.*, II: 129-30. [2] *S.B.*, II: 133. [3] *S.B.*, II: 138.

February Mackay had written to Sir Robert from Dornoch in Sutherland, and also from Portskerra, Tongue and Durness along the north coast of Strathnaver.[1] When Mackay had decided to sell Edderachillis, he had met the Tutor of Kintail, and then had ridden south to Edinburgh. Probably he visited Munro of Foulis on the way, with whom he was reported to have 'fallen in exceeding great.' It was from Edinburgh that he had written to his uncle in April, offering him the first refusal of Edderachillis. He wrote no more letters to Sir Robert (who appears to have hoarded his correspondence with care) until the announcement of the Sinclair marriage at the New Year.

What Sir Robert discovered about the intervening eight months fills several vitriolic pages of the history he wrote some years later. The Earl of Caithness, he stated, possessed 'old writs of certain lands in Strathnaver' which would enable Mackay 'to free himself from the Earl of Sutherland's superiority.' Mackay travelled straight from Edinburgh to Caithness to examine these. The Earl of Caithness asked Mackay in return to help him to bring to justice the Gunns who had confessed to the burning of the corn at Dounreay, to which Mackay consented.[2]

It was not easy to bring these men to justice. They still enjoyed the hospitality of Dunrobin castle while they waited to be called as witnesses in Edinburgh. Sir Robin stated that Mackay actually came to reconnoitre in the neighbourhood of Dunrobin with the object of abducting the Gunns, but that he was forced to abandon the project. It is hard to divine whether this was one of the passages in his history in which Sir Robert was able to chronicle the truth. The Earl of Caithness and Mackay, he concluded his account of this incident, then expelled other Gunns from their homes, and the Tutor of Sutherland was obliged to find hospitality for a larger number of witnesses than he required. Such was the situation (as Sir Robert later described it) when he received news of the Sinclair marriage from Rossal. It was followed by a second during 1619, when Mackay's younger brother John married the daughter of Sir James Sinclair of Murkle, another kinsman of the Earl of Caithness, and was presented by his brother with the estate of Strathy. John Mackay had been reared by Sir Robert Gordon, sent to

[1] Gordonstoun MSS. 59, 60, 61, 62. [2] Gordon 1813: 351.

Europe, recommended for a knighthood by the Earl of Sutherland; while he was heir to the Chiefship. But now that the Chief had a son, John Mackay was able to retire from the political arena, and to lead the untroubled life of founding the dynasty of the Mackays of Strathy. It was to be an uneventful dynasty, save that among all the younger sons of its younger sons, it was to produce the most justly celebrated tasksman in Gaelic poetry, Iain Mac Eachainn.[1]

What Mackay found among the writs of the Earl of Caithness, or what engendered his sudden and total distrust of his uncle the Tutor can only be surmised. Sir Robert's history suggests that the latter was occasioned by the Mackay properties in the earldom of Sutherland. They were described exactly in the royal charter to Mackay in 1499, and contained in Queen Mary's gift of the superiority of Mackay's possessions to the Earl of Huntly. Uisdean Mackay recovered them in 1570, subject to this superiority, and a charter under the great seal confirmed them to him in 1608, subject to the superiority of Sutherland.[2] When Sir Donald Mackay had sought to enlarge these properties in Sutherland, his uncle had objected and he had given way. But Sir Robert stated in his history that he did not stop there: he questioned Mackay's title to any property in Sutherland—'his pretences within Sutherland,' as he called Mackay's title.[3] He harassed Mackay's tenants in Sutherland until they appealed to Mackay for help.

During 1619 he also countered Mackay's reconciliation with Caithness, by making overtures to the Earl himself. The Gordons had last used this device to destroy the amity between Mackay and Caithness in 1588, over thirty years before. The Earl of Caithness had then been a young, inexperienced man, but the lesson of what followed might have lasted a wiser man a lifetime. The Earl of Caithness seems to have lacked judgment, though he wrote elegant and graphic letters, took an interest in architecture, and enjoyed brief success as a military commander at Kirkwall. He sealed his own doom when he accepted Sir Robert's invitation to Dunrobin, and especially when he invited Sir Robert to spend four nights at Girnigo, where the muniments of Caithness were almost certainly kept. The Earl of Caithness was at this time unable to stir out of his country

[1] Mackay 1906: 315. [2] Mackay 1906: 412-3. [3] Gordon 1813: 323.

for fear of his creditors, while his son, Lord Berriedale, was imprisoned in Edinburgh for their joint debts.[1] His susceptibility to the blandishments of such an influential neighbour as the Tutor of Sutherland must be assessed in the light of these circumstances.

Gordon asked Caithness to act as arbiter between the house of Sutherland and their recalcitrant vassals the Mackays, and it will be seen that the Earl accepted this charge from his lifelong enemy. When Mackay first discovered his new role, he had just taken pains to clarify his own position. In July 1619 he wrote to his grandmother the Countess from Letterinie, to protest that while he distrusted and feared the Tutor, he wished no harm to the young Earl. Indeed he looked forward eagerly to the day when the Earl would take over the management from his uncle. In the meantime he would continue 'that duty to his lordship in his minority that shall make me blameless with his lordship before his best friends when his lordship come to perfect age. For I protest to God that I never craved nor crave not a foot of ground that pertains to the Earl of Sutherland. Neither have I troubled none of his lordship's friends or dependents with putting them to any trouble or expenses; but press [ ] the best I may to defend myself till the Earl of Sutherland be an man.' He offered a fresh agreement with the Tutor. 'I am willing to bide by all the heads of the compromise at Tain and to bide by the same friends and oversman. If that submission be not extant, it is but the writing of it again. Therefore your ladyship shall advertise me with diligence . . .' So great was his distrust of his uncle that he told his grandmother he was keeping a copy of this letter: 'for the copy of this letter will bear me witness sometime of my willingness to keep duty to the Earl of Sutherland.'[2] Evidently the Countess forwarded this letter to the Tutor, since it remains amongst his correspondence.

Mackay then departed for Loch Stack in the Reay forest, as it was later to be called. Avuncular missives from the Earl of Caithness cannot have improved his sport. He replied to the Earl in his vein of dry sarcasm, thanking him for his 'pains taken with my uncle for settling me. I was ever and shall be blameless with my uncles; and no man knows better than your lordship

[1] *R.P.C.*, XI: 68, 209, 583. [2] Gordonstoun MS. 90.

what duty I reserved to them.' Gratified by this reply, and heedless of its warning, the Earl of Caithness forwarded the evidence of his diplomacy to Sir Robert Gordon. He had suggested a tryst with Sir Robert, which Mackay eyed warily. 'Before I received your lordship's letter, I got an letter from my Lord Forbes written at Sir Robert's desire, as I think, desiring an free communing with me at Elgin the 22nd of the next month, which I will keep, for I rather have an free communing first, that I may know what Sir Robert would be at.'[1]

The Earl of Caithness lacked the faintest perception of what Sir Robert was at. In October 1619 he wrote to assure the Tutor once more of 'the respect I carry for the weal and honour of my Lord Sutherland (I hope time shall try me). God grant that this tryst take effect, and however it shall fall forth, I shall leave nothing undone that my works or power can to have it going betwixt the house of Sutherland and Mackay as it ought betwixt an superior and an vassal. For it's no good pendicle that will harm the principal.'[2] It would have seemed almost inconceivable that Caithness could already have forgotten, despite Mackay's reminder to him, what had been the invariable role of Sutherland's vassal. But at least the anonymous author of the *Conflicts Among the Clans* shared the optimism and trust of the Earl of Caithness. He ended his story in the year 1619 with the unlucky prophecy: 'all particulars betwixt the houses of Sutherland and Caithness were finally settled: and then went both of them familiarly to either's houses, whose perfect reconciliation will doubtless tend to the peace and quiet of these parts of the kingdom.'[3]

That October Sir Robert Gordon's father-in-law the Dean of Salisbury died, and he was compelled to travel not only to England but also to France to settle the affairs of the Dean: who was a Gordon also.[4] Before he left, he sounded Mackay as to whether he could count on the vassal army to invade Caithness, and the reply was unpromising. 'As concerning the commission which the Council has desired you to take against the Earl of Caithness,' Mackay advised his uncle, 'the Earl of Caithness did know thereof long since and is on his guard, and

[1] *S.B.*, II: 140. [2] Gordonstoun MS. 68. [3] *Conflicts* 1780: 86.
[4] Gordon 1813: 362.

has provided for his own safety: so that in my opinion it will be an longsome business, evil and hurtful for the countries and without profit to yourself.'[1] Sir Robert knew how well Caithness was on his guard, and could assess Mackay's obstructiveness accordingly. It is not easy to establish whether the failure of the case of the burnt corn at Dounreay was due to Mackay's recalcitrance, or to the busy Tutor's concern with other affairs outside Scotland. In February 1621, the Privy Council made the case available to Sir Robert after its five years' hiatus, by enquiring why no conclusion had been reached in the action brought by Lord Forbes in April 1616.[2] But by the spring of 1621 Sir Robert Gordon had found a fresh pretext.

It concerned a certain Thomas Lindsay, who became involved in a quarrel with James Sinclair of Durran in Thurso, and who died of his wounds. Lindsay was a half-brother of Robert Munro, Commissioner of the diocese of Caithness: it was through this connection that Lindsay had become tenant of a diocesan property that was almost certainly the subject of his quarrel with Sinclair.[3] Sir Robert Gordon left the Commissioner of Caithness to bring his charge in Edinburgh against Sinclair of Durran 'and his master the Earl of Caithness', and did not even suggest later in his chronicle that without the help of the Gordons, the Commissioner 'could do little herein.'[4] Gordon appeared to have no part in this sudden misfortune that had befallen his friend the Earl of Caithness, only a few days after his own return to the north, except through what the King wrote from Windsor to his Scottish Privy Council on the 25th May 1621.

'By the Godless and beastly behaviour of the said Earl, the country is come to that estate, as not only our subjects of the more civil disposition are oppressed and enforced to leave it, but likewise is so evil disordered as no part of the Highlands, or most remote islands of that our kingdom, were ever more barbarous.' The King's language is misleadingly violent: he habitually referred in such terms as these to his Highland subjects. On this occasion he ordered the course of action that Arthur Smith and the Dounreay corn had failed to elicit. 'We can think of no more ready course to be taken in that business

[1] *S.B.*, II: 139. [2] *R.P.C.*, XII: 415-6.
[3] Gordon 1813: 366-7. Mackay 1829: 207-8. [4] Gordon 1813: 366-7. 334.

than to give commission to some discreet party, not only to apprehend the person of the said Earl, but likewise to take his houses . . . and for that intent, no person occurreth to our memory more fit than our servant Sir Robert Gordon, Tutor of Sutherland: who, being warranted by our commission and assisted by the forces of the adjoining sheriffdoms of Inverness and Orkney, may conveniently perform that service.'[1]

But now that the Tutor was at last offered a commission of fire and sword against Caithness, he lacked the support of Mackay to enforce it. He would himself be forced to enter Caithness and face an angry Earl with three strong castles: Sir Robert Gordon refused the commission.[2] He offered fresh concessions for an agreement with Mackay, while the Earl of Caithness prepared for the danger that he might be forced to travel to Edinburgh, by trying to reach agreement with his creditors. Thus a year passed, until Gordon signed his humiliating contract with Mackay in June 1622. 'All controversies between them depending at law were continued until the Earl of Sutherlands' majority.' Sir Donald need have no further dealings with his uncle.[3] But the Earl of Sutherland's grandfather the Chancellor, Lord Dunfermline, died, and his successor refused to support the Gordon vendetta. Sir Robert hurried to tell James VI in person that the unparalleled barbarities of the Earl of Caithness remained unpunished, and returned in the spring of 1623 with royal instructions that the case was to be reopened.

The Earl was given until the 10th August to appear before the Lords of Council in Edinburgh, and having lost interest in his creditors by this time, he was unable to do so. This was anticipated, for his denunciation as a rebel and the lengthy commission of fire and sword for Sir Robert Gordon, were drafted in the Privy Council in July. The commission named Mackay, and called upon 'earls, lords, barons, substantious feuars and landed gentlemen' of all the northern counties to lend assistance, with 'their men tenants and servants.'[4] Gordon did not refuse this commission. But he took with him the heir of the Earl of Caithness, Lord Berriedale, for use in parley with his father: he asked for and was promised 'a piece of battery'

[1] Gordon 1813: 368. *R.P.C.*, XII: 503. [2] Gordon 1813: 369.
[3] Gordon 1813: 373. [4] *R.P.C.*, XIII: 280–4.

from Edinburgh: and special measures were adopted to ensure that the population of Caithness was disarmed in advance.[1] In all of these matters, Mackay was implicated by name, and in all he was restored to his correct and ancient title as 'Sir Donald Mackay of Strathnaver.'

The Earl of Caithness was apparently so confused by all these preparations that he saw nothing but creditors advancing upon him. He sent a commissioner to Sir Robert Gordon, and 'desired him to remember that he was a nobleman, a peer of the kingdom . . . that nothing could be laid justly to his charge but civil matters, which concerned only his creditors, all other crimes alleged against him being mere calumnies; that he was the first nobleman that ever was proclaimed a rebel or challenged a traitor for debt.' Gordon appears to have paraphrased a communication in the graphic style of the Earl of Caithness, so unlike his own.[2]

Caithness acted with belated wisdom at this critical moment: he did not oppose the royal authority, but retired to Orkney, leaving Sir Robert and his huge armament to advance into a disarmed and undefended country. Mackay heard indirectly in Durness on the 22nd August of what was afoot, and was exasperated. 'Right honourable and loving uncle. This day I am informed by Mr Robert Munro our Minister that all your people is warned to go to Caithness on Monday next, and that yourself goes in person; whereof I cannot but marvel.' Sir Donald's father had been denounced by James VI as a rebel for failing to act in similar circumstances, concerning the Western Isles. Sir Donald pointed out that he had been left in ignorance of a royal commission in which he was named, and asked his uncle 'to advertise me where you think to remain, or where I shall meet your worship . . . I shall be at Farr on Wednesday night to await your worship.' He concluded that 'I rest and shall ever remain, although I be not well used, your worship's loving nephew ready to serve you.'[3] But on arrival at Helmsdale, where his grandfather had been poisoned, Sir Robert Gordon did not march up the strath of Kildonan to meet Mackay in Strathnaver. Finding a disarmed populace without a leader, he sent word to Mackay, forbidding him to enter Caithness, while he marched

[1] *R.P.C.*, XIII: 332-3, 312-3, 379. [2] Gordon 1813: 376-7.
[3] Gordonstoun MS. 123.

boldly over the Ord himself. He informed Mackay that his clansmen might cause unnecessary disturbance.

The Chief of Mackay was sufficiently angry to abandon his invariable practice of addressing Sir Robert as his loving uncle, and signing himself his loving nephew. He wrote on the 6th September from Strath Halladale: 'very honourable, I received your letter the 6th instant, showing that you think it fit that I retire myself and my forces at this time. Forbye that I have received your letter before I convened my men, I should be very willing to have stayed. But you may be assured that my company shall not be troublesome to the country of Caithness more than any others that has gone.' He added that he had every intention of coming to Caithness, where 'I shall attend your advertisments at Thurso the morn, at night, and desire you to appoint me an place of meeting.'[1]

They met at Wick, after Sir Robert Gordon had already taken possession of all the castles of the Earl of Caithness. It cannot be proved that it was Gordon who destroyed the entire muniments of the earldom, the charters dating from the time when a Norwegian King had authorised the Sinclair expedition to Greenland, the correspondence, the administrative documents. There is no trace of those writs that the Earl had shewn to Mackay 'to free himself from the Earl of Sutherland's superiority.' From the Saga period to the seventeenth century the history of Caithness is virtually a blank: and this blank is perhaps the most formidable achievement of Sir Robert Gordon's destructive genius.

The evident object of Gordon's actions was to win the Caithness earldom for himself in the same way as a younger brother of the Earl of Huntly had seized the Sutherland earldom a century earlier. It was now foiled by the failure of the Earl of Caithness to offer treasonable resistance to the King's forces. He was permitted to return to Caithness, and to live on an annuity, stripped of all his powers and responsibilities but still the Earl in name.

Meanwhile, Mackay was able to complete the transaction which had begun with the burning of the corn at Sandside. During 1624 he acquired from Lord Forbes the lands of Reay and Dounreay, thus extending the bounds of Strathnaver several

[1] Gordonstoun MS. 124.

miles east of the cleft rock that had formerly marked the boundary. He also formed an association with neighbours who included his brother-in-law, newly created Earl of Seaforth, for the relief of the Earl of Caithness.[1] In December 1625 a 'most loving nephew to serve you' was once again writing from Tongue to his 'right honourable and loving uncle', but the tone of the letter did not much support these expressions, while the protestations of goodwill for the young Earl of Sutherland appear quite deliberately contemptuous of his uncle. 'I hope by time to approve myself an better friend to his lordship than you take me to be.'[2]

These were the circumstances in which Mackay made one of the most fateful decisions in the history of the chiefship, described thus by Sir Robert Gordon. 'Sir Donald Mackay (a gentleman of a stirring spirit), finding himself crossed at home . . . takes resolution to leave the kingdom. And to this end he causeth his friends to deal at court with the King for a licence to transport men to Count Mansfeld into Germany. Upon the first motion of the business, his Majesty gave liberty to deal with the Count Mansfeld's agent resident at the court of England. The articles and covenant being agreed upon, they were sent into Scotland in the month of March 1626 to Sir Donald Mackay, together with a license to levy and take up men to that effect.'[3] It is not known that Mackay possessed any friend at court other than Sir Robert Gordon, able to speed his business. Gordon would not have helped Mackay in this way unless he had decided to dispense in future with the undependable services of his vassal, and the 3,000 men whom it was apparently estimated that Mackay could still call to arms among his clansmen. If Gordon had made such a decision, it was natural that he should wish to see such a reserve of power removed altogether from the north, lest it should be used in the interests of anyone else there. Sir Robert stated that Mackay 'assembled in a few months about the number of three thousand men', and this was the number permitted by the royal warrant.[4]

Fortunately for Mackay's regiment, it was not raised in time to serve under Mansfeld. In April 1626 that unlucky general was defeated by Wallenstein. He moved into Silesia with what

[1] Gordon 1813: 399. [2] Gordonstoun MS. 141. [3] Gordon 1813: 401.
[4] Reay MS. 153.

remained of his army, and by the autumn he was on his way, with only a few followers, to the Dalmatian coast. Somewhere near Sarajevo he died, leaving his men to starvation and captivity.[1] Christian IV of Denmark, the last Protestant champion still in the field, was defeated by Tilly in August. The cause appeared to many to be lost and there were defections in Germany, and consternation in Britain. Christian IV retreated northwards to the mouth of the Elbe and here, at this dismal but opportune moment, Mackay's regiment arrived to reinforce his army.[2] Colonel Mackay was prevented by illness at the last moment from sailing with his men.

But he was present at Cromarty in September 1626, from where they embarked, to sign agreements with the creditors who had advanced money to equip the regiment.[3] Unfortunately the muster rolls of those who sailed do not survive, as in the case of MacNaughton's Highlanders who sailed from Loch Carron in 1627; whose piper, harper and *scriver* can all be identified[4] still. But Mackay's regiment did not sail without either a Chief or a *scriver*. Robert Munro of Foulis, the Black Baron, accompanied the expedition without rank, having squandered his patrimony. His junior cousin Robert Munro held a commission, who was to give his companions that unique memorial, *Monro His Expedition with the Worthy Scots Regiment* (*Called Mac-Keyes Regiment*), 'the memory whereof shall never be forgotten, but shall live inspite of time.' The soldier wrote: 'if you ask why I wrote these observations, it was because I loved my comrades; if why I published them, know it was for my friends.'[5]

It is partly owing to Munro's labour of love that the clansmen of the Chiefs of Mackay can be studied in greater detail from the moment they sailed from Cromarty, than during the whole previous period of their recorded history in Strathnaver.

[1] Wedgwood 1957: 185-9. Poyntz 1908: 50.
[2] Roberts 1958: 328. Wedgwood 1957: 188.
[3] Reay MSS. 9/1, 28/2b. [4] Gregory 1831: 254. [5] Munro 1637: ii.

5

Clan Mackay as a Military Unit

THE men of Mackay's regiment may be presumed to have reached Holstein, wearing the clothes in which they were portrayed four years later in Germany.[1] These show variants of a costume whose earliest relevant description was written in Gaelic in 1594 by Lughaidh O'Clerigh, commenting upon the appearance of Hebrideans. 'They were recognised . . . by the distinction of their arms and clothing, their habits and language, for their exterior dress was mottled cloaks of many colours with a fringe to their shins and calves; their belts were over their loins outside their cloaks.'[2] Of engraving number 104 of the men of Mackays' regiment, McClintock has commented: 'the man on the left has a long coat to the knees, opening in front, made of tartan cloth with plain sleeves, and with a belt at the waist. The second wears what have been described as trews, but are more probably an imitation in tartan cloth of the baggy knee-breeches then popular on the Continent. The third man has a belted-plaid with the upper part covering the shoulders and arms; and the fourth has a belted-plaid similarly arranged except that the plaid has been thrown off the left arm and shoulder. Number three has bare legs. Numbers one and four appear to be wearing tattered trews of light-coloured, unpatterned cloth. The men in the background have belted-plaids or kilts to the knee; and all the men wear flat bonnets of the familiar pattern.'[3]

The description beneath this picture stated in German that

[1] B.M. *Tracts* 1750 b29: 95, 104, 105. [2] O'Clerigh 1948: 73.
[3] McClintock 1949: 21-2.

'besides muskets, they have their bows and arrows and long knives.' Of the Hebrideans, O'Clerigh observed: 'other of them had bows of carved wood strong for use, with well-seasoned strings of hemp, and arrows sharp-pointed, whizzing in flight.' The bow was already an obsolescent weapon in Europe, and was used for the last time as an offensive weapon in a British battle by Highlanders at Tibbermore in July 1644: unless notice is also taken of a clan conflict in 1688 between Mackintosh and Macdonald of Keppoch.[1]

The question of the regimental colours occasioned the first strain in Dano-Scottish relations. From this it appears that the Mackays did not bring their own colours with them. It has already been noticed that they have preserved the oldest clan banner in existence, the *Bratach Bhàn*, now housed in the Scottish National Museum of Antiquities.[2] In Holstein the regiment received Danish colours from Christian IV, upon which Robert Munro recorded: 'The regiment mustered received colours, wherein his Majesty would have the officers to carry the Danish cross, which the officers refusing, they were summoned to compear before his Majesty . . . to know the reasons of their refusals.'[3] They were perhaps ignorant that the *Danebrog*, a white cross upon a red ground, was no ordinary emblem like those of St Andrew or St George. It was less ordinary even than *Bratach Mhic Leòid*, the bunting which had been bestowed on a Chief of Macleod, as everyone knew, by a fairy.[4] The *Danebrog* had been lowered from heaven by God to Bishop Absalon at Reval in the year 1219.[5] It is little wonder that, at the meeting with Christian IV, 'none would adventure, fearing his Majesty's indignation, to gainstand openly his Majesty's will.' They hit upon the expedient of referring the matter to their own King, Charles I, a notorious stickler in matters of ceremonial and symbol. But Charles I was anxious to avoid financial commitment in a war that had been begun ostensibly to recover a throne for his sister, and this may have governed his attitude. 'Answer was returned, they should obey their will under whose pay they were, in a matter so indifferent.'[6]

Mackay's second in command, Lieutenant-Colonel Arthur

[1] Gregory 1831: 251. [2] Mackay 1906: 273-6. [3] Munro 1637: I, 2.
[4] Grant 1959: 85-7. [5] Schultz 1941: 678. [6] Munro 1637: I, 2.

Forbes, died soon after the regiment's arrival in Holstein, and was replaced by Alexander Seton in the continuing absence of the Colonel. Thus early is it made clear that the higher ranks were by no means the perquisites of the Chief's clan, while Munro's chronicle perhaps gives an exaggerated impression of the proportion of Munros in positions of rank. They may have enjoyed advantages when Munro became the regiment's commanding officer, but in the autumn of 1626 the Chief of the Munros himself was without rank, even if he could live with the extravagance that he enjoyed. 'The Baron of Foulis coming over a volunteer was allowed a free table to entertain an Earl, being ordinarily above sixteen persons at table: his visitors, horses and servants entertained accordingly.'[1]

Mackay, Forbes, Seton and Munro were by no means the first Scots to serve as mercenary officers in the European war. Hepburn, Gray and Alexander Leslie were at this time winning fresh laurels under the Swedish banners in Poland.[2] But these were English-speaking Lowlanders, and the men under their command, where they were Scots, were not their clansmen. The nearest equivalent to the men of Mackay's regiment among the armies of Europe were the Irish mercenaries: and it was natural that the Mackays should have been called 'Irish' in Europe, as they were still described in Strathnaver. But in their organisation as a Celtic clan regiment they were unique, just as they were unique in the entire annals of the Thirty Years War in possessing their own regimental chronicler.

The first months in a foreign camp were spent in training for the campaign of the next spring. 'During the tedious winter the regiment was well exercised and put under good discipline, as well the particular companies as the whole regiment, so that mine eyes did never see a more complete regiment for bodies of men and valient soldiers.' They were enjoying a luxury that few of them would ever again experience: but they were also awaiting their first trial before the eyes of strangers, 'the land of Holstein full of prosperity at this time, having all things in a golden swim and waving carelessly in a swallowing plenty, having her heart full of pleasures, disdaining what was to come.'[3]

[1] Munro 1637: I, 1. [2] Grant 1851: 39-44. Terry 1899: 17-8.
[3] Munro 1637: I, 2.

The New Year broke stormily on the north coast of Europe, heralding the tenth year of the Thirty Years War. In Vienna the Emperor, inflated by the successes of the previous year, planned to gain control of the Baltic sea. His general, Wallenstein, had increased his army to nearly 140,000 men, which he marched in the spring into neutral Brandenburg. Its Calvinist Elector raised a small force to defend Berlin, but its Lutheran citizens pelted them out of the town with cobblestones, fearing that their Elector was attempting to impose Calvinism on them by force. In vain Christian IV awaited ships and subsidies from Britain: Charles I chose this emergency to declare war on France. But Colonel Mackay arrived in March, and was despatched with five companies to join an English force on the Weser commanded by General Morgan. In July, Christian IV recalled them to the Elbe theatre for Tilly was advancing to join the huge army of Wallenstein in an onslaught down the Elbe to annihilate the Danish King.[1]

Mackay was ordered to march up the Elbe to its confluence with the Boitze stream, and to defend the town of Boitzenburg at this spot. It was a tense march in the direction of the advancing enemy, without reliable intelligence. 'The next day our march continuing, in the morning our fore-troops having gotten alarm, retired on us. Whereupon we, drawing into battle, resolved to fight and provided ourselves accordingly for the enemy's coming; which being found but a false conception, nothing followed on it but the continuance of our march without further interruption . . . The next night we lying in quarters, our guards orderly disposed, before day we had another alarm. Our duty duly discharged of all, both horse and foot, if the enemy had come we were provided. But the alarm proving false we brake up, continuing our march.'[2] Robert Munro's prose is interesting. John Eldar had written fluent English prose to Henry VIII in about 1542 after a Scottish university education. The Chief of Mackay wrote English letters of increasing fluency and containing an enlarging vocabulary, by constant practice with his Gordon relatives. But Munro's style shows evidence of neither of these advantages. He was utterly unskilled in the English language's use of relative and other subordinate clauses, and he used verbs as a Gaelic speaker would do, especially if he

[1] Wedgwood 1957: 192-9. Munro 1637: I, 4-7. [2] Munro 1637: I, 8.

had learned to read and write Latin. It will be demonstrated that this was precisely what Munro was required to do as soon as he obtained military command in Europe.

Mackay's regiment soon experienced the feelings of the European peasantry who were looted, murdered, tortured and pressed into service by the mercenary armies that swept over their fields in the course of this terrible war. Munro assumed they should be grateful, because he fought to save them from the Catholics. The Catholics fought to save them from the Calvinists, and the Lutherans to save them from both: or so the rulers who employed these mercenaries proclaimed. And the country people starved while their saviours consumed their provisions, or hid in the woods while their saviours quartered in their homes. They were fortunate if they suffered no worse fate. Munro called them 'Boors' after the German *Bauer*: which Fuller explained, when the term was in common use among English speaking people, 'Germany hath her Boors, like our Yeomen.' The first boorish incident occurred on the march to Weser. 'On this expedition towards the Weser stream, unfortunately Captain Boswell, coming after the regiment, was killed by a number of villainous boors, ever enemies to soldiers. The cavalier's death was much regretted of all that knew him, and no reparation had for his death. But the boors being fled, the dorp was burnt off.' Munro here adopted the German *Dorfe* for *Baile* or *Village*.[1]

Before Mackay reached Boitzenburg, a lighter incident occurred in the course of dealing with the local people. 'Being quartered a mile from Lauenburg in a dorp where the boor for fear quit his lodging, so that for want of provision we were forced to send our sutler called John Matheson towards Lauenburg: in his absence our boys made use of his rug to cover their faces in drowning of bee-hives. The rug being rough did lodge a number of bees, which, when the boys had drowned the bee-hives, they threw away. The sutler coming late home, we being abed, went to rest; and putting off his clothes, drew his rug to cover him. But as soon as the bees found the warmness of his skin, they began to punish him for his long stay, that he was forced roaring like a madman to rise and throw off his rug, not knowing (though well he felt) the smart of his sudden enemies.

[1] Munro 1637: I, 4.

We called to him, asking if he was mad. He made no answer, but still cried the Devil had bewitched him in piercing him in a thousand parts, still rubbing and scratching, crying with pain, not knowing the reason; till a candle was lighted, and seeing the bees, threw his rug into a draw-well.'[1]

At Boitzenburg, Colonel Mackay received instructions to continue his advance along the Elbe to Brandenburg with seven companies, leaving Major Dunbar to defend Boitzenburg with four companies. Munro the chronicler accompanied his Colonel. Munro was critical of this division of his regiment, writing after he knew what Christian IV had not yet learned, that the army of Tilly was approaching in strength. 'Our orders were to divide our regiment again, and to leave Major Dunbar with four companies to beset Boitzenburg sconce, the enemy's army being then within five miles of it, ten thousand strong of foot besides horse.' This army arrived within two days of Mackay's departure 'and lay down within a cannon-shot of the sconce. And having begun his lines of approach, the first night the Major made an out-fall, where having bravely shown their courage and resolution, returned again without great loss. The enemy longing to be repaired of this their bravado, resolved to storm the sconce at all quarters. But finding resolution joined with valour against him, after long fighting in vain, he is beat off from the walls and forced to retire at that time, with the loss of five hundred men at least. But having redoubled his forces the next time, sets on with greater fury than before; but is beat off the second time also, with loss. The third time he adventured and, as was reported, the Scots defenders as is well known behaved themselves so well that, the enemy storming the walls, the defenders for want of powder threw sand in their enemies' eyes, knocking them down with the butts of muskets . . . At last the enemy is forced to retire without effectuating anything.' This first action by a few hundred men of Mackay's regiment against an army of thousands founded a reputation for personal courage which was never lost.[2]

It also taught the men that their enemies in the field were not necessarily foreigners. 'There was also a Scottish gentleman under the enemy who, coming to scale the walls, said aloud, "have with you gentlemen; think not now you are on the

[1] Munro 1637: I, 10. [2] Munro 1637: I, 10-1.

streets of Edinburgh bravading." One of his countrymen thrusting him through the body with a pike, he ended there.'

Dunbar's resistance could not stem the Imperialist flood. Tilly's forces crossed the Elbe at a lower point, and Christian IV ordered Dunbar to retire northwards. In September, Tilly and Wallenstein converged for the thrust down the Elbe that drove Christian through Holstein, into Denmark itself.[1] Mackay's seven companies in Brandenburg were cut off. 'Our retreat towards the King's army in Holstein was hindered, the passages being all beset by the enemies' forces, so that there was no other passage free for our army to pass through, but only to retire towards the Baltic Sea.'[2]

Here, on the east side of the Danish peninsula, they found the same plenty that Holstein had offered the previous autumn on the west side; and now offered no longer. 'In this Lager we had abundance of flesh and of drink, but we were slightly provided of bread and salt, where a soldier had but one pound of bread allowed him in ten days, if that he took it not off the field. Our Scottish Highlanders called this Lager the flesh Lager, and justly, for the soldiers were so cloyed with flesh that oxen flesh was let lie on the ground, the hides taken off by the soldiers and sold for a can of beer a hide, the whole body left on the place untouched; and at last, the soldiers weary of mutton also, eating only the heads and feet, being boiled with wheat brought off the fields. In all this necessity the town of Wismar did prove very discourteous to us.'[2] The local inhabitants had invited no army to strip their fields, slaughter their stock and commandeer their homes, nor were they concerned because the sister of Charles I and her Calvinist husband had lost the throne of Bohemia. Their discourtesy is not difficult to account for.[3]

The remainder of the regiment's present service in Germany was courageous and tragic. Major Dunbar was ordered to defend the castle of Bredenburg in Holstein with his four companies, which he did until they were annihilated. 'The enemy sends a trumpeter summoning to surrender the place, which was refused: whereupon they entered to approach, and the defender resists. The service thus begun comedian-like ends very tragically, the whole court and lodgings running with blood,

[1] Wedgwood 1957: 199. [2] Munro 1637: I, 15. [3] Roberts 1958: 346.

with which the walls and pavements are sprinkled with our Scottish blood, to be viewed and seen to this day.' Munro lost about four hundred of his companions at Bredenburg.

Colonel Mackay's seven companies barely escaped the same fate. They extracted themselves by sea from the flesh Lager, and returned to Holstein through the Danish peninsula. Here they were ordered to hold the pass of Oldenburg against the advancing army of Tilly. They reached the pass such a short time before the enemy that they had no leisure to fortify it. 'Our Lager was drawn out into the most convenient part for maintaining of the pass, where the first night we begin to work in the trenches, and continue working the whole night and the next day, till noon that the enemy was seen marching towards the pass in full battalions of horse and foot; which before three o'clock had planted batteries to play with cannon on our Lager and to force a passage over the pass.'[1]

Munro indicates vaguely that there was a Danish general present with some German troops under his command in addition to the Highlanders. He called them *Dutch*, which was his word for *Deutsch*, or German: he did not specify the nationality of the General. At dawn the next day the action began and the General ordered Mackay to advance into the pass with half of his regiment. 'The enemy's cannon played continually on the Colours, which were torn with the cannon,' and for two hours Mackay held the pass with great loss of men while the German troops who had accompanied them 'all fled but the Captain.' Mackay himself barely escaped. 'In time of this hot service, powder being distributed amongst soldiers, a whole barrel was blown up, whereby the Colonel was burnt in the face and many soldiers spoiled.' Mackay was reinforced by Lieutenant Colonel Seton with the remainder of his regiment, and all day the men fought on 'till night that it grew dark, and then darkness, the enemy of valour, made the service to cease.' At this moment refreshment arrived for the weary men. 'There is a barrel of beer sent us from the Lager. The officers for haste caused to beat out the head of it, that every man might come unto it with his hat or head-piece. They flocking about the wagon whereon the barrel lay, the enemy's cannonier gives a volley to their beer, which, by God's providence, though shot amongst the

[1] Munro 1637: I, 17.

midst of them, did no more harm but blew barrel and beer in the air.' It was harm enough. But that same night they were relieved by the Duke of Weimar, 'and we having deserved best were first brought off, getting orders to march in the night to ships.'[1]

When they reached the port at 10 p.m. undisciplined cavalry filled the harbour, and the terrified sailors refused to bring their ships within range of the confusion that reigned there. Munro attacked. 'I advanced with our Colours alongst the pier. Our pikes charged. We cleared the pier of horsemen, suffering them to save themselves from drowning where they found the channel most shallow; and advancing thus to the end of the pier we seized upon one ship with some horses in it, where we set our Colours. And making the ship launch off a little from the shore for fear of being aground, having manned the ship-boat with an officer and some musketeers, we sent to force other ships out of the road to launch in and serve us; until such time as the most part of our regiment were shipped. Inevitably, 'some villains who were gone a-plundering in the town, but not knowing the danger they were in, they stayed all night from us and were taken by the enemy the next morning.'[2]

The last to come aboard were already being attacked by the pursuing cavalry. 'A gentleman born in the Isles of Scotland called Alexander Mac Worche, being wounded in the head and shot in the arm, the enemy's horsemen shooting at him with pistols, he leaps from the shore with his clothes on, notwithstanding those wounds, and swims to my cousin Captain Munro's boat; and being brought in, died the next day.' In his spelling of the name Mac Mhurchaidh, Munro revealed what a seventeenth-century manuscript from Ross-shire reveals also: in this part of Scotland the knowledge of literary Gaelic rules was moribund.[3]

Less than nine hundred men of Mackay's regiment escaped by sea to take up their winter quarters in the Danish island of Fyn, of whom a hundred and fifty men were wounded, besides officers.[4] It was exactly a year since about two thousand men had sailed from Cromarty. Wallenstein swept into Jutland, leaving Christian only his islands and his undestroyed command

[1] Munro 1637: I, 17-9. [2] Munro 1637: I, 27. [3] Macrae 1923.
[4] Munro 1637: I, 33.

of the sea. On the 19th October, Mackay was commissioned by him to return to Scotland, to make up the numbers of his regiment by fresh recruitment.[1] The Danish Chancery issued instructions on the 18th October that a ship was to be made available to carry him to England.[2] Lieutenant-Colonel Seton went on leave to the United Provinces. Munro the chronicler was promoted Major in place of Dunbar, and thus found himself acting Commanding Officer of the regiment. In November, Christian ordered Major Munro to occupy the island of Laaland with four companies. It was little more than a token gesture by the Sea-King, as Wallenstein occupied or threatened each Baltic port; and Munro's winter duties were unremarkable.

In the spring the Imperialists laid siege to the Hanseatic port of Stralsund, in pursuit of their plan to gain control of the Baltic, and its leading burgomaster appealed both to Christian IV of Denmark, and to his former enemy Gustav Adolf of Sweden, for help. In the defence of Stralsund, Denmark and Sweden at last found a cause to unite them.[3] It was Christian IV who first sent troops to the menaced city. 'The 28th of May 1628,' Munro recorded, 'not without danger both by water and from the land, we entered the town of Stralsund, the Imperial army lying before it, having their batteries near the water. At our incoming they shot our mast. Having grounded before our incoming, we ran the hazard both of drowning and killing; but being again without hurt come off, our comrades wearied of watching, immediately after our entry we relieved the watch at Franckendor, being the only post in the town most pursued by the enemy.'[4] This relieving force consisted of about a thousand men composed of one German company and seven companies of Mackay's regiment. They were commanded in Mackay's absence by Lieutenant-Colonel Seton, who served under the Danish commander, Henrik Holck.[5]

Munro described vividly the dangers of his regiment's new post. It lay 'without the walls on scurvy outworks which were but slightly fortified with a dry moat. The enemy lying strong before us, and approaching near, we fearing a sudden onfall, those that were relieved of the watch by 5 o'clock were ordained again to meet by 9 o'clock in the morning; whereof the one

[1] Grimble 1961: 26-7. [2] *Kancelliets* Brevbøger 1627-9: 211.
[3] Roberts 1958: 358-63. [4] Munro 1637: I, 64. [5] *Sveriges Krig*: III, 76.

half were appointed to lie in readiness at their arms without the port near the works, whileas the other half were appointed also to lie in readiness at their arms on the Market Place, to attend all occasions of alarums, either within or without the town. And thus we watched nightly, relieving one another, for the space of six weeks.[1]

Munro's anger over the town's failure to provide proper accommodation for men engaged in such stringent duties had better justification at Stralsund than at Wismar in the previous year. 'Notwithstanding of this our great nightly watch and duty kept, the burghers of the city did prove very ungrateful and unthankful to us, in not quartering our soldiers as they ought to do.' Some of the troops took matters into their own hands. 'Captain Munro's company did lie on the streets four nights unquartered; till the fortnight that they came off the watch, unknown to their officers, they went to the burgomaster's own house and said they would quarter with him, if there were not orders taken for their quartering. But receiving a soft answer they retired for that night.'

The incident illustrates the manner in which military discipline was enforced. 'In the meantime the burgomaster did complain to Colonel Holck, then Governor, who did cause to assemble a Council of War, where the Lieutenant and company were both accused as mutineers. The Lieutenant proved he knew nothing of it, and that the soldiers had done it without his knowledge, he was assoiled and made free by the sentence of the Council of War. But the company were ordained, being divided into three corporalships, that out of every corporalship one should be hanged; who were to draw billets out of a hat, which were all blanks till one had the gallows on it . . . Of the three ordained to be executed it was concluded, by the intercession of the officers, made to the Governor, that one might suffer; who again being two Scots and a Dane, having drawn lots, it fell to the Dane to be hanged. The Governor himself being a Dane also, he could not of his credit frustrate justice, seeing before he was so earnest to see our nation punished for a fault whereof he was rather guilty himself, not having appointed them quarters as he ought; so that the Dane suffered justly for a Dane's fault.'[2] Gustav Adolf of Sweden had as

[1] Munro 1637: I, 64. [2] Munro 1637: I, 64-5.

yet sent nothing more than a consignment of gunpowder for the relief of Stralsund. Unlike Christian IV, he was not at war with the Emperor, his country was not overrun by Imperial armies; and he was preparing to attack Poland. But by the 23rd June he had landed 600 men in Stralsund despite his other commitments. One of their two commanders was James MacDougall, known in the Swedish records as Jakob Duvall.[1]

They arrived just in time. 'The 26th of June 1628 the Duke of Friedland, Wallenstein, General to the Imperial army, having come to visit the beleaguering and finding Field Marshal Arnim had lain six weeks and not gotten it in, the General being offended, at his coming he did recconnoitre the whole town; and finding our post to be the weakest part thereof by reason of the situation and of the insufficiency of the works, the wall not exceeding the height of a man, he resolved to pursue it by storm, swearing out of a passion, he would take it in three nights, though it were hanging with iron chains betwixt earth and the heavens.' Munro mentioned with gratitude that the Swedish reinforcements were sent to his sector. In particular, 'Lieutenant Colonel MacDougall and his Major, called Semple, with four-score musketeers, voluntarily did come to succur and help our nation; who at his first coming received death wounds, whereof he died shortly after.' Munro referred to Semple. 'His Lieutenant Colonel also was taken prisoner, and was missing for six months, we not knowing whether he was dead or alive.'[2]

In the fury of that night assault the frail defences were 'almost ruined' and Munro himself was helped into the town, 'wearied and grown stiff with my wounds', which included a bullet in the knee. Seton came to visit him the next day, 'being unable to stir out of my bed,' and the conference was an anxious one. Seton was not only acting Colonel of Mackay's regiment in the continued absence of its Commanding Officer: he was also acting Governor during Holck's absence in Denmark on a recruiting mission similar to Mackay's.[3]

Munro's advice was that the survivors of the regiment should 'be all put under the Colonel's company till such time as the recruits should come from Scotland, and then every man should be suffered to serve again under their own companies as before.'

[1] Roberts 1958: 364. Fischer 1907: 87.
[2] Munro 1637: I, 67, 69. *Sveriges Krig*: III, 89.
[3] Munro 1637: I, 74, 68, 73.

The regiment was reformed in this way, before it entered on the second night's battle in the corpse-strewn rubble of the outpost. 'The night thus passed furiously on both sides, not without great loss . . . In the morning our soldiers, some of them being armed with corslets, head-pieces, with half pikes, morgensterns,' (i.e. clubs with spiked heads) 'and swords, being led with resolute officers, they fall out pell-mell amongst the enemies and chase them quite out of the works again; and retiring with credit, maintained still the triangle or ravelin. The enemy considering the loss and how little he had gained, the town also being not void of fear . . . the enemy sends a trumpeter, to know if they will treat for conditions.'[1]

This was the respite for which Lieutenant Colonel Seton craved. He agreed to a fortnight's truce, while articles of capitulation were drawn up which the burghers of Stralsund were perhaps eager enough to sign, lest a worse fate should befall them. But on the 2nd July, 400 Danish reinforcements reached the port, and a week later Holck himself returned with a regiment of over a thousand men, recruited by Spynie in the north of Scotland. The proposed treaty was denounced, and Wallenstein had already retired before Gustav Adolf's commander, Alexander Leslie, arrived on the 17th July with the main body of Swedish relief.[2]

For many years the Stewarts had encouraged recruitment for Christian IV, whose sister was the wife of James VI, and had frowned ineffectually upon those who took service under his enemy Gustav Adolf. Now at last the armies of the two Scandinavian Kings met in Stralsund in a common cause, and the men who followed James MacDougall and Alexander Leslie, Spynie and Mackay, met as allies among the mercenaries of many nations. But during their six weeks' defence of Stralsund, five hundred more of Mackay's regiment had been killed. Of the two thousand men who had sailed from Cromarty in 1626, less than four hundred remained alive to enjoy the reputation they had already earned throughout Europe.[3]

Even these few did not return to Denmark in safety. After negotiations between the Danes, the Swedes and the Stralsunders, this Hanseatic port became Gustav Adolf's first German

[1] Munro 1637: I, 74. [2] Roberts 1958: 364-5. Munro 1637: I, 74-5.
[3] Munro 1637: I, 80.

ally, and Alexander Leslie its first Swedish commander. Stralsund's defending force consisted in July 1628 of slightly over 4,000 men, of whom 1,000 were Stralsunders, 1,200 at most were Swedes, and the remainder were troops of the King of Denmark. These troops, between 1,500 and 2,000, including the remnant of the Mackays and the new Spynie regiment, Christian IV led out of the town to be the companions of his final disaster. It was at Wolgast on the coast east of Stralsund that he fell into Wallenstein's trap. In the action on the 2nd September, all were slaughtered who did not surrender or flee, and only a remnant of Spynie's new regiment escaped by ship to Denmark. Of Mackay's regiment Munro observed: 'I do not think one hundred were free from wounds received honourably.'[1]

So it was not an impressive number who 'met with their Colonel, being come from Scotland with the recruits.' Mackay had last seen his regiment five months previously, when a thousand men would have restored it to its original strength. He arrived with something less than a thousand men—Spynie's activities perhaps account for this—but twice as many would have been required in the regiment's present plight. Several officers had returned home, and decided to remain there. 'Sir Patrick Mackay having stayed in Scotland, his company was cashiered, and Captain Annan's also . . . Lieutenant Stewart being married, and having stayed in Scotland with his wife, his place was given to Eye Mac-Key.'[2] (Munro's spelling conceals a late adherent of the old form of the clan patronymic, Aodh Mac Aoidh, which was henceforth more usually rendered in the anglicised form of Hugh Mackay.) The mutilated Spynie regiment was reduced, and its men were drafted into Mackay's. Robert Munro was promoted Lieutenant Colonel on the retirement of Alexander Seton.[3] His Chief, the Black Baron 'of Foulis having levied a company in Scotland, joined also to the regiment'. Colonel Mackay had returned to Denmark a peer.

He had also brought with him his sons John and Angus, to put them to school in Denmark.[4] These boys represented the second generation of Mackay gentry who were sent abroad for their education. The first was represented by their uncle John Mackay of Strathy, who had been sent to the fashionable resort

[1] Munro 1637: I, 80. Wedgwood 1957: 210. Roberts 1958: 366-8. *Sveriges Krig*: III, 110.
[2] Munro 1637: I, 80, 82. [3] Grimble 1961: 28. [4] Mackay 1906: 142.

of Saumur, under the influence of his Gordon relations. Lord Reay's sons followed an ancient practice of their Sinclair relations: the present Earl of Caithness had received a part of his education in Scandinavia.

On the 29th September 1628, the month of the Wolgast disaster, the Danish Chancery noted that 'the noble Sir Donald Mackay, Baron of Reay and Lord of Strathnaver' desired that his two sons should be admitted to Sorø Academy. Orders were to be sent to the Academy to comply with his wishes, and to direct that the two youths should be placed under the same discipline and treated in the same manner as the other boys of noble birth there.[1] John, Master of Reay, wrote in October 1628 from Copenhagen that 'his Majesty has directed us to an university called Sorø, which is eight Dutch mile laying from this town, and there we three get free meat and chamber, our father furnishing the rest of our necessaries.'[2] Either John Mackay had not yet learned the distance between Copenhagen and Sorø, or he was ignorant of the measurement of a German mile. One of his school-fellows was Jens, son of Jørgen Rosenkrantz, who wrote that Sorø Academy contained Germans, Poles, Scots, Swedes, and even Catholics. In mentioning Scots, Rosenkrantz referred to John and Angus Mackay, who were the only Scots at Sorø during the academic year 1628-9.[3]

They witnessed the operation of Christian IV's Danish educational policy, which was in complete contrast with that of his Scottish brother-in-law James VI. James had ruled over Celtic and English subjects, and had attempted to anglicise his Celtic subjects by ordaining an English education for the sons of their leaders in Scotland. Christian IV ruled over Danish and German subjects, and he designed Sorø Academy as a school in which the sons of the Danish nobility might be protected from Germanisation by receiving a Danish education.

After Mackay had attended to the affairs of his regiment and of his sons in Denmark, he returned again to Britain. Robert Munro acted as Commanding Officer as 'the garrisons lay in quiet all winter, during which time his Majesty's commissioners lay at Lübeck, treating for a peace with the Emperor.'[4] Gustav Adolf was preparing to enter the war as Christian IV abandoned

[1] *Kancelliets Brevbøger* 1627-9: 513. [2] *H.M.C.* 6th Report: 685.
[3] Mackeprang 1923: 411. [4] Munro 1637: I, 83.

it, and the Danish King turned this circumstance to his advantage. He invited Gustav Adolf to visit him in February 1629, thus presenting an appearance of Norse solidarity which helped him to extract more favourable terms from Wallenstein.[1] The Peace of Lübeck was signed in June, and in the same month the Danish Chancery was recording its arrangements for the reduction of Mackay's regiment. 'We were one thousand four hundred strong, besides officers, and having lain at Angle till the peace was concluded, his Majesty did thank off or dismiss his army, save a few number that was kept a month longer till the enemy had marched out of the country.' Lieutenant-Colonel Munro supervised the final reckoning with the Danish authorities, 'leaving the Colonel, being absent, to make his own reckoning thereafter with his Majesty.' The regiment enjoyed free quarters until 'the ships were ready to sail.'[2]

But Munro waited neither for the ships to sail nor for his Colonel to return. 'My Colonel being in England, I hearing his Majesty of Sweden . . . did stand in great need of a supply of foot, thought then it was a fit time for me, being out of service, to offer my service unto his Majesty of Sweden.' Gustav Adolf accepted, and 'despatcheth my commissioner back again with a commission, and moneys to me in the Colonel's name; and in his absence I did direct as a beginning of the regiment, Foulis, Captain Munro and my own captain, being three captains of the regiment, unto Spruce, before the Colonel's coming from England.'[3] This must have occurred in July 1629, when the first entry for Mackay's regiment occurs in the Swedish military records. The regiment's strength was then 260 men, of whom 30 were German, divided into four companies under Lieutenant-Colonel Munro, Captain John Munro, and two under Captain Robert Munro of Foulis.[4]

The Swedish plans for an offensive in Germany the following year required an army of 75,000 men, of whom no more than 45,000 were already on their muster-rolls in the autumn of 1629. It also happened that the mercenary market was tight during this year.[5] Gustav Adolf had often looked to Scotland for troops in the past, both Highland and Lowland, and a Swedish memorial of the 29th December is one of many evidences that Robert

[1] Roberts 1958: 372-85. Wedgwood 1957: 221-3. [2] Munro 1637: I, 85.
[3] Munro 1637: II, 1. [4] S.R. 1629/14: ff. 231-45. [5] Roberts 1958: 414, 377.

Munro was only one of many Scots whom he added to his Colours. Sir James Spens of Wormiston is mentioned in it, whose Swedish service dated back to the reign of Gustav Adolf's father, and whose name was now borne by Spens Scots and Spens English.[1] Spens had once recommended a certain John Campbell to Gustav Adolf on the grounds that he would bring a knowledge of Gaelic to the task of drilling recruits, and this solitary allusion proves that the Swedish King faced the Highland language problem before Mackay's men entered his service.[2] It was only one of many: in January 1630 an embassy reached Stockholm, bearing a message that none could read, and that was subsequently discovered to be in the Tartar tongue.[3]

In the melting-pot of races that was the Swedish army, Mackay's regiment soon began to lose its national identity. By August 1629 it was at Braunsberg, its strength increased to about 370. Its four companies had been slightly enlarged, and a new company under Major David Signot had been added, composed of Swedes and Germans.[4] By October, Captain John Munro's company had been transferred to Ruthven's regiment, and replaced by a Scots-German company under Captain John Learmonth. The proportion of Scots to other nationalities in Mackay's regiment was thus further diminished.[5] By December, the total strength was just over 300, of whom the Scots were not much more than half.[6] But early in 1630 Captain John Munro returned with his company from Ruthven's regiment, bringing the total numbers of Mackay's regiment to nearly 400 men, and the proportion of Scots to nearly three-quarters.[7]

What remained of Mackay's regiment was becoming in fact Munro's regiment. The Chief, Captain Munro of Foulis, was in Sweden by December.[6] It may have been he who organised the transport of separate detachments of his regiment to Sweden, according to a plan prepared on the 13th December 1629. They were to be disembarked at Göteborg in January, encamp briefly in Västergotland, and then proceed to Närke, Västmanland and Uppland. Here, the towns of Örebro, Västerås, Uppsala and Enköping were to be prepared for their reception.[8]

[1] *Sveriges Krig*: III, 239, 246. [2] Fischer 1907: 95. [3] Roberts 1958: 571.
[4] S.R., 1629/16: ff. 175-185v. [5] S.R. 1629/18: ff. 244-7, 263-75.
[6] S.R. 1630/22: ff. 271-83. [7] S.R. 1630/28: ff. 146-80.
[8] *Sveriges Krig*: III, 246-7, 251.

But early in 1630 the Chief of Mackay arrived for the third and last time with new levies, over 800 men of whom the majority were Scots, although there were also some Germans, English and Irish in his ranks. The Colonel's company was the largest, containing 168 men, all of whom were Scots. His company commanders were Lieutenant Colonel John Lindsay, Captain John Sinclair, Captain John Moncrief, Captain John Innes and Captain John Beaton. Captain Signot was included in the list to make a seventh company, but he was also shewn on the strength of Munro's remnant of Mackay's regiment.[1]

In February 1630, Mackay crossed the Sound in the company of Munro the chronicler, and travelled through Skåne, whose churches still attest the Danish domination that the Vasa kings destroyed. Perhaps it was in Gustav Vasa's great castle on the coast at Varberg that they were 'nobly and courteously entertained by the Governor.' Munro called it Warden Castle, describing how they set out from there to Göteborg, 'mounted with the Governor's best horses, being conveyed by his servants.' They visited Colonel Alexander Hamilton on their journey, who was employed 'in making of cannon and fireworks for his Majesty of Sweden', and they stayed with one Captain Sinclair over Easter. After Mackay reached Stockholm, the Lion of the North held a feast 'where thirteen cavaliers of our nation did sit at his Majesty's table, and were royally entertained.'[2]

Between May and August, the various companies of Mackay's regiment were shipped to Germany. Their total strength appears to have been just over a thousand men.[3] Colonel Mackay himself left Stockholm in April and spent some weeks living aboard his ship; except when he landed 'in an isle.'[4] But it was he, and not Munro the chronicler, who was present on that memorable day when the King of Sweden landed with his army in Pomerania.[5]

But Colonel Mackay and the detachment that accompanied him found a substitute for their absent chronicler in a Swedish Intelligencer whose record was published four years later, and who proves that the Highlanders had news-value, even when there was so much else to report. He described how Gustav

[1] S.R. 1630/37: ff. 6, 167-210. 1630/38: ff. 1-20, 196-210.
[2] Munro 1637: II, 2. [3] *Sveriges Krig*: III, 392, 569. [4] *State Trials* III: 446-9.
[5] Roberts 1958: 417. Wedgwood 1957: 238.

Adolf travelled up the Oder River to Stettin, twelve days after landing. He was accompanied by three Scottish Colonels, Mackay, Spens and MacDougall, 'with their three Scottish regiments.' On the 26th July they reached Stettin, 'and now the King landing his men at a castle within an English mile of the town about 10 a.m., presently puts them into battaglia. Graf Neels and the Lord of Reay commanding 400 musketeers that day had the vanguard . . . While this was a-doing, all the ladies and gentlewomen were in the windows and upon the leads, looking upon the King and his people.'

Gustav Adolf demanded entrance by a trumpeter, but the Duke of Pomerania, who commanded the town, came out to plead with the Swedish King for neutrality. ' "Cousin," says he to the Duke, "if you mean to keep me out of the town, you must set other manner of people to guard it than these ladies." . . . The Duke, perceiving his Majesty, though pleasant, yet earnest, desires leave to go again into the town. The King consents unto the motion, but sent order withal unto the Lord Reay to guard the Duke's person thitherward; and that when the drawbridge was let down and the ports set open for the Duke's coach, to enter the town together with it; and if it were possible, to make good the port.' Thus two hundred of Mackay's regiment took Stettin without a shot. The Colonel 'so disposes his musketeers (which were Scottish) that 200 of them marched before the coach, and must needs therefore enter before the Duke's coach could. . . . The Duke seeing this dismisses his own forces, which he had till then kept in garrison: who thereupon took present oath and pay for the King's service.' The Duke himself, however, took the precaution of writing an abject letter to the Emperor, explaining that he had yielded to compulsion.[1]

A week later, Munro the chronicler and his contingent were wrecked as they sailed for the Pomeranian coast. They struck a shoal of sand at 11 p.m. on the 3rd August, and two men who tried to swim ashore through the surf were drowned. The chronicler identified one of them as Murdo Piper, which establishes only that a regimental piper was lost, and that his name was not Munro. Next, the two ship's boats were lowered and lost. But Munro supervised the construction of a raft from

[1] *Swedish Intelligencer* 1634: 49-50. Wedgwood 1957: 244.

the masts and cross-yards, and with its aid 'the most part' of the troops were landed with their arms, though without ammunition or baggage. Despite this, they captured Rugenwalde by surprise, and held it until Gustav Adolf sent Sir John Hepburn to relieve them.[1]

A maternity case added to the night's adventures. 'In the very moment when our ship did break on ground, there was a sergeant's wife a-shipboard who, without the help of any women, was delivered of a boy which all the time of the tempest she carefully did preserve; and being come ashore, the next day she marched four English miles, with that in her arms which was in her belly the night before.' There was a Minister on board also, to handle such contingencies, so that the child 'was christened the next Sunday after sermon, being the day of our thanksgiving for our deliverance.' Whether this pun was Munro's own, or that of 'our preacher Mr Murdo Mackenzie, a worthy and religious young man,' is not clear.[2]

The presence of the Rev. Murdo Mackenzie in Mackay's regiment raises several questions. Number 13 of Gustav Adolf's Articles of War laid down: 'all priests and ministers that are to be in our camp or league shall be appointed by the bishop of the same diocese or land from whence the soldiers come whom he is to be among. No colonel or captain shall take what minister he shall think good, but shall be content with whom the bishop shall appoint him.' This English text of the Swedish Articles of War was actually published from 'a Journal book of that expedition by a Scottish gentleman then in that service: the copy whereof was communicated unto me by the right honourable the Lord Reay.'[3] The Colonel of Mackay's regiment knew the religious regulations of the Lutheran King of Sweden, regulations that the Episcopalian King of Britain would have approved. Nor can it be assumed that Mackay or his clansmen held theological views different from Charles I or Gustav Adolf at this time.

The Swedes already possessed a record of tolerance towards Calvinism, despite widespread detestation of 'that dangerous creed.' During the spring of 1630 John Durie had resumed his negotiations with Sir James Spens for a *rapprochement* between

[1] Munro 1637: II, 4. Roberts 1958: 443. *Sveriges Krig*: III, 426.
[2] Munro 1637: II, 6. [3] *Swedish Discipline* 1632: II, 69.

Lutherans and Calvinists, but they proved fruitless.[1] The Rev. Murdo Mackenzie was presumably an orthodox Calvinist by the time he became one of the Commissioners of the General Assembly of the Church of Scotland, between 1643 and 1649. But the nature of his views in 1630, as of his appointment, remains an enigma.[2]

During the autumn of 1630 Gustav Adolf confined his military operations to limited objectives, in which both Mackay and Munro took part with their separate companies.[3] By December, Mackay had again left to raise recruits for his regiment; and to supervise the raising of two other regiments in addition. When he left Stettin, never to set eyes on his regiment again, Lieutenant Colonel Munro was moved into the town in his place.[4]

In January 1631 Gustav Adolf signed a treaty with France and embarked on his winter campaign in Mecklenburg, the state which shared with Pomerania the German coast of the Baltic Sea. 'We brake up from Stettin, taking our march towards New Brandenburg,' Munro recorded, 'the earth clad over with a great storm of snow, being hard frost.' At a castle a few miles north of New Brandenburg 'the soldiers and officers that first entered made good booty . . . gold chains and money in abundance, by reason the Imperialists had lain long there.'[5] New Brandenburg was held by Knyphausen with only 750 men, including six companies of Mackay's regiment, but he was ordered by Gustav Adolf to defend the town to the last. Munro himself 'and my squadron of foot' were directed to Malchin, over twenty miles away. So the Mackay companies in New Brandenburg lacked the presence of their Commanding Officer and chronicler when Tilly stormed the town on the 9th March.[6]

It was widely believed by Swedes at the time that the entire defending force of New Brandenburg was slaughtered by the victors. In fact some 250 were killed while 500 prisoners were taken.[7] This may have been all one to Gustav Adolf when he wrote to Mackay in London to inform that his men were almost all cut off at the loss of New Brandenburg.[8] Munro spoke of 'the cruelty and inhumanity used here by Tilly's army.'[9] It was

[1] Fischer 1907: 63. Wedgwood 1957: 240.
[2] Mackay 1885: 97n. [3] Roberts 1958: 446-52. [4] Munro 1637: II, 7–13.
[5] Roberts 1958: 469-76. Wedgwood 1957: 245-6. Munro 1637: II, 14–5.
[6] Roberts 1958: 477. Munro 1637: II, 19. [7] Roberts 1958: 477.
[8] Reay MS. 181. [9] Munro 1637: II, 28.

revenged within the month, when Munro took part in the massacre of over 3,000 soldiers at Frankfurt on Palm Sunday, 'in repaying of their former barbarity and cruelty, used by them at New Brandenburg, where we see the Lord repayeth their wickedness.'[1]

With the loss of New Brandenburg on the 9th March 1631, the Mackay regiment ceased to exist, save in name.[2] The Swedish King incorporated the survivors in one of the four regiments of the new Green Brigade, commanded by Colonel Sir John Hepburn, and was confident that Mackay would return a fourth time with fresh recruits.[3] In 1632 a new Mackay regiment was formed with Munro the chronicler as its Commanding Officer, John Sinclair promoted to Lieutenant Colonel, Major William Stewart, Captain Patrick Innes, Captain David Munro, Captain Lauchlan Ross, and Captain George Heitel. The regiment possessed little more than five hundred men, and although Scots were in the majority, there were also large numbers of Germans and some Englishmen among them.[4] At the same time another regiment was called after Colonel Munro, having Hector Munro as its Lieutenant Colonel, but only about 150 Scots in its ranks.[5] These are the last references to Mackay's regiment in the Swedish military records.

But before its disappearance, it received a last bizarre tribute in the sheets that were published in Germany in 1631. One of these has been described already.[6] In number 95, a Highlander (who must be presumed to be a member of Mackay's regiment) is shewn in the symbolic role of chastiser of the Imperialists. He stands in his belted tartan cloak and flat bonnet, holding aloft a winnowing fan above the buttocks of members of 'the most detestable Popish League'. These kneel over a low table scattered with loot, and appear to have been interrupted as they were cramming it, coins and all, into their mouths. Nine quatrains of crude German verse, printed beneath, are presumably addressed to the guzzlers between strokes of the winnowing fan. They are unredeemed by translation, as verse 4 fairly exemplifies: 'Welcome to you, you fine guests, you shaven-heads, you rough branches. The dainties will taste bitter, the nuts harder than a stone.'

[1] Munro 1637: II, 36. Roberts 1958: 481. [2] *Sveriges Krig*: VI, 198-201.
[3] Grant 1851: 65, 231. [4] S.R. 1632/28: ff. 109-45.
[5] S.R. 1632/28 ff. 369-85. [6] B.M. *Tracts* 1750 b29: 104.

The poetry of the sheet number 105 is both larger in quantity and higher in quality, while the theme is more arresting. 'Strange conversation,' runs the superscription, 'held in the royal Swedish camp between two foreign nations, a Lap and a Gael (Irrlander) in the same predicament and war.' The illustration shows these two men standing in thoughtful conversation with their port of arrival behind them, to which ships are sailing before a rising sun. Both the Lap and the familiar Gael carry bow, quiver and musket: while a Finn stands silently listening to one side, armed only with a musket.

'What have we to seek here?' asks the Lap, his hand outstretched towards the Highlander, 'here in this foreign country? Is it not shameful, is it not disgraceful that we cannot sit peacefully at home, and must sweat abroad? What devil began this war? I wish it were ended already so that it was not necessary for me to hasten hundreds of miles to here, to this country.' Then the Lap recalls the life he has left. 'I sit at home in the forests, pious and quiet with my fur. I think the people should see us here, who live in such strife and lay waste their own country, nearly every inch of ground.'

It is now that the Lap observes the Highlander. 'But wait; what do I see that I never saw before? For someone has come wandering here. Good wishes to my friend: it seems to me that they haven't much place here, because you have so strangely, wonderfully joined in also, just like myself.'

The Highlander confesses that he is no better informed than the Lap as to what the circumstances are in Germany: 'that we poor Gaels should have to be sent here, so far over water and land. Indeed, I have never heard a single word concerning this place. You who have already been here longer, explain the situation to me.'

This pretended ignorance suited the literary purposes of the anonymous poet: the Lap was required to provide the facts for the Gael to comment upon.

He told the Highlander that although he did not know who had begun the war, the enemy was now Tilly, backed by the Jesuits and the Popish League. It was not their religious errors or intolerance to which the Lap objected, but their greed and lust for conquest.

Gustav Adolf was indeed represented as the champion of God

and his Word, but primarily as the King who resisted paying tribute. 'To them our King will now give neither a halfpenny nor penny, but will overthrow them and teach them that God and his Word are of more worth; therefore, and for these reasons has he summoned us here.'

The Gael agreed that it was extremely lamentable, and provoked the Lap into making comparisons. 'That is true and regrettable. Oh, we poor Lap peasants, although the whole world holds brave and worthy people like us, on that account we are now gentle and mild, not so bald and wild by far that we would bring our own land to shame and disgrace, and break our country's own limbs, neighbours, friend, and our brothers, in that manner, and make the children into warriors. I know for certain that in your case that does not happen in your country: yes, in the very wilds of Tartary I have never seen that.'

The Gael, hitherto a good listener, began to out-talk the Lap after this last, rather tactless comparison. He supplied the information that the Holy Roman Empire had formerly been a land of righteousness, of 'power and might without war and strife,' until there arose in it 'a tyranny worse than that of the Turks.'

Where the Lap had given only a subordinate place to the religious issue, the Gael did not refer to it at all. He named Tilly, the League and the Spaniards as the enemy, but not the Jesuits or the Papists or the Italians, as the Lap did. He had come to Germany to correct tyranny, and 'woe to the country', he said that must be taught such lessons by a Lap and a Gael.

'Yes indeed, my dear Highlander', responds the Lap, and 'Quite right, my dear Highlandman.' The Thirty Years War could not have lasted long if the potentates of Europe had shown half the talent for agreement of these outlandish peasants of the German poet's imagination.

These sheets would appear to belong to the political propaganda of the Swedes, were there any evidence that the Swedes were organising, subsidising, or in any way encouraging this form of propaganda.[1] In the absence of such evidence the sheets can only be read as expressions of German interests and religious and political attitudes in Stettin, the year after

[1] Rystad 1960.

Mackay's regiment astonished the town, by its dress, and by the manner in which it captured the town without bloodshed. Many members of the regiment who wore the dress which appears in the illustrations must have acquired German as their second language after Gaelic, by the time these sheets were published. They were accustomed to poetic flytings and discussions: these were a staple of their Gaelic literature for centuries to come. It may be supposed that every member of Mackay's regiment still in Stettin when these sheets were published must have laughed at their likenesses, and heard their versified opinions recited. It is even possible that the German rhymester based his doggerels on actual arguments that took place in broken German in the taverns.

The actual voices of the Mackays and their comrades in arms, expressing their thoughts in their own language, cannot be recovered. Their second language must have been German or English, or a little of both, and in these may be read the gerundive prose of Munro and the rough-cast verse of the broadsheets. But a third language also preserves an echo of their voices: the Latin in which administrators sought to preserve order in this tower of Babel. In order to interpret what the soldiers of Mackay's regiment were reported in Latin to have said, it is necessary to examine the administrative and financial basis upon which this regiment was founded.

6

Take-Over Bids in the Mackay Country

FROM Mackay's early attempt to add to his properties in Sutherland, and from his acquisition of the estate of Reay, it may be assumed that Uisdean his father left his affairs in a prosperous state. Donald Mackay's other principal outlays after succeeding to the chiefship consisted of the marriage portions of his two sisters, and of the fine for his escapade with Mary Lindsay. He wrote of his sales in the Edderachillis area in this connection, and he also alienated the lands of Strathy to his younger brother John.[1] Their father Uisdean had done the same when he settled Scourie upon his brother. Between Donald's succession in 1614 and his application to raise a regiment in 1625, it does not appear that he acted with improvidence, or that he was compelled to seek his fortune abroad for the same reasons that persuaded the Chief of the Munros to do so. Sir Robert Gordon gave as the explanation that Mackay was 'of a stirring spirit' and that he was 'crossed at home.'[2] Mackay also possessed an uncle to encourage him, and to advance his application in the venal Stewart court.

The profession of arms was natural to Highland Chiefs, and through a historical anachronism they were able to raise men in the seventeenth century by the machinery of mediaeval feudalism, reinforced by the sentiment of tribal paternalism. In addition, Mackay had witnessed Lowland example in this field of enterprise. After the failure of the Fife Adventurers in Lewis, James VI in 1607 permitted James Spens, who was of their company, to begin his more prosperous career in Sweden.[3] In

[1] Reay MS. 129. [2] Gordon 1813: 401. [3] Fischer 1907: 71.

1612, Colonel George Sinclair made the fatal march through Gudbrandsdal, so famous in Norwegian song, in his attempt to join the Swedish service.[1] In the same year, Robert Stewart sold Orcadian vassals to the Swedes in exchange for copper.[2] By 1625, James VI was restricting emigration, which strengthens an assumption that Sir Robert Gordon's part in securing a permit for Mackay was an important one.[3]

The evidence available to Mackay showed him that this enterprise, for which he was peculiarly well suited by temperament and by social position, was a profitable if hazardous one. The agreement into which he entered on the 4th March 1626 gave him £150 sterling a month as Colonel, and an allowance of 20 shillings sterling for every man whom he levied and transported from Scotland in his regiment.[4] In April 1626 an approach was made to the elderly Lord Treasurer of England, the Earl of Marlborough, for an advance. 'The taxation of Scotland,' Marlborough was informed, 'intended for this service, is employed by his Majesty's direction to the defence of the country, so that we stand in need of present money for the transportation of the regiment, which we beseech your Lordship to give order for.'[5] By the 15th May, Mackay had assembled 3,600 men, ready to sail.[6] But by the 6th July no money had materialised, and 'Colonel Mackay having out of his generous disposition to his Majesty's obedience and service listed an regiment of 3,000 men, to have been employed in service according to the instructions given unto him, and he having them [in] readiness to be transported,' a thousand of these men had already 'disbanded themselves' in desperation. The Scottish Privy Council ordered the immediate payment to Mackay of £500 sterling, lest the remainder should desert also. A fortnight later Charles I wrote to approve this allowance, and ordered the payment to Mackay of a further £2,000 sterling.[7] In August the Scottish Privy Council added to Mackay's regiment a handful of prisoners from the Tolbooth 'sometimes called MacGregors.'[8] On the 22nd August it was arranged that Dutch ships should transport the regiment at a rate of 5 merks scots for each soldier.[6]

But whether or not Mackay received any of the money due

[1] Michell 1882. [2] Fischer 1907: 84. [3] *R.P.C.*, XIII: 702.
[4] Reay MS. 149. [5] *C.S.P.D.* 1625–49 Add. 122. [6] *R.P.C.* (NS) I: 389.
[7] *R.P.C.* (NS) I: 320, 347. [8] *R.P.C.* (NS) I: 385.

to him under his agreement of March 1626 before his regiment sailed in October, it was not enough to save him from the necessity of mortgaging portions of *Duthaich 'Ic Aoidh* as security for the debts he had incurred. For instance, on the 28th September, he infefted his brother-in-law Colin, Earl of Seaforth in the lands of Skelpick and Rhinnivie at the mouth of the Naver river, in the barony of Farr. In return, Seaforth bound himself as cautioner for Mackay's debt of 7,000 merks, of which 5,500 were advanced by Robert Munro, Minister at Durness and Farr, while £1,000 had been advanced by James Haliburton, an Edinburgh merchant. The yearly tack duty of Skelpick and Rhinnivie was stated to be 700 merks.[1]

Soon after Mackay rejoined his regiment in March 1627, he received the first complaints from his men. They spent ten weeks by the Weser with the English forces under General Morgan, whose better conditions of service did not improve the morale of the Scottish regiment. 'Seeing the English regiment did get weekly means, whereas we were entertained on proviant bread, bere and bacon,' Mackay petitioned Christian IV for the arrears of payment due to his men.[2] 'Nothing procures more faithful service than a Master's liberality. This magnanimous King's liberality we could not complain of, having paid us in money and with assignation of moneys on our own King.' Writing in the lifetime of both monarchs, Munro did not mention that Charles honoured his debts in similar fashion, nor pay his own King any other form of compliment. 'The want of pay at the Weser made our soldiers a little discontent, seeing the English get due weekly pay. Nevertheless I did never hear of our nation's mutiny, nor of their refusal to fight when they saw their enemies, though I have seen other nations call for geld before going before their enemy to fight; a thing very disallowable in either officer or soldier, to prefer a little money to a world of credit.'[3]

It was on the 10th May 1627 that Mackay wrote to Christian IV in Latin, informing him that he had not received the promised payment, with the result that his affairs at home were embarrassed, while his officers blamed him and his soldiers demanded to be fed and paid.[4] Munro of Obsdell carried a letter

[1] Reay MS. 28/2b. [2] Munro 1637: I, 5. [3] Munro 1637: I, 7.
[4] Reay MS. 160.

personally from Mackay to Christian, dated the 28th May, in which Mackay complained that although he had now written twice, he had received no reply.[1] But the Commissioners for War sent information to Mackay in German on the 29th May that 4,000 Imperial dollars had been forwarded towards the money due to his regiment. They added that full regular monthly payment was not at present possible.[2] Christian IV wrote to Mackay in Latin on the 3rd June to apologise for the delay caused by the exigencies of war, and promised to pay Mackay's private outlays within a fortnight, and the wages due to his soldiers before the end of the month.[3] From Stade, seat of the Commissioners of War, Field Marshal Erskin confirmed on the 5th June that a month's pay had been forwarded to Mackay for his regiment.[4] Mackay had also taken the useless step of appealing to Frederick V, husband of Charles I's sister the Winter Queen.[5]

On the 12th June Mackay wrote to Lord Forbes that if Christian IV 'opens not his purse, I will seek another master; the King of Spain is an true man and an good payer.'[6] In this remark Mackay revealed that the religious issue was of no more concern to him than it was represented by the German rhymester of Stettin as having meant to the Highlander in his regiment. Christian IV had some excuse for delay in making punctual payment, as he prepared to meet the combined armies of Tilly and Wallenstein, yet he did provide a month's pay for Mackay's men before 400 of them were killed at Bredenburg, and another 400 fell in the pass of Oldenburg. It appears to have been paid to the survivors when they reached their quarters in the island of Fyn: while the officers received two months' pay.[7]

Nor did death invariably cancel all debts. In about 1633, Mackay was reminded by the widow of William Welch that he owed £272 for her husband's two years of service as a surgeon to his regiment under the Danish flag, besides the £20 disbursed in furnishing a surgeon's chest.[8]

On the 19th October 1627, Mackay was commissioned by Christian IV to recruit another 1,000 men in Scotland, to make up the losses in his regiment, in circumstances explained in Latin

[1] Reay MS. 161. [2] Reay MS. 162. [3] Reay MS. 163. [4] Reay MS. 164.
[5] Reay MS. 167. [6] *H.M.C.*, 2nd Report: 195. [7] Munro 1637: I, 30, 34.
[8] *C.S.P.D.*, 1633–4: 375–6.

as follows, over Mackay's signature: 'to the end that I may obtain enough money, he has given me letters of credit to the Most Serene and Puissant Prince and Lord, the Lord Charles, King of Great Britain, France and Ireland.'[1] At this time, Mackay was created a Baronet by Charles I, which raises the question, whether the King considered this to be a partial, or even a total, payment of his earlier debts to Mackay, and whether Mackay accepted the honour on these terms. On the 19th February 1628, Mackay was created Lord Reay, which raises a similar question involving the King's fresh debts. On this recruiting mission Mackay received no money payment according to the terms of Christian IV's commission, though various subsequent admissions of liability by servants of Charles I will be examined.

Recruitment in the north was made more difficult for Mackay by the fact that others had been harvesting the same fields during 1627. Alexander, Lord Spynie had been empowered to impress all 'strong, able and counterfeit limmers, called Egyptians . . . sturdy beggars and vagabonds, masterless men and idle loiterers . . . as also, fugitive soldiers who received pay and were enrolled under Colonel Mackay.'[2] The Scottish Privy Council had also commissioned James Sinclair of Murkle to raise 3,000 men for the King of Denmark, specifying that he might seize fugitives from Mackay's regiment.[3] Charles I himself wrote that Highlanders should be pressed into service, at the same time as he defaulted in his payment for such service.[4]

Mackay returned to Denmark with his levies in 1628, in time to fall into Wallenstein's trap at Wolgast on the 2nd September, in company with the veterans of his regiment. Their acting Commanding Officer, Alexander Seton, had already resigned from his command after the relief of Stralsund.

Seton gave his reasons in a letter apparently composed by himself, and certainly in his own hand, in ungrammatical French.[5] He submitted to Christian IV that his company was bankrupt, and begged the King to pay his 600 men the money due to them on enlistment, and two month's wages. The letter is undated, but perhaps he had not yet met his Colonel on Mackay's return to Europe, for he added: 'il se contente de le

[1] Grimble 1961: 26-7. [2] *R.P.C.* (NS) I: 542. [3] *R.P.C.* (NS) I: 547.
[4] *R.P.C.* (NS) I: 1900. [5] Grimble 1961: 28.

recevoir de Sa Majeste de la Grand Britaignie.' Seton's petition was followed by a more professional composition, drawn up for Mackay in Latin and presented to Christian IV on behalf of himself and of his surviving troops.[1]

'Before the said Colonel set forth into Britain, His Serene Majesty contracted with the said Colonel by writ confirmed with signature and seal, that payment would be made in several months to the veteran companies which he had left in Denmark. Yet up to the present day (except one half-week's pay) they have received not a penny, and now ten months have passed, nor clothes, although my lieutenant (who held supreme command over my men in my absence) repeatedly demanded the fulfilment of his Majesty's promise. He has continually received only this reply, that payment would be made before my return. Now however, since by divine assistance I have returned hither and earnestly requested the fulfilment of the royal promise made to me, nothing is done to meet it. And the soldiers, wounded and maimed, and the remainder fighting persistently against the enemy run to me and beg I recompense them in some way for their own suffering and bloodshed, for the death of their friends, the mutilation of their limbs; or that I give permission for them to return to their country, to their homes and friends. For this reason, in virtue of his Majesty's agreement with me, I humbly ask that two months' pay be given to my officers and myself; and to remedy the present lack of shoes and linen shirts and army boots, the veteran soldiers should receive one month's pay. And as to the rest, that the accounts be examined and passed with me for the remainder of the pay, and letters be sent to the most Serene King of the Britons, in which he is requested to deign to give me the remainder of the pay.' He submitted an account for 1,922 Imperial dollars for the 306 men of his new levy; and for 1,301 Imperial dollars in respect of the 190 men of the Laird of Foulis' body of men.

According to Munro, Christian IV fulfilled his part of the bargain. The regiment was reformed with the help of Mackay's new recruits, and probably of Spynie's survivors and other detachments of different nationality. 'The regiment thus complete was mustered, and received a month's means together with a reckoning of their bye-past rests, with an assignation on

[1] Grimble 1961: 29.

his Majesty of Great Britain for the payment of the moneys.'[1] The earliest such assignation that survives among the Reay papers is dated 11th May 1629, and states that the debt of Charles I was £4,576 sterling.[2] In that very month, the debt was formally recognised for the first time: but this was a recognition of part of the debt assigned by Christian IV, not of the original debts that had led to mortgages of the Mackay country. A warrant was drawn up for the payment to Mackay of £3,000, assigned to him by Christian IV, while another £1,000 was to be paid to Mackay personally: the significances of such a distinction is obscure when the whole amounts to less than the original assignation. But while Mackay was instructed to raise a third contingent of men, this money was not paid to him until after May 1630.[3] By then, the Chief of Mackay had become involved in a new and even more costly imbroglio.

After his return to Denmark with the third contingent of men, Mackay travelled to Sweden with his Lieutenant Colonel, Munro the chronicler, in February 1630. Here they visited Colonel Alexander Hamilton, and Mackay was able to return this hospitality soon after he left Stockholm in April, for Colonel Hamilton found it convenient to reside in Mackay's ship while he awaited orders from Gustav Adolf. Hamilton was the brother of the Earl of Haddington, whose son Sir James Hamilton was Mackay's guest in the ship also. The party was completed by David Ramsay, an emissary of the head of their family, the Marquess of Hamilton, who was arranging to raise an army of 6,000 men for the Swedish service. 'And one night drinking healths,' Mackay deposed a year later, 'amongst the rest the Marquess's health coming by course, I asked Colonel Hamilton the Marquess's Christian name. He answered me "James, by the grace of God." Sir James added, "King of Scotland." Therefore his health did pass under that name till I did take exceptions.'[4]

The Hamiltons had been heirs to the Scottish throne with only a single life separating them from it from the death of James V in 1542 until an heir was born to James VI. They lacked the necessary Tudor blood to follow the Stewarts in succession to the English throne, so that Sir James Hamilton's facetious answer to the newly ennobled Gael who did not know

[1] Munro 1637: I, 82. [2] Reay MS. 173. [3] *C.S.P.D.*, 1628-9: 555.
[4] *State Trials*, III: 447.

the personal name of the great Marquess of Hamilton contained a kernel of accuracy. Mackay deposed that Sir James 'did laugh' at his host's humourless response to what sounds like the family joke. Perhaps the whole Hamilton Plot which they thereupon disclosed to him was the joke of urbane Lowlanders, bored by the pomposity of the Highlander, slightly out of his social depth. They undoubtedly invited Mackay to join the Marquess of Hamilton's service. But the serious purpose of augmenting Hamilton's continental army would not have been inconsistent with the joke that it was to be used to place the crown of Scotland upon the head of the Marquess.

Surrounded by solicitous Hamiltons and their agent, Mackay confessed to having made a proposal that reveals something of his motives as he transported more and more men into the carnage of the Thirty Years War, without any longer remaining to fight with them. He had not as yet enriched himself, but he had reached the baronage, and it is evident that he was playing for high stakes. 'I told him I had a mind to seek the reversion of Orkney from the King my master, if the Marquess would mediate with my master. . . . He said, by God it was to be thought upon; and he did desire me to give him leave to think upon it that night. On the morrow he and Alexander Hamilton did desire me to write a general letter to the Marquess with the two Colonel Hamiltons, with great assurances of true friendship from their master, if I would continue constant in resolution. I did give them my letter, and so we parted.'[1] Mackay is revealed in his own deposition to have been torn between cupidity and suspicion, of which the second was amply fed by the conversation of foreign courts and camps.

At Stettin in July 1630 Mackay encountered a cousin of David Ramsay, the Hamilton agent, called Meldrum. According to Mackay, Meldrum told him 'he was writing a declaration of the justness of the Marquess's quarrel, with the tyrannical using and suffering of the Church under King James in his last days, and now worse groaning under his son; with the Hamiltons' clear title to the Crown.' Meldrum was alleged to have said that Charles I's sister, the Winter Queen living in exile at the Hague, had promised her daughter to the Marquess, so that the two dynasties would be united.[1]

[1] *State Trials*, III: 448.

The widespread gossip and suspicion of which Mackay's is a reflection began to take root from 1629 onwards, when Charles I began his government without Parliament. So far from being able to support his sister at the Hague or the Protestant cause in Germany, he became himself financially dependent upon foreign aid. This need would increase if he were ever to require a domestic army to enforce his episcopal religious policy: while the foreign subsidies he received already came from Catholic Spain. In return for them, English ships carried the bullion for payment of Spanish troops in the Low Countries, and the Dutch were thus prevented from severing the vital lifeline which maintained foreign forces upon their soil. The Winter Queen's Dutch hosts might plot against her brother Charles I, both as Calvinists, and as enemies of Spain. In Scotland there were Calvinists to share their aspirations, and a nobility threatened by Charles I's declared intention to recover the Church property which they had seized. Charles I was permitting recruitment in Britain of levies for the Protestant champion from Sweden: but the suspicion grew in Mackay's mind that Hamilton intended to use these to deprive Charles I of his Scottish throne.[1]

Mackay was commissioned by Gustav Adolf in the autumn of 1630, not only to make up the numbers of his own regiment, but to supervise the creation of a second under the command of Munro of Obsdell, and of a third composed of Englishmen under Sir Thomas Conway.[2] Gustav Adolf commissioned the Marquess of Hamilton likewise, and envisaged a 'fifth army' under Hamilton as part of his plans for 1631.[3] But being a more intelligent King than Charles I, he soon became suspicious of the only Scottish officer he ever distrusted.[4] In October 1630, Gustav Adolf wrote to Sir Alexander Hamilton, saying it was commonly reported that Charles I was giving him assistance, but he had no certain information about Hamilton's success in raising an army. He requested that some fit person might be sent to give details and discuss future plans. In December he wrote again from Stettin, to the Marquess himself, saying that he had discussed Hamilton's conditions with Sir Arthur Rankin and Mackay. In January 1631, Gustav Adolf wrote to the Marquess that Mackay had communicated fully to him what

[1] Wedgwood 1960: 186-90. [2] Munro 1637: II, 12-3. Mackay 1885: 232-3.
[3] Roberts 1958: 450. [4] Fischer 1907: 89.

was in the mind of Charles, and he commended Mackay himself as a fit and faithful man.[1]

On the very same day, Mackay himself wrote to the Marquess from Elsinore. He explained that he had powers from Gustav Adolf to conclude all the arrangements with Hamilton. He announced that Hamilton's army would be assured a free passage through Denmark despite the machinations of the Imperial ambassador. Mackay was transparently pleased with his diplomatic success, and with his skill in communicating what was in the minds of Kings. 'The King hearing that I was of mind to join your Lordship, he would prevent me, with heaping more honours and profit on me than any ever had in his army. His Majesty has given me three regiments, and has made me Captain of his own Guards, which now must all be Scottish gentlemen. I could not refuse his Majesty's offers, but that your Excellency shall see how far I am ready to be your Lordship's servant, I will leave all that, and trail a pike under you if I cannot serve to no better use.'[2]

Thus cupidity and suspicion contended in the mind of a man who thought he could expound the thoughts of Charles I, though he could not assess the worth of Hamilton. At some time after December 1630, Mackay confided to the Master of Forbes (so the latter deposed), that Hamilton had no intention of entering the Swedish service, 'but these levies were intended for some other purpose which would break out in its own time. Withal he enquired of me, what the Marquess meant by bringing home so many arms to Scotland, and what meant his making so many cannons and muskets in Scotland, and what meant his making all his chief officers Scotsmen? "Well," said he, "you will hear news of this ere long." '[3] In March 1631, Mackay returned to Britain through the Calvinist Low Countries, and during the eight days that he spent at Amsterdam in the company of David Ramsay, he received the final confirmation of his suspicions. He had offered his military services to Hamilton in return for Orkney, and Ramsay brought him word of the manner in which these would be required. 'I did ask him where our forces should meet. He said, upon the sea and thereafter land in Scotland or England. He would tell me no more: but that for my business

[1] *H.M.C.*, 11th Report: 70. [2] *H.M.C.*, 11th Report: 70-1.
[3] *H.M.C.*, 2nd Report: 194. *State Trials* III: 430.

of Orkney, I might have it better cheap than to pay the duties of it. And he told me that when I should meet with the Marquess, he would infuse in me that which he durst not, since he would have the Marquess to take the thanks to himself.'[1]

Mackay's subsequent actions support the supposition that he hoped to earn the earldom of Orkney through Hamilton's influence with Charles I, by helping the Marquess to raise the 6,000 men whom he had undertaken to lead in the army of Gustav Adolf. Once he had decided (rightly or wrongly) that Hamilton's intentions were treasonable, he hastened impetuously to disclose his information, however damaging to himself. Ignorant as he was of the court intrigue that Charles I mistook for government, Mackay unfolded his story to Lord Ochiltree, a Stewart of the royal house, consequently antagonistic to Hamilton. He told Ochiltree of the conversations in his ship in the Baltic, at Stettin, at Amsterdam: and Ochiltree passed the plot to the Lord Treasurer in the form that provoked such an uproar, and that led to the summoning of the Court of Chivalry.

While Mackay waited for the Court to meet, he spent the summer of 1631 in recruiting. An official in London noted on the 21st July that his regiment 'was almost all cut off at the loss of New Brandenburg'[2] of which Gustav Adolf wrote to Mackay in Latin. He told Mackay of his anxiety that the three regiments for which he was responsible should be brought to full strength, and of the difficulty of accomplishing this in Germany. He hoped that recruitment in Scotland would repair his losses, and assured Mackay that the expenses of the levy would be met promptly. 'We are also willing to reward the excellent fidelity and promptitude therein with our royal favour and grace.'[3]

On May Day Mackay informed the Swedish King that he was attending to recruitment, and asked for subsidies, since he had no means of his own with which to meet his expenses.[4] By July, Sir Thomas Conway had raised 800 men in England, while Mackay applied for a warrant to transport these to the continent.[5] Conway was to 'be allowed 8 riks dollars for every man, 20 shillings in hand, and good security to receive the rest at their landing at Stralsund, where they shall be presently received into the King's pay, and transported to the rest of the regiment

[1] *State Trials*, III: 450-1. [2] *C.S.P.D.* 1625-9 Add.: 414.
[3] Reay MS. 181. Mackay 1885: 233. [4] Reay MS. 184.
[5] *C.S.P.D.* 1631-3: 124.

which is already there.'[1] In August Mackay was still begging the servants of Charles I for Conway's warrant, and was informed that Dorchester 'makes no doubt that when the King shall return from Woodstock, Sir Thomas Conway will have the warrant.' At Oatlands the King revoked his permission to recruit in Ireland, 'for some reasons best known to his Majesty.'[2] But Gustav Adolf had replied in July that 'we have also given orders to our Commissary Larsson that he should pay to you 9,600 Imperial dollars for the enlisting of your regiment. And we request of you that if we should be a little tardy in paying, you should nevertheless prosecute the levy by your means and be persuaded that the money advanced by you in this business will be immediately repaid by us.'[3] Conway's companies left England in October.[4] The companies formed into Colonel John Munro of Obsdell's new regiment sailed from Cromarty in June, July and October.[5]

It was fortunate for all these men that they did not serve under Hamilton, as Mackay had at one time intended. The Marquess did raise the force of 6,000 men which Gustav Adolf had commissioned, but although they reached the continent, they did not survive to fight under the Swedish flag. In December 1631 they simply perished by maladministration in Hamilton's hands.[6]

During the summer of 1631, Mackay had a third preoccupation, besides his appeal of treason against Ramsay and his recruiting responsibilities. He was left a widower by Lady Barbara Mackenzie after she had borne him six children, of whom five survived. The date of her death is uncertain, as also the date of Mackay's association in London with Rachel Winterfield, or Harrison. Sir Robert Gordon concluded his History in the year 1630, presumably without having heard of Rachel: but it seems likely that Mackay contracted a secret liaison with her as early as 1629. By 1631 the friendship was over, and Mackay was applying for a warrant 'for apprehending that woman who calls herself the writer's wife,' and Secretary Dorchester cooperated in instituting a 'search after the woman mentioned by him.'[7] Sir Robert Gordon's continuator later explained that Mackay had married Rachel, but had obtained a sentence of

[1] *C.S.P.D.* 1625-9 Add.: 414. [2] *C.S.P.D.* 1631-3: 129, 131, 132.
[3] Reay MS. 184. Mackay 1885: 233-5. [4] Reay MS. 188. [5] Reay MS. 189.
[6] *C.S.P.D.* 1631-3: 202. [7] *C.S.P.D.* 1631-3: 124, 131.

nullity on learning that she had another husband living in Ireland. In the interval she had borne a son to Mackay, called Donald.[1] It was not an auspicious time for Mackay to have exposed himself to such claims, even though the claimant does not appear to have found a powerful protector at this time.

Mackay's domestic circumstances became more complicated still in the spring of 1632. He had found lodgings in Greenwich on his return to London in the summer of 1631, and it was from there that he addressed his correspondence concerning the raising of new levies. He was detained in London throughout the winter by the trial, and until May 1632 by the abortive combat. In Greenwich, between the date of the trial and that fixed for the combat, Mackay married Elizabeth Thomson, whose father, Robert Thomson, was keeper of the Queen's wardrobe.[2] He did so, according to Gilbert Gordon, Sir Robert's continuator, 'without the knowledge of any friend of quality.' Gordon states that it was 'imputed to the Lord Reay as a matter of great weakness that a man of his reputation in the world should have married a woman without birth, without means, without friendship; and chiefly at such a time, whenas his honour, life and fortune lay at the stake, and he being uncertain every day when he should have been called to fight against David Ramsay. But in matters of love the wisest are to seek.'[3]

So the Chief of Mackay returned home to Strathnaver in 1632 with a woman whose right to be termed his wife was contested by another; without the financial means to lift the mortgages from parcels of the Mackay country; with influential enemies, and apparently without friends.

There had been changes at Dunrobin since Mackay had assured his grandmother the Countess of Sutherland of his goodwill to the young Earl, and had safeguarded himself against further dealings with the house of Sutherland until the Earl came of age to manage his own affairs. The aged Countess died on the 14th May 1629, a Catholic to the last.[4] In the following year Sir Robert Gordon surrendered his control of the earldom, according to the terms of his commission as Tutor.[5] The transactions were completed in the summer of 1630.[6] But the Earl agreed that Sir Robert Gordon should take part in the feudal

[1] Gordon 1813: 458. [2] G.E.C. X: 754. [3] Gordon 1813: 458-9.
[4] *S.B.* I: 169. [5] Gordon 1813: 382. [6] *S.B.* I: 216-7.

procedures now required between Mackay as a vassal and the Earl as his superior.[1] 'You write that you would wish to be with me when I settle with my Lord Reay. Truly I should be glad of it,' the Earl told his uncle.

Gordon had already written detailed instructions for the young Earl, before he laid down the responsibilities of Tutor. The Earl must keep a spy in Strathnaver 'whom you shall entertain as your secret pensioner, that he may still advertise you of all things either spoken or devised.' He must strengthen his hold upon the long disputed border between the earldom and the Mackay country: 'fail not to place the trustiest men you have, and in whom you confide most, upon the borders of your country.' The superiority of Strathnaver was admitted privately by Sir Robert Gordon to be based upon a hoax. It had been bestowed on Bishop Reid by Regent Mary. Gordon of Huntly had contested the grant and obtained another in his own favour from the Regent's daughter. He had purported to pass his right of superiority to Gordon of Sutherland without Mackay's consent. Sir Robert told his nephew: 'Bishop Reid of Orkney obtained a gift of Strathnaver before the Earl of Huntly by reason of Donald Mackay's bastardy, which gift of Huntly's is the ground of Aodh Mackay's claim. This former right was bought by your father from Bishop Reid's heirs, and the gift was taken in my name. Keep this right quiet until you do see yourself straited by the other, and then defend yourself thereby as you can.' The Earl was thus instructed how to make one good title out of two bad ones.[2]

Sir Robert Gordon's History, also completed by 1630, appears to have been intended for a wider public, since it tells the story quite differently from the advice to the young Earl. The Chiefs of Mackay, Sir Robert informed posterity, were only infefted with some lands in Strathnaver called Farr. 'And ever since that infeftment, they did write themselves, in all contracts and obligations, Mackay of Farr; till now of late that Sir Donald Mackay did write himself (upon what ground I know not) Mackay of Strathnaver, which also he hath again relinquished since he was created Lord Reay, seeing the Earl of Sutherland's eldest son is called Lord of Strathnaver.'[3] The Mackay title is preserved in the state documents of two centuries: the Gordon

[1] *S.B.* II: 157. [2] *S.B.* II: 337-68. [3] Gordon 1813: 305.

title, as a rank in the nobility rather than a feudal superiority, was never made valid by letters patent, and was abruptly dropped by every party to the disputed succession in the 18th century.

The very superiority, so dubious in its origins, was further weakened by a warrandice that Mackay held from the young Earl's own father. 'I doubt not but Mackay by virtue of this warrandice will press to deprive you, if he can, of the superiority of Strathnaver,' ran Sir Robert's private advice. Mackay must be compelled to surrender this document at all costs. 'If he do not, then do you remove him from the lands of Durness, whereof he has no right as yet but a little ticket of your father's subscribed by him upon his death bed, which will not avail much by law.' All this and much more in Sir Robert's letter to his nephew reveals their deep interest in Mackay's embarrassments, and the means by which they planned to increase them, before anyone advised Mackay to bring his costly appeal of treason, or anyone had heard of Rachel Winterfield.[1]

The principal objective was to secure the superiority of Strathnaver. 'Use Mackay rather as your vassal than as your companion, and because they are usually proud and arrogant let them know that you are their superior. Let Mackay's pencil never be displayed where your is . . . Let him have his pencil folded up when yours is displayed.' But Gordon gave close attention to the next objective, which was to acquire the *dominium utile*, the heritable use of Strathnaver, and to settle Gordons in its lands. 'If you shall happen to buy or purchase any lands in Strathnaver, use kindly the natives you find upon the land, that thereby you may purchase their love and alienate their minds from Mackay.' Kindness was to be temporary only, designed to deceive the inhabitants. 'Be not too hard-handed to them at first, for by a little freeness and liberality you may gain them, which is the nature of all Highlanders. Yet by progress of time I wish you to send some of your own people to dwell amongst them.' The acquisition of the Chief's titles to the clan lands, the undermining of clan loyalties through bribery, agents and pockets of settlement by Lowlanders, these were the principal weapons of expropriation. But there were other bulwarks of racial pride and identity, of which the Highland

[1] *S.B.* II: 337-68.

language and dress were the most obvious. 'Use your diligence to take away the relics of the Irish barbarity which as yet remains in your country, to wit, the Irish language and the habit. Purge your country piece by piece from that uncivil kind of clothes, such as plaids, mantles, trews and blue bonnets. Make severe acts against those that shall wear them. Cause the inhabitants of the country to clothe themselves as the most civil provinces of the kingdom do, with doublet, hose, cloaks and hats, which they may do with less charges than the other. It is no excuse which some would pretend, alleging that uncivil habit to be lightest among the mountains.'

As for the other symbol of barbarity, 'the Irish language cannot so soon be extinguished. To help this, plant schools in every corner in the country to instruct the youth to speak English. Let your chief schools for learning be at Dornoch.'[1] That this part of the Gordon policy did not succeed in Strathnaver for another three centuries was partly the achievement of the Munro ministry, and in particular of Alexander Munro, whose sacred poetry is the earliest surviving vernacular literature in Strathnaver. In addition to succeeding Robert Munro of Coull as sole Minister in the Mackay country at some time after 1635[2] Alexander Munro acted as a Justice of the Peace during the decade of the 1630s, in which he was joined by two other Munro ministers of the sheriffdom of Sutherland and Strathnaver.[3] His signature survives on legal documents, such as one which he witnessed in Durness in 1636.[4] The poetry in which he reintroduced the Bible story to a people still without a Bible in their own tongue was preserved in the Fernaig manuscript.[5]

> The wonder of the works of the Creator
> Made by him at the beginning of time;
> This is an epistle each man may read,
> The might of God, written in the universe.[6]

While Sir Robert Gordon sought to promote the English civility in Strathnaver, the Irish barbarity was represented there by the Rev. Alexander Munro.

It boded ill for Mackay that when he returned to the north,

[1] *S.B.* II: 337-68. [2] *Fasti* VII: 106. [3] *R.P.C.* (NS) V: 388-9. [4] Reay MS. 3/5. [5] Macrae 1923: 23-41. [6] MacInnes 1951: 268.

his most well-disposed Gordon relative, Sir Alexander of Navidale was preparing to emigrate. Sir Alexander had remained resident in Sutherland while his brother the Tutor and courtier hurried to and fro between court and earldom: which was wise, since Sir Alexander was a Catholic. As soon as the young Earl came of age in 1630 he redeemed his uncle's lands, and so deprived him of much of his livelihood. 'I think I may say it without offence,' Sir Alexander complained to his brother, 'that there was never any man so unnaturally dealt withal for good service.'[1]

One other change that greeted Mackay on his return remains to be noticed. In 1631 Charles I erected a sheriffdom of Sutherland, including Strathnaver, in favour of its Earl: the creation was ratified by the Scottish Parliament in 1633.[2] It assembled for Charles I's first visit to his northern kingdom, where, at his coronation on the 17th June 'and at the ensuing Parliament, Sir Robert Gordon, knight baronet, being Vice-Chamberlain of Scotland, carried the King's train from the castle where his Majesty lay the night preceding, to the abbey, together with four Earls' eldest sons.'[3] Charles I had acted as godfather to Sir Robert Gordon's son in the previous year.[4] Even if Mackay had been solvent and surrounded by friends, it would have been difficult for him to resist a family to which the King granted such favours. When Sir Robert travelled from Edinburgh to Dunrobin in 1633, Mackay capitulated to him.

He surrendered the all-important warrandice, and received a feu charter for Durness in place of the 'little ticket.'[5] He bound himself as the Earl's vassal to attend him at all Parliaments, to obey his call to arms, to pass beneath his banner: as men had done in England before 1485.[6]

Other transactions into which Mackay entered during this decade illustrate the means by which he tried to evade bankruptcy. In 1633, the year in which he obtained the charter to Durness, he issued a charter of confirmation to his brother John Mackay for the lands of Strathy.[7] In 1634 he completed the implementation of his sister Mary's marriage contract of 1618[8] Her husband Sir Hector Munro was by this time Laird of Foulis in succession to the Black Baron. Their 'apparent heir male'

[1] *S.B.* II: 154. [2] *S.B.* I: 218-9. [3] Gordon 1813: 462.
[4] *H.M.C.*, 6th Report: 683. [5] Reay MS. 144 f. 178. [6] Gordon 1813: 463.
[7] Reay MS. 129. [8] Reay MS. 8/1.

was Colonel John Munro of Obsdell, who had carried Mackay's complaints to Christian IV in 1627. Munro of Obsdell died in 1634,[1] leaving a younger brother Robert Munro, subsequently of Achness.[3] The property dealings of Munro of Achness by Loch Shin are thus linked, however tenuously, with Mackay's original provision for his sister.[3]

In May 1634 Hector Munro of Pitfure obtained from Mackay a charter to the lands of Eriboll, Hope, and West Moine, for the sum of 10,000 merks.[4] Three days later, Mackay bestowed on his son Hugh, who had formerly possessed Eriboll, some lands at Edderachilis.[5] Hugh Mackay, the Chief's son who had thus been deprived of his patrimony, died after 1650 without heirs.[6]

In 1637, Mackay disposed of the greater part of the barony of Reay to William Innes, who had been tenant of Sandside under Lord Forbes in 1616 when the action for arson had been brought in Edinburgh.[7] In April 1637 the lands of Sandside were erected into a separate barony in favour of Innes.[8] The barony of Reay was redefined in its shrunken condition.[9] In June the £1,000 borrowed from Haliburton in Edinburgh in 1626 had been repaid, and also the 5,500 merks owed to the Rev. Robert Munro of Coull, Minister of Durness.[4] But in July, Mackay and his son registered an obligation to George, Earl of Seaforth for 2,288 merks.[10] A debt of 5,225 merks incurred in 1624 had been registered in 1636, so that Mackay's sales do not appear to have brought him within reach of solvency by 1637.[11]

It was essential to the Gordon plan of expropriation that this should be so, and by 1642 it had succeeded. 'The year of God 1642,' recorded the Gordon chronicler, 'the Earl of Sutherland perfected and finished that bargain which he had formerly begun with the Lord Reay for the lands of Strathnaver, and bought them even from Mudale to Invernaver; and at Whitsunday this year 1642 the Earl did set these lands to such tenants as he pleased . . . So now by joining the strath of Strathnaver to the Earl's property in Sutherland . . . the Earl is become mighty both in manred and otherways.'[12] These were the lands of the

[1] Reay MS. 8/2. [2] Reay MS. 8/3. [3] Reay MS. 17/1b. [4] Reay MS. 18/2b.
[5] Reay MS. 12/4. [6] A.P.S. VI, Part 2: 623. [7] *R.P.C.* XII: 415-6.
[8] Henderson 1884: 245-6. [9] *R.G.S.* 1634-51: no. 700. [10] Reay MS. 18/1b.
[11] Reay MS. 12/1b. [12] Gordon 1813: 509.

Abrach Mackays, including Mudale to the west of Loch Naver, and Achness and Rossal to its east: and the twenty-five-mile valley of the Naver which runs north into the barony of Farr and the north Atlantic. They remained in Gordon hands, except for one brief interval, until the sale of 'manred' to fight Britain's wars ceased to be profitable, when the last Gordon ruler evicted the inhabitants to speculate in sheep instead.

It remains to examine the pressures that forced Mackay into a transaction he was evidently so anxious to avoid.

The first of these was an expectation of money owed to him by Charles I which was not paid, and which can best be estimated from the random disclosures of the King's servants. On the 3rd August 1632, Lord Treasurer Weston ordered the officers of the Exchequer to pay Mackay £200, part of the £3,000 assigned to him by the King of Denmark, to be defalked out of money borrowed from Christian IV by James VI.[1] An account of payments by way of anticipation as they stood on the 19th November 1634, charged upon current payments of future revenue, included the sum of £1,210 against the name of Mackay.[2] It appears from a warrant of the 16th March 1638 that Mackay may have helped himself by writing I.O.U.s on the Exchequer, for it refers to £145 'which was due out of the Exchequer by an assignment of Lord Reay for his diet and lodging during his confinement at Greenwich.'[3]

By May 1638, the remaining liability was being undermined by prevarication. 'I do not think it would be well to send the Privy Seals,' wrote one royal servant to another, 'for they mention that the payment is for maintenance, or a month's pay granted to the King of Denmark, which would bind his Majesty to the agreement, whereas I hold that he is not bound. The auditors refuse to give up the original receipts, but I will have copies made that we may know concerning Lord Reay's part. As to the other monies for soldiers, a certificate must be got from the auditor to say what maintenance of soldiers has mounted to the sums with which the King is charged, for there is a closed account for maintenance disbursed by the Treasurer for the troops. . . .'[4]

A second pressure was provided by the patrons of Rachel

[1] *C.S.P.D.* 1631-3: 397. [2] *C.S.P.D.* 1634-5: 298. [3] *C.S.P.D.* 1637-8: 309.
[4] *C.S.P.D.* 1625-49: 577.

Winterfield, or Harrison. Mackay's association with her had been concluded by 1630, when Sir Robert Gordon appears to have been ignorant of her existence. In 1631 she was in hiding from successive warrants for her arrest. But on the 1st April 1637 Charles I wrote to his Scottish Privy Council that Mackay was not to be given a licence to go abroad until he had made satisfactory provision for 'her who is now found to be his wife.'[1] In August the Scottish Privy Council designated her 'Dame Rachel Harrison, Lady Reay . . . as an decreet given hereanent by certain judges delegate by his Majesty for trial of the same of the date the 16th of May 1636 bears: and after the said marriage she, having borne divers children to the said Lord,' (only a son Donald is mentioned in connection with maintenance, and any others would have had to be twins) . . . 'nevertheless it is of truth that in the year of God 1631, and against the strict bands of matrimonial conjunction and laws of church and policy, he withdrew himself from her company and society, and took to wife one Elizabeth Thomson, with whom he has now lived by the space of six years and begotten divers children on her, to the great offence of God, neglecting of the complainer his lawful spouse, and Donald Mackay his son, and putting them to beggary amongst their friends.' These bizarre inventions of the Scottish Privy Council Register, so reminiscent of Sir Robert Gordon's approach to contemporary history, make contentious comparisons between Rachel, of whose origins nothing is known, and Elizabeth Thomson, whose family background in Greenwich and opportunities for meeting her future husband are both accounted for.

But it was no invention that Rachel had acquired friends since 1632, friends moreover with influence in Scotland. 'Her friends have directed the said lady to this kingdom, to sue for justice before the Lords of the Privy Council.' Her friends also helped her to draw up an account of her expenses, larger than those admitted by the King's servants for Mackay's regiment. 'She had been at the charge of £4,000 sterling upon the entertainment of herself, her son and family,' (the identity of this additional family is unexplained) 'and upon suits of law these six years and a half bygone.' She, or her representatives, shewed Mackay's rental to be 50,000 merks a year. The Lords of the

[1] *R.P.C.* (NS) VI: 440.

Privy Council voted her £2,000 and an annual income of £400 sterling, which should be reduced to £300 if Mackay should take custody of his son. These amounts may be multiplied by fifty to approximate them to their modern sterling value.

The judgment of the Privy Council in Edinburgh in presenting such a colossal bill in 1637 was based explicitly on the judgment of 'certain judges' in London in 1636 that Rachel had been Mackay's wife all this time. Such a judgment required evidence that had not been available when Mackay obtained the successive warrants for Rachel's arrest; and the Privy Council stated that this evidence came exclusively from Mackay himself: 'his own declaration all written with his own hand at London the 23rd of April 1631.'[1] Such alleged carelessness on the part of Mackay raises the question, who actually found, possessed, and submitted the incriminating document. If Rachel had owned it in 1631, she could have used it when her alleged husband was in London, and surrounded by people eager to be revenged on him.

Mackay himself was in no doubt as to who produced the mysterious instrument designed to complete his ruin. He opened his mind on the subject to Sir Alexander Gordon of Navidale, and although his letter is much taken up with other matters such as providing men to serve under Sir Alexander's son, it is necessary to read it as a whole. For if Mackay is to be believed, his indictment is a grave one indeed. 'As for men to your son, I had some thirty in roll that we might want, and would do any company good, and I thought to have sent my son Hugh with them. After meeting with my friends, they all in one voice absolutely have refused to suffer any men go out of this country till they see the event of these plots hatched by your brother Sir Robert Gordon for all our ruins, as is alleged: and I am sorry there is too much evidence thereof. I am but one, and let never earth bear me but I would do for your son as for my own. But I pray you, uncle, excuse me that I must now follow part of the advice of them that thinks to die for my defence, and in defence of their fathers' lands. I am sorry that I know not in whom to trust, my own uncle betraying me. The world would not make me believe it, if I had not seen his hand.

'The particulars were these. I was advertised that the letters

[1] *R.P.C.* (NS) VI: 502-4.

I sent to the Council and to some Councillors, being my friends, part were upholden and part written over, and my hand counterfeit, and closed with my own seal which I sent with William Innes.' It was William Innes of Sandside who had represented Mackay before the Scottish Privy Council . . . 'Yet I did not accuse Sir Robert thereof at Dornoch because I sent the letters with William Innes and not with him. Yet in Tongue I caused Sir Robert Gordon and Robert Munro of Assynt to accuse Sandside. He first freed Sir Robert, but in end confessed Sir Robert made him do it, and produced a draft or copy of a letter written all by Sir Robert's hands, which letter Sir Robert, as he alleged, made him write over and counterfeit my name to it. Then they closed up and delivered it to the Council as from me, a letter that confessed more than Mistress Harrison herself alleged . . . O miserable world, where there is no faith, trust nor credit, to take away a man's means and then betray him. The Lord forgive them. What could the Council do but as they did, having my letter as their warrant? I know you nor no honest heart will never believe there is so much falsehood in man.' Sir Alexander, with the loyalty to which his family owed their success in such measure, sent the letter to his brother Sir Robert, adding that he found it 'not noways pleasant as will appear by my answer to him.'[1]

In 1638 Mackay was put to the horn at the instance of Rachel, for having failed to pay either the capital or interest due to her. In July 1642 he was convicted of having ignored this threat also, and was ordered to Blackness castle where Lord Ochiltree was a prisoner, on pain of treason.[2] This was the year in which Mackay completed his sales to the Earl of Sutherland, just as the great rebellion broke over the head of Charles I. The Gordons, gorged with royal powers and favours, joined the King's enemies: Mackay remained impotently loyal to the King who had ruined him.

[1] *S.B.* II: 152-3. [2] *R.P.C.* (NS) VII: 309.

7

The Fight for Survival

THE Stewarts were originally French officials who settled in Shropshire. They contracted a fortunate marriage into the Norman baronial family of Bruce, which successfully acquired the Scottish crown, and then died out, leaving the succession to a Stewart. In the sixteenth century Hector Boece, Principal of King's College, Aberdeen, invented a Celtic pedigree for the Stewarts, saying that they descended from Banquo, murdered by King Macbeth, whose son escaped to Wales, beside the Shropshire border.[1] But if this pedigree pleased James VI, the Celtic people did not, and it does not appear that Charles I escaped the inheritance of his father's anti-Gaelic prejudices, although he never expressed them with such extravagance.

When the English subjects of Charles I rebelled against his rule, both in Scotland and in England, an inevitable pressure resulted, forcing him to seek support from his Celtic subjects. His English subjects accused him of seeking such support, illogically identifying it with Strafford's army in Ireland. But while his interests were damaged by such accusations, they were not strongly served by actual Celtic support, partly because of the weaknesses and divisions within the Celtic world, partly because of the King's reluctance to accept such support.

In 1638, the year in which Mackay was put to the horn for his failure to meet Rachel Harrison's expense account, the Marquess of Hamilton was sent by Charles as his commissioner to Scotland, to negotiate with the opponents of his episcopal policy. As a distrust for Hamilton grew in Edinburgh, men re-

[1] Boece 1941, II: 144.

membered the charges which Mackay had brought against him in London seven years earlier. James Gordon, Parson of Rothiemay, remarked that Charles had appointed his cousin commissioner 'because he knew him to be a zealous patriot towards his native country: and herein he was not mistaken, for if the Lord Reay spoke truth, before that Scotland had been harmed by the King's misgovernment, he had rather been King himself.'[1] In the same year the Parson of Rothiemay recorded that while the Earl of Sutherland had joined the Covenanters, Charles retained loyal support 'in the north of Scotland, the Lord Reay and the highlands of Strathnaver and the most part of the west isles.'[2]

The first attempt to wean Mackay from his loyalty to the King was despatched by Montrose, Home, Boyd, Loudoun and Balmarino early in 1638. On the 26th March they all signed a letter saying, 'we did write unto you that in consideration of the weighty business now in hand (whereby our religion, lives and liberty are in evident danger) you would repair to Edinburgh with all convenient speed, that you might be truly informed of the estate of our affairs and give your concurrence and advice how these innovations of the Service Book, High Commission canons and other abuses so much threatening the overthrow of religion and law might be removed.' The Chief of Mackay was threatened by more immediate dangers at this time than innovations in a Service Book (that would have to be translated into Gaelic before it could menace his countrymen). As he could not venture into Edinburgh for fear of Rachel Harrison's friends there, he had presumably ignored the earlier invitation.

'And now having thought it a fitter way for your ease, and sparing your pains in so long a journey to send some of our number from this to meet at Inverness upon the 25th of April next with the Earl of Sutherland, Lord Lovat, Master of Berriedale, Laird of Grant, Balnagown and other barons and gentlemen of quality; we do earnestly desire that you will be pleased to be present at the said meeting, where our commissioners shall treat with you in all respective manner, informing you how legally we have proceeded from the beginning, what care we have had to maintain religion according to the pattern of our

[1] Gordon 1841: I, 59. [2] Gordon 1841: I, 61.

worthy and pious reformers, with what respect to the person and authority of his sacred Majesty and obedience to the laws and statutes of this kingdom made in favours thereof; and to clear all doubts and scruples that may arise in the mind of any man not truly informed nor conceiving aright these matters.'

Mackay was thus informed that his non-attendance at Inverness would be in defiance of his feudal superior, but that the King's northern Lieutenant, the Marquess of Huntly, and the Earl of Seaforth were not yet Covenanters. As for a dispute over ecclesiastical organisation, there had been so little of any kind in the Mackay country for so many generations that it could scarcely be considered of much relevance there. As for Mackay's 'zeal to the purity of religion, your love to your native country and maintenance of the laws we have happily lived under,' the subscribing noblemen were perhaps not the best judges of the happiness of the Mackays in the laws they lived under, or of the manner in which their love of country was recognised in Edinburgh. The issue for Mackay was that if he made an unwise or an unlucky response, he could be more deeply ruined than he had been already.[1]

Mackay attended the meeting in Inverness on the 25th April, and there he followed his superior's example by signing the National Covenant. The leaders reported: 'we have communicated the same with the whole gentry, ministers and burghs of the shires of Caithness, Sutherland, Inverness, Cromartie.' They called a meeting at Forres in Moray on the following day where they expected to receive 'the like satisfaction.'[2] The Covenanting leaders had outflanked the Marquess of Huntly, and the largely Episcopalian or Catholic region which he controlled. But Mackay sent his son John, Master of Reay, to wait upon the King's Lieutenant.[3] He ordered arms for Strathnaver.[4] Mackay's sole motive seems to have been that his clan should not lose the remainder of its lands because its Chief had been tricked into treason in the course of a dispute between the King and his Scottish magnates over stolen church property.

In March 1639 the newly appointed Covenanting General, Alexander Leslie, captured Edinburgh, and in the following month Montrose entered Aberdeen, where he made prisoners

[1] Reay MS. 194. [2] *S.B.* I: 228-9. II: 169. [3] Spalding 1850: I, 137.
[4] Spalding 1850: I, 163.

of the Marquess of Huntly and the son of Mackay. In the same month 'there was also taken by the Covenanters . . . certain carbines, muskets, pikes, corslets and ammunition pertaining to the Lord Reay, and taken out of an barque happening by chance to come to Peterhead, as she was carrying them to Strathnaver, to the said Lord's country.' It must have occurred before Montrose had sent John Mackay a prisoner to Edinburgh, for 'the Master of Reay, being in this country, and hearing of this wrong, went and told the Earl Marshal how his father's arms were plundered in his bounds by the Covenanters. The Earl gave him no contentment, but seemed to allow the same wrong, saying his father was not an good Covenanter.'[1]

In Mackay's next act there may have been an intention to recover his arms and his son: it is impossible to interpret with certainty. At the end of May 1639 'there was about 4,000 brave men on horse and foot coming out of Caithness, Strathnaver, Sutherland, Ross and Moray; the Earl of Seaforth, the Lord Lovat, the Lord of Reay, the Sheriff of Moray' and many other notables 'upon their journey to Aberdeen to have joined with the army there.' But they met opposition by the river Spey, which resulted in a parley, and it seems to have been Seaforth who agreed to take his men from the north home again, 'whereat great exception was taken.'[2] Spalding appears to suggest that this army was intended for Montrose and the Covenant. Seaforth played a part so ambivalent at this time that only an intention to survive a dispute which he found irrelevant to the north of Scotland is discernible in his behaviour. The purpose of Mackay's and Seaforth's demonstration remains obscure.

But in June 1639 the two Highland Chiefs sought protection from this time of troubles in a bond for 'the keeping of peace and tranquility in the places where we live and have our being.' They trusted 'that our friendship under God and our sovereign lord the King's Majesty may very much conduce to the particular weal and standing of either our houses and families, and to the good of all our friends, vassals and tenants.'[3] While Seaforth signed this bond in Ross-shire, Charles I entered into peace negotiations at Berwick with the Scots whom he had not

[1] Spalding 1850: I, 137, 163-4. [2] Spalding 1850: I, 194.
[3] Mackay 1906: 431-3.

the strength to defeat. Edinburgh castle was handed over to Hamilton, so that Huntly was able to hurry from his captivity to the royal presence, while the Master of Reay returned to Strathnaver with a recital of these events.[1]

When the Scottish Covenanters marched into England for the second time, and again forced the King to capitulate to them in October 1640, Sir Robert Gordon received a disquieting message. It was sent by the Earl of Sutherland's younger brother George Gordon, who accompanied the Scottish army to Newcastle in the capacity of a lay Elder of the General Assembly. He alerted his uncle at court: 'ye are charged by the Estates (amongst others of our countrymen who are for the present abroad from their country) to compere before our Parliament at the next session thereof to answer such things as shall be laid to your worship's charge, under pain of forfaultry. What the particulars of your accusations will be I cannot learn . . . My opinion to you is that ye strive by all means possible to keep the diet. This much I thought was incumbant to me to let you know, it coming to my ears, lest ye should be surprised on a worse.' George Gordon also attempted a phrase in the language which his uncle was so anxious to eradicate. 'Sleight Toine Vaighe is become our competitors of late, who within these few ages thought it no discredit to be servants to our ancestors.' He must have been referring to a Celtic people; and of none could this claim ever have been true. It belongs to the Lowland folk-belief that the Highlander looked upon the Lowlander with admiration as his elder brother. If the remark was intended to refer to Sliochd Cloinne 'Ic Aoidh, the people of Clan Mackay, it was particularly far-fetched.[2]

The factors which faced Sir Robert Gordon were these. The Scottish Commissioners treated with the English Parliament for the terms of their withdrawal from English soil, with £300,000 in compensation. The Earl of Sutherland was consequently closer to substantial emoluments than the Marquess of Huntly, who had remained inertly loyal to the King. Sir Robert saw Strafford attainted by Parliament and betrayed to execution by his master. He saw Archbishop Laud impeached and imprisoned, while Lord Keeper Finch and Secretary Windebanke, those less worthy servants, escaped abroad. But the

[1] Wedgwood 1955: 269, 275-7. [2] *S.B.* I: 170, II: 170-1.

emergence of Pym in the English Parliament as a subject wielding power comparable to that of Argyll in Scotland had consequences of which Sir Robert Gordon made one final bid to extract advantage. For Charles decided that he would rather capitulate to the Scots than to the English, to Argyll rather than to Pym.

In August 1641 Charles returned to Edinburgh, bringing with him the Elector Palatine his nephew, in whose name he hoped to persuade the Scots to hand their army to him: to raise an army in Britain upon the pretext of the European war, but for use in Britain, was what Mackay had suspected Hamilton of intending, ten years before. Charles intended it on this occasion, but nobody in Edinburgh trusted him, and his cousin Hamilton betrayed him.[1] In October a rebellion broke out in Ireland, in which Irish Gaels claimed the King as their leader, just as the Scottish Covenanters and the English Parliamentarians had claimed.[2] Of the three nations, it was the Scots who possessed the victorious army, led by Alexander Leslie and controlled by Argyll. Charles created Leslie Earl of Leven and Argyll a Marquess, while Campbell of Loudoun was appointed Chancellor. Sir Robert Gordon was nominated a Councillor on the 13th November, the Earl of Sutherland a Lord of the Privy Council on the 16th.[3]

But they were just too late to grasp the fruits of this situation. Mackay was ordered a prisoner to Blackness castle in July 1642; not for any sin against the Covenant, but for his failure to support Rachel Harrison.[4] He sold the Naver valley to the Earl of Sutherland 'even from Mudale to Invernaver.'[5] Sir Robert Gordon returned with the King to London, who erected the lands that Sir Robert had purchased in Moray into a barony called Gordonstoun. Charles was selling baronetcies at a discount at this time, in his desperate need for money, so it does not appear that Gordon would have had any difficulty in buying a peerage. But the title which the Gordons desired (since they continued to use it without right) was that of Strathnaver: and it appears that Mackay's sale was too slow for Sir Robert Gordon, waiting in England to complete this work before he deserted the King. In 1642 he returned to Scotland for the

[1] Wedgwood 1955: 455-66. [2] Wedgwood 1955: 469-74.
[3] *A.P.S.* V: 388, 405. [4] *R.P.C.* (NS) VII: 309. [5] Gordon 1813: 509.

last time, to guard his properties for the remaining twelve years of his life, a baronet to the last.[1]

When Charles I raised his standard at Nottingham in August 1642, the Celtic Chief who had once raised regiments of fighting thousands was now crippled beyond any capacity to support his King. The Gordon family whom the King had favoured was actually recruiting in the Mackay country for the service of the King's enemies. In April 1642 Argyll had commissioned Mackay's former adjutant and chronicler, Robert Munro, to command an army of 2,500 men in Ireland, which was joined in May by Captain George Gordon the Earl's brother and lay Elder, with a company of 160 men from Sutherland and Strathnaver.[2] Its purpose was to strengthen the Presbyterian enclave in Ulster against the revenge of the Catholic Irish Gaels, so that the Catholic Sir Alexander Gordon of Navidale may not have been pleased when his son John joined Munro's army. His eldest son made his way to the royal army in England, in which he died at the battle of Edgehill, in company with Colonel John Munro, son of Hector Munro of Assynt.[3]

At some time between the Privy Council judgment of 1637 and that of 1642 concerning Rachel Harrison, Mackay was left a widower for the second time, by the death of Elizabeth Thomson from Greenwich. Ignoring the claims of Rachel, he thereupon married Marjory, daughter of Francis Sinclair of Stirkoke, by whom he begot another five children. Five children survived from his first marriage, and a daughter from his second, in addition to the two sons of Mary Lindsay and Rachel Harrison, who bore his name.[4] John, Master of Reay had likewise married a Sinclair as his first wife in 1636, who died after having borne him two children. When he re-married to Barbara Mackay of Scourie, his second cousin, it was the first time a future Chief of Mackay had ever possessed a wife of his own name, within historical memory.[5]

It is impossible to assess the effect of these marriages upon the financial burdens of the estate, since the marriage contracts do not survive. But evidently Mackay was restored to solvency neither by the sales of the 1630s, nor by that of 1642. The new decade offered opportunities for fresh speculations, amongst

[1] *S.B.* I: 201-2. [2] Wedgwood 1958: 89. *S.B.* I: 235. Gordon 1813: 509-10.
[3] Gordon 1813: 511. [4] Mackay 1906: 142-3. Henderson 1884: 104.
[5] Mackay 1906: 157.

which may be seen those of the future Sir Robert Farquhar of Mounie. Farquhar was in Mackay's company in Germany in 1627, as paymaster to his Regiment.[1] It was to him that the Master of Reay had written from Copenhagen in 1628, addressing him as his 'loving foster-father.' Farquhar possessed only two daughters, and one of these co-heiresses was married to Ludovick, eldest son of Sir Robert Gordon.[2] Farquhar's interest in Strathnaver is seen in Mackay's sales to Hector Munro of Pitfure in 1634, which Farquhar witnessed at Tain.[3] He was described as a 'merchant burgess of Aberdeen' in 1635.[4] He lent 700 merks in 1636 to Hugh Mackay of Scourie, whose daughter married the Master of Reay.[5] He lent 500 merks to Mackay in 1637.[6] Mackay was in correspondence with Farquhar during the sales of 1642, and one of the letters to Farquhar reached the files of Sir Robert Gordon.[7] When Farquhar was in Edinburgh on the 24th February 1642, he was described as 'bailie of Aberdeen.'[8] Farquhar enjoyed the advantage that should any misfortune befall Sir Robert, his heir would still inherit half of Farquhar's fortune; which it was consequently in Gordon interests to augment. By 1644 the debts of Mackay to Farquhar were registered by the Master of Reay as amounting to 2,500 merks.[9] Such were the stages by which Farquhar advanced to the grant registered in his favour under the Great Seal of Scotland in January 1650. He received the lands and barony of Farr, including the townships of Achnambat, Borgie, Achina, Crask, Swordly and Kirtomy, with the Naver fishings: the coastal townships, in fact, beyond the limits of the Earl of Sutherland's property in the Naver valley. To this was added the town and lands of Forsinard, through debts stated to have been incurred by William Mackay of Bighouse.[10] All of these properties were conveyed by Robert Farquhar to Sir Robert Gordon of Gordonstoun in 1651.[11]

While the documentary processes of expropriation may thus be studied, it is less easy to assess the success with which Sir Robert Gordon's plan was implemented in the lands mentioned in these documents.

[1] *H.M.C.*, 2nd Report: 195. 6th Report: 686. [2] *H.M.C.*, 6th Report: 685.
[3] Reay MS. 18/2b. [4] *R.P.C.* (NS) V: 517. [5] Reay MS. 13/9.
[6] Reay MS. 13/12. [7] Gordonstoun MS. 401. [8] *R.P.C.* (NS) VII: 208.
[9] Reay MS. 9/3. [10] *R.G.S.* 1634-51: no. 2168. Reay MS. 9/4.
[11] Reay MS. 9/8.

The men of the Mackay country were armed, and as their Chief had written, they were prepared to die 'in defence of their fathers' lands.'[1] Sir Robert recorded how he was given a commission 'for punishing the wearers of pistols' in 1623. He had summoned offenders to Dornoch from as far afield as Durness, Edderachillis and Assynt, and fined them.[2] But in 1627, 'although the wearing of hagbuts and pistols is forbidden, and the slaughter of deer, roe and venizon, yet Alexander Mackay of Langwell, Neil Mac Angus in Easter Lairg, and Kenneth Mac Ian 'Ic Ivan'—and doubtless many others—'with hagbuts and guns shot and slew a great number of deer, roe and venizon in the said forests.' The accused killed a cow belonging to Neil Mackay, living at Skaill, who was perhaps employed as a forester, since he instituted the summons against them.[3]

In 1647 it was reported in a newsletter from Edinburgh that 'the Highlanders in the shire of Strathnaver . . . are a wild people and go naked, only wearing a kind of aprons, and their weapons are bows and arrows. The arrows are forked, that where they stick there is no getting them out but by lancing, and they are a considerable party . . .'[4] The capital of Scotland was as likely to have derived its information from the German broadsheet as from first-hand information of Strathnaver at this time, but it is not unlikely that the weapon depicted at Stettin in 1631 was still in use in the north of Scotland in 1647.

The erection of the new sheriffdom of Sutherland in 1631, comprehending Strathnaver, does not seem to have led to any immediate increase of Gordon control over the Mackay country. In 1634, commissions were issued against 'broken and lawless limmars' and 'sorners'. They bestowed powers to 'apprehend and cause justice to be administered upon these limmars, and for this cause to hold courts etc. with power of fire and sword, and permission to bear hagbuts and pistols in the execution of this commission.' In Ross-shire there were named the Earl of Seaforth amongst twelve Mackenzies, while Lord Lovat was named amongst four Frasers. There were ten Munros and twelve Rosses. In Strathnaver five Mackays were named: the Chief, his brother John of Strathy, his sons the Master of Reay and Hugh of Eriboll, and Mackay of Bighouse. Yet the Earl of

[1] *S.B.* II: 152-3. [2] Gordon 1813: 383. [3] *R.P.C.* (NS) VIII: 444.
[4] *C.S.P.D.* 1645-7: 568.

Sutherland was one of only three Gordons.[1] On the other hand, the roll of Justices of the Peace for 1634 shows a tilting of the balance. In the sheriffdom of Sutherland and Strathnaver there were three Gordons and two Mackays; John of Strathy and Hugh of Eriboll. Three Munro ministers were nominated Justices, including Alexander the poet in Durness, and another Alexander Munro at Golspie. There were also two Munro ministers enrolled as Justices in Caithness, one of them at Latheron, the other, the Rev. John Munro, minister at Reay.[2]

In 1624, the Privy Council named the senior Abrach Mackay 'William Mackay of Achness.'[3] This topographical place-name occurs also beside Loch Shin, where the younger brother of John Munro of Obsdell was designated 'Robert Munro of Achness' in September 1637. The Achness of which William Mackay was to be the last Abrach proprietor lay beside Loch Naver, close to where the river emerged from it to pursue its journey north. His son was designated John Williamson and stated to be living in 'Carnache.'[4] If this was Carn Achaidh, part of the lands of Mudale which Mackay sold to the Earl of Sutherland in 1637 for 52,000 merks,[5] then John Williamson may have been dispossessed there also. He was already a burgess of Thurso in 1636,[6] while a 'John McWilliam in Carnach' appears in a document of 1666.[7] Murdo, brother of William Mackay of Achness, was designated 'of Gnubmoir' in 1636.[8] This was the township of Gnub Mór, which lies to the south of Loch Naver and within sight of Achness. Murdo's son John married a daughter of the Rev. Alexander Munro the poet. There was still a Murdo Mackay living in the neighbouring township of Trudirscaig in 1678, but there is no evidence and little likelihood that it was the same man.[9] In 1712 there lived beneath Ben Klibreck an Angus Mackay who was heir to the deceased Murdo in Achness.[10] The old names continued in this area, although Gordon wrote that in 1642 'the Earl did set these lands to such tenants as he pleased,'[11] and Sage wrote of the Gordons whom he found on his appointment as Minister in Achness in 1816, 'who were placed there by the Earl of Sutherland when he purchased the lands of Strathnaver from Donald, first Lord Reay.'[12]

[1] *R.P.C.* (NS) V: 224-5. [2] *R.P.C.* (NS) V: 388-9. [3] *R.P.C.* XIII: 510.
[4] Reay MS. 3/6. [5] Reay MS. 6. [6] Reay MS. 3/5. Mackay 1906: 258.
[7] Reay MS. 21/2b. [8] Mackay 1906: 246-7. [9] Reay MSS. 21/5b, 21/6b.
[10] Reay MS. 22/10b. [11] Gordon 1813: 509. [12] Sage 1889: 279.

Sufficient evidence of the Gordon plantations in their new territories is lacking, But there are faint intimations that Sir Robert Gordon's plan was not easily implemented in the circumstances of 1642.

In 1643 Mackay left his affairs in the hands of his son John, Master of Reay, and sailed to Denmark. It is possible that he intended to raise troops for Charles I in the kingdom of his uncle Christian IV: it is possible that he intended his exile to save the Mackay country from the colossal claims of Rachel. There is no surviving evidence beyond the bare statement of Spalding: 'Upon the 17th day of July the Lord of Reay shipped at Aberdeen and went to Denmark, who had lain a long time before at Torry. He was the King's man.'[1] Assuming that Sir Robert Gordon preserved all Mackay's letters (which is probable), Mackay had last written to his uncle from Durness in 1639. In this letter he showed himself to be indeed the King's man, but he also betrayed the first symptoms of declining health, as well as of despondency. 'I have been ever sickly since I did depart from Dunrobin last . . . I shall be glad to see you . . . if I be able to travel, which I hope I shall for I am an great deal better. I am your nephew and servant D. Reay.'[2] In the spring of 1643 in which Mackay sailed to Denmark, Charles I offered the Orkney Islands to Christian IV in return for Danish assistance.[3] Mackay received letters patent from Christian IV in November 1643, ordering him to raise a regiment of foot soldiers in Scotland, and to transport them for the service of the King.[4] It does appear that Mackay and Christian intended to use the still-continuing Thirty Years War as a pretext for raising men for Charles I, although Christian protested to the Scottish Parliament in 1645 that this was not so.[5]

In March 1644 the Gordon country rose in the rear of the Covenanting army, and when Sir John Gordon of Haddo took Aberdeen, the King's Lieutenant, the Marquess of Huntly bustled to the city to enjoy the credit. But the approach of Argyll soon induced Huntly to retire.[6] Indeed, a fear of Argyll carried Huntly to extraordinary lengths. 'Ye hear how the Marquess of Huntly had left the town of Aberdeen, contrary to the expectation of many, upon the last of April, leaving his whole

[1] Spalding 1850: II, 259. [2] Gordonstoun MS. 223. [3] Wedgwood 1958: 213.
[4] Reay MS. 197. [5] Reay MS. 199. [6] Wedgwood 1958: 316-6.

friends within the town in great fear and melancholy.' He moved about Aberdeenshire for some days, then made for the coast, where he 'ships and lands in Sutherland.' There he spent the night in the home of a Gordon. 'Upon the morn he, with his man, rides to Caithness, stays with his cousin german Frances Sinclair that night . . . takes order with his trunks . . . and himself, with his man, upon the morn horses, and to Strathnaver goes he.' Thus the Master of Reay received the head of all the Gordons a fugitive in his home beside the Kyle of Tongue.[1] By the time Montrose at last arrived in the Highlands with the King's commission, in July 1644, the man who could have raised the royalist Gordons was hiding in Tongue. The former Colonel of Mackay's regiment was ruined and in exile, his most populous recruiting grounds along the Naver river the property of the Covenanting Earl of Sutherland.

But the victory of Montrose at Tibbermore, with the eleven hundred Macdonalds led by Alasdair Mac Colla Ciotach, caused a crisis in which the Earl of Sutherland was instantly involved.[2]

Sutherland was not only a member of the Committee for the Defence of the Kingdom: he had also held a colonelcy of horse and foot since 1643, of which he had made, as yet, no active use.[3] He was no sooner called upon for service than he made it clear that his horse and foot were designed solely for service against his private enemies. 'There needs nothing be expected from us here,' he wrote to Lord Elcho on the 14th August 1644, 'till the slowness of Caithness and malignancy of Strathnaver and Assynt, which are within our division, be taken course with.' Strathnaver, which had recently been claimed as an integral part of Sutherland, was now explained to be an independent region over which the Earl himself, exercising the triple functions of superior, sheriff and colonel, stated that he had no control. The aged Earl of Caithness, ruined by the Gordons, had died in the previous year, leaving his great-grandson as the heir whose malignancy now frightened the Earl of Sutherland. Donald Macleod of Assynt had written an abject letter to Sir Robert Gordon as far back as 1633.[4] Subsequent transactions prove him to have been paralysed by insolvency.[5] The Chief of Mackay was in exile. Such were the phantoms

[1] Spalding 1850: II, 353, 367. [2] Wedgwood 1958: 364:6. [3] *S.B.* I: 236.
[4] Gordonstoun MS. 210. [5] Reay MS. 11/15.

with which the Earl of Sutherland sought to explain his reluctance to leave his properties.

He added others at random. 'The Laird of Murkle in Caithness, who is convener of their committee of war, doth always foreslow them in that shire, and not only hinder them, but by his reports of vasion of my Lord of Reay and others by sea, and through the fears of the Clan Donald from the west, puts all others in such fears as there will hardly be any men at all gotten to be levied out of their fields.' Gradually the blame spread its ripples until these lapped the head of the Gordons in Tongue. 'It is no wonder that the Master of Reay doth give no obedience to the Estates' orders, when in despite of them he doth keep an open table to the Marquess of Huntly in his fields, and as they report, doth go openly to their churches' (an excessively foolish slander) 'which I admire the Estates should so long suffer.'[1] In addition to the powers of his other offices, the Earl was armed with two separate writs for the arrest of Mackay. In the second of these, the Committee of Both Kingdoms in London ordered their 'officers in the north', to make Mackay prisoner.[2]

Nevertheless, Mackay returned from Denmark in time to take part in the royalist defence of Newcastle in 1644, and to be taken prisoner at its capture by his former companion in arms, Alexander Leslie, Earl of Leven. 'Upon the 12th of October General Leslie took the town of Newcastle, plundered the same, took divers prisoners both English and Scots . . . The Earl of Crawford, Lord Reay and some others were taken there also, and the Lord Ogilvie taken elsewhere, who were all sent in to Edinburgh and warded, there to abide trial conform to our Scots laws.' Such had been the King's commissions to Leven and Argyll when he hoped to obtain their army that all these men could be convicted of treason, and Mackay could expect forfeiture, if not execution.[3]

By this time the Earl of Sutherland was astir. He had joined Seaforth and Lovat in Ross-shire, the three men united by fear of the Catholic Macdonalds whom Montrose led. They marched in a body to the Spey where Argyll met them at the end of October, and entrusted Sutherland with the defence of the north.[4]

The march to the Spey and the new commission have the

[1] *S.B.* II: 171-2. [2] *C.S.P.D.* 1644: 18-9. [3] Spalding 1850: II, 425, 430.
[4] *S.B.* I: 239. Gordon 1813: 521.

appearance of a bid to protect the new Gordon plantation in Moray, the barony of Gordonstoun beside the Spey. Beyond it could be seen the foothills of the Grampian range, into which the army of Montrose had recently vanished. Sir Robert Gordon of Gordonstoun was exposed to Montrose by the claims of gratitude in addition to proximity, and to his consternation he had been reminded of this fact. Montrose had written to him, urging him to 'be ready to advance his Majesty's service by all possible means, both openly and in secret, as occasion shall offer.'[1] Occasion now offered in the most alarming manner, so that Sir Robert wailed on the 26th November 1644: 'we are in such a fright here that we cannot think of any particular business: for Montrose strives to make his winter quarters here in Moray. He hath been these sixteen days at Speyside, about Rothiemurchus, and now he is in Badenoch. We expect him daily in Moray.'[2] But Montrose took his army of Catholic Macdonalds to winter in the country of the Presbyterian Campbells.

1645 was the year of his wonderful victories. Since Charles I had by this time suffered virtually total defeat by his English subjects, he was left dependent upon the arms of his still victorious Gaelic subjects in Ireland and Scotland. The Gaels possessed at last the royal authority to revenge themselves upon the people who were expropriating them and reducing them to servitude. Jacobitism had been born, which sounded the death-knell of the Stewart dynasty, and which it took the English-speakers of Britain over a century to destroy, using every weapon of genocide.

The issue was seen in these terms by Gaelic spokesmen of the day, just as it had been seen by John Eldar a century earlier. A bard sang of Macdonald of Antrim: 'until the spoils of war avenge the exile and the agony of Ulster, foster under thy wing, O Creator, the blood of kings whose mark is Tara.'[3] Niall Mac Mhuirich chronicled the campaigns of Montrose in one of Scotland's last sustained exercises in the ancient literary prose.[4] On the 25th January 1645 Montrose won the victory over Argyll at Inverlochy which Ian Lom celebrated. 'Early on Sunday morning I climbed the brae above the castle of Inver-

[1] *H.M.C.*, 6th Report: 681. [2] *H.M.C.*, 6th Report: 683. [3] Flower 1926: 118.
[4] Cameron 1891: II, 137-339.

lochy. I saw the army arraying for battle and victory on the field was with Clan Donald.'[1] The English speakers of the Lowlands could expect the first Celtic avalanche since the day of the Red Harlaw in 1411.

This exact parallel was noticed in the Mearns, as Niall Mac Mhuirich recorded. 'They met an honourable old man who was telling them stories and historical affairs, and along with the other stories he told them, he said that the Mearns had not been spoiled since the time it was spoiled by Donald of Isla, the year he fought the battle of Garioch or Harlaw against Duke Murdo; "and I suppose, young man, that you are descended of him, if you be the captain of Clan Ranald." '[2]

Montrose approached the Mearns in a recruiting sweep up the great glen to Inverness and thence into Moray. The ambivalent Earl of Seaforth was flirting with the Covenanters at this time, concerned, perhaps over his title to Lewis, which was claimed by Argyll. He retired from Elgin on the 17th February, just in time before Montrose entered Moray's capital. There, two of Huntly's sons made amends for their father, still hiding in Tongue, by joining the royal standard. Seaforth returned to sign a bond with Montrose before returning to his own country.[3] In nearby Gordonstoun, Sir Robert kept a careful record of the damage done to his estate; since the machinery of Edinburgh might yet serve to repair these losses.[4]

Montrose marched south to capture Dundee. He was surprised by General Baillie while his men were roaming the town, and brought them to the safety of the hills in a feat of countermarching for three days and two nights. 'I have often heard those who were esteemed the most experienced officers, not in Britain only, but in France and Germany, prefer this march to his most celebrated victories.' The terror of the Lowlanders increased when it was seen that he could capture the strongest town with impunity. In Edinburgh, Mackay and the other prisoners in the Tolbooth were condemned to death, but the sentences were not executed, perhaps for fear of reprisals.[5]

The Covenanting officer Sir John Hurry had hastened north to ensure that reinforcements from this large and uncertain area should serve the Covenant rather than Montrose. Hurry

[1] Mackenzie 1955: 10-3, 18. [2] Cameron 1891: II, 196-7.
[3] Napier 1856: II, 491-4. [4] *S.B.* I: 202-3. [5] Napier 1856: II, 495-7.

summoned the Earls of Sutherland, Seaforth and Findlater to join his colours, and thus these men were trapped into facing Montrose at Auldearn on the 8th May 1645. Montrose was joined by a third son of Huntly: Seaforth had brought conscripts from his disputed lordship of Lewis, originally to honour his bond with Montrose, but finally to die at the hands of their fellow-Gaels while the three Earls fled safely from the field. Niall Mac Mhuirich could not have been old enough to witness this latest victory, as Ian Lom had witnessed Inverlochy, but since his is the most graphic and circumstantial account that survives, it is likely to have been taken from an eye-witness.[1]

The Master of Reay never stirred from Tongue in support of either side. The Gordon chronicler stated that Sutherland left him unmolested out of family affection. 'The Master of Reay, being within the Earl of Sutherland's division, never joined with him, paid no loan nor tax, nor any contribution whatsoever of men or money to the public. Neither did he give his personal appearance to any committee. Yet the Earl of Sutherland, out of love and favour to him, did pass all this in silence, he being so near of kin to that Earl'. This hardly agrees with Sutherland's own excuse, that he was prevented from moving out of his sheriffdom by the malignancy of his cousin. 'And (as I do believe), since the Marquess of Huntly repaired thither, he spared the Master of Reay more for his sake, and did forbear (so far as he could) to trouble him, although he was his vassal and bound by many ties to follow him. The Earl of Sutherland sent a message to the Master of Reay that if he would be a quiet and good neighbour, he needed not fear any harm from him; which the Master of Reay promised to perform.' The most effective sanction was that his father lay in the Tolbooth, under sentence of forfeiture and death. The Gordon chronicler did not mention this, but he referred to another: 'the Earl of Sutherland did oversee him, knowing (as the Master of Reay did also pretend) that a little charge would sink him who was already overburdened with debt.'[2]

In December 1644 the Master of Reay registered the debt of 2,500 merks to Robert Farquhar[3], which led to the transfer of the barony of Farr to Farquhar in 1650, and to Sir Robert

[1] Napier 1856: II, 497-505. Cameron 1891: 184-93. [2] Gordon 1813: 527.
[3] Reay MS. 9/3.

Gordon in 1651.[1] In March 1644 the Master of Reay sold Kinlochbervie and other lands to Robert Munro of Achness for 12,000 merks.[2] This transaction may be the culmination of the letters of apprising which Munro obtained against Mackay in 1637, followed by a decreet in 1638.[3] In 1643 Robert Munro made a contract with his son Hugh, who in 1673 assigned the decreet of apprising against Mackay to the son of Sir Robert Gordon and son-in-law of Farquhar.[4] Many of Mackay's clansmen had lent him small sums during the previous decade, without being enabled to acquire any titles to land.[5] But in 1644 the Master of Reay alienated to Duncan Mackay of Syre the town and davoch lands of Skerray and Ribigill for 4,000 merks.[6]

On the 27th February 1645 the Scottish Parliament ordered 'John, Earl of Sutherland to raise and lift the eighth man of his division for strengthening of his own regiment, and for this effect ordains the committee of war with the Earl of Sutherland's division to be assisting him in the lifting and out-putting . . . and to put all Acts and Orders formerly made anent deficients and runaways . . . to due execution.'[7] But Sutherland does not appear to have made any attempt to raise an army in the rear of Montrose. At Letterlyell on the 10th June 1645, the Master of Reay entered into a pact with his uncle of Strathy, Mackay of Bighouse, Hector Munro of Eriboll and three Mackays without designation. 'Whereas we underscribers are deeply sensible of the unconveniency that may result upon us through the misery of the present times, wherein we are like to be enforced either to partake the rebellious course of others against our dread Sovereign, or to undergo the violence of those men who would constrain us to share in their disloyalties, have therefore resolved unanimously not to comply any more with any disloyal procedure, but from henceforth heartily and readily to join and concur by ourselves and followers wheresoever we shall happen to be required; not only for defence of our persons, lands and goods against all and whomsoever, without exception, who shall endeavour to molest us as said is, but likewise to repair our loss upon the occasioners of them as the case shall require.'[8] It was an ultimatum to their feudal superior, sheriff, and colonel.

[1] Reay MSS. 9/4, 9/8. [2] Reay MSS 17/1b. [3] Reay MSS. 3/1b, 3/2b.
[4] Reay MSS. 4/11, 4/12. [5] Reay MSS. 3/6, 3/8, 3/9, 3/10.
[6] Reay MS. 20/1b. [7] *A.P.S.* VI Part 1: 355. [8] Reay MS. 200.

While the Chief of Mackay lay in Edinburgh, under sentence of death and forfeiture, Christian IV wrote to the Scottish Parliament from Copenhagen in May 1645, asking for his release on the grounds that he had returned to Scotland as a Colonel, with a mandate to raise another regiment for the Danish service. It was an accident that Newcastle was being besieged during his arrival there.[1] But in August Montrose entered Edinburgh in triumph, and Mackay had been released with all the other prisoners before the great Marquess met his defeat on the 13th September.[2] Mackay returned to Strathnaver in October 1645, a year after his capture: Huntly left Tongue just in time to avoid an embarrassing meeting with its owner, after having spent over a year there.[3]

Mackay flung himself into the cause in which the interests of Charles I and of the Gaels were now united, despite the defeat of Montrose, and the apparently unassailable position of the Earl of Sutherland and the Covenanters. 'After the Lord Reay's arrival, pretending some commissions from his Majesty and his General Montrose (but not from Huntly), he convenes his countrymen in November 1645. He forces his son and special friends to join with him, comes to a part of Strathnaver which he had formerly sold to the Earl of Sutherland, takes up all the rents thereof (the tenants for the most part being Sliochd Iain Abraich, of his own kin), and takes away the Earl's own proper ky out of Badenloch, distributing them amongst his friends and followers.'[4] A Scottish Parliament convened at St Andrews lost no time in compensating Sutherland for his alleged losses, and in rewarding his negligible services. On the 10th January 1646 they met the first of his supplications with a grant of 1,600 dollars.[5] At the same time, peace was made for the remainder of the winter between Sutherland and Strathnaver: 'seeing there had no blood yet happened betwixt these two countries, neutral friends dealt betwixt them for a truce during the winter following.'[6] The fact that they were still two countries ensured that the truce could not last.

Huntly also was suddenly active on behalf of the ruined King. From Aberdeen he wrote to Mackay on the 19th February 1646: 'My Lord and loving Cousin, your Lordship's son is so well

[1] Reay MS. 199. [2] Wedgwood 1958: 479, 482, 487, 490-7. [3] *S.B.* I: 243.
[4] Gordon 1813: 530. [5] *A.P.S.* VI Part 1: 505, 597.
[6] Spalding 1850: II, 367.

informed of all I have lately heard from England, and hath been such an eye-witness to our late proceedings here that for this time I remit all to his relation. Only know that our arms are by this time shipped at London, and I expect them within a week. Also, the King doth assuredly hold his journey to York in the beginning of April, and I hear that the people are cooling everywhere in the south. Within few days I may perhaps know more, whereof you shall be advertised.'[1] Two days later, Huntly was at Auldearn, eighty miles further north. 'My Lord, at this time I will only recommend unto you what I formerly advised anent your wariness in not joining with any man into any by-courses, but to keep your self upon the sure ground of obeying his Majesty's orders; and let others do as they please. Only do what you can to hinder Sutherland from coming forth.'[2] This was what the Master of Reay had practised during the year which Huntly spent in Tongue; and what the Gordon historian was at pains to state that Mackay did without Huntly's authority. It would have been hard for Mackay to prevent Sutherland from coming forth once the prizes were being distributed by the Scottish Parliament. The Committee of Estates ordered him to bring his troops also: but Sutherland left these behind.[3]

Mackay, Huntly and Montrose were all planning to take the offensive in the spring. But in the spring the net closed round Charles I at Oxford, and on the 6th May he fled, to surrender to the Scottish army at Newark.[4] Before the news of this event, let alone of its consequences, could penetrate to the north coast, Mackay had completed several of his dispositions at Tongue. On the 21st May 1646 he commissioned his son: 'I, Donald Lord Reay, his Majesty's Lieutenant Governor of these northern shires of the kingdom of Scotland, ordains and commands you, John, Master of Reay, Colonel of the Strathnaver regiment presently in his Majesty's service, to convocate and convene the said regiment, with all other forces of the counties of Sutherland and Caithness that shall be willing to adhere and join with you, and that you draw to a head all the forces you may, either in an entire body or by division, as you find occasion, to the marches of Sutherland, and if the said counties sends any forces over

[1] Reay MS. 201. [2] Reay MS. 202. [3] *S.B.* I: 243-4.
[4] Wedgwood 1958: 552.

Portincullter to join with Middleton and his associate rebels, do your best endeavour to stop and stay their march. Or of you hear that any forces be marching to invade Caithness or this country of Strathnaver, in either of these two cases you shall invade the county of Sutherland with fire, sword and all other hostility you may, as likewise to stop the said ferry to your uttermost power. And for your further help in this expedition these presents gives you full power to give order unto all others that shall join unto his Majesty's service. This you fail not to do, and all your under officers, as you shall answer upon your highest peril, providing always that the eight days of the cessation and assurance be expired betwixt me and Sutherland.'[1]

'Now the Parliament drew on at Edinburgh,' related the Gordon historian. 'The Earl of Sutherland addressed himself thither, not only to assist at the Parliament, but also to prosecute his civil actions against the Lord Reay, which were divers. First, whereas the lands of Durness are held by the Lord Reay of the Earl of Sutherland in feu, for the payment of a certain yearly feu-duty, and other irritant causes, that land now fell into the Earl of Sutherland's hands, for not-payment of that duty. Secondly, he had an action of ejection against him, for possessing himself of the lands of Strathnaver which he had formerly sold to the Earl of Sutherland. Thirdly, he had an action against him for the rest of his lands, for rising in arms against him, being his superior in all the lands he hath.'[2] He was assisted by Charles I, who was required to make two concessions by his Scottish captors. The first, that he should establish Presbyterianism throughout his kingdoms, he refused. But he consented to order Montrose to lay down his arms and to leave the country.

The first concern of Montrose was the personal safety of those who had risked their lives in the King's service. 'I cannot be so base nor dishonourable,' he wrote to Mackay in June 1646, 'to leave all who have engaged in the King's service in the mire, but at least desire that they may have immunity for what is past, and be assured of their lives and fortunes in time coming (which is so just that none who carries the name of a Christian can refuse).' He was wrong. The Earl of Sutherland was not alone in seeking to ensure the opposite. Montrose told Mackay that

[1] Reay MS. 203. [2] Gordon 1813: 535.

he had sent for such an assurance, but Charles had withdrawn his commission without terms, so that he no longer possessed the authority to negotiate. 'Meanwhile though I be to do no hostile act, I resolve not [to] abandon you and Seaforth and all other friends who are engaged, until I see you honourably secured.'[1]

Montrose was totally alienated from Argyll because he had led Macdonalds to defeat him, from Covenanters because he had led Catholics to defeat them, from the Lowland magnates, because he had brought an army of Gaels into the Lowlands. Even the royalist Huntly, whom he had once taken a prisoner, was reluctant to deal with him, as Montrose told Mackay. He had asked Huntly whether 'I might come to the Bog to him (in regard I went lately to it before, but he took his horse and fled the house.' Huntly 'absolutely refused all.'[2] But at last Montrose found a man of honour in Scotland, in General Middleton, who came to him with a soldier's terms. The Committee of the 'Kirk' declared them contrary to the Covenant, the ministers thundered excommunications from their pulpits, but the followers of Montrose, including Mackay, were for the present safe.[3]

Huntly tried to add to their immunity. 'These are to certify,' he wrote from the Bog of Gight in September 1646, 'that Donald Lord Reay and John, Master of Reay with their friends and followers have faithfully adhered to the King's service under my command, I being (at that time) his Majesty's Lieutenant of and in the northern parts of this his Majesty's kingdom; and therefore do desire that (according to his Majesty's ordinance thereanent) they and every of them may be secured in their persons and goods from any trouble or molestation upon pretext of what warrant soever which shall not be approved by his Majesty's immediate assent or authority.'[4]

Sir Robert Gordon was abroad once more. 'My noble Lord,' he wrote to Huntly on the 5th November, 'my stay at Aberdeen was longer than I did expect, being hindered by a fourteen days' sickness. I am now (I thank God) returned home . . . and unable any more for winter journeys. I called at the Bog in my return, but in regard of your Lordship's absence I did not

[1] Mackay 1941: 310-1. [2] Mackay 1941: 311. [3] Napier 1856: II, 639-40.
[4] Reay MS. 205.

stay. I did see no man at Aberdeen, but kept me within doors. I was neither summoned nor enquired after to my knowledge. Only I spoke with the Earl of Sutherland and Provost Farquhar, at whose house I lay.'[1]

Sir Robert Gordon had owed much of his success to the assiduous correspondence, both at home and abroad, through which he had kept himself so well informed. Colonel John Munro of Obsdell had written to him in 1632 of events in Europe, and Colonel Robert Munro had done the same in 1635 from Hamburg.[2] He still continued this practice. 'I have herewith sent to your Lordship,' he told Huntly, 'a letter directed by General Major Munro out of Ireland the 26th of September last to the Earl of Sutherland, which showeth that the Irish have declared themselves for the Pope and the King of Spain, having rejected his Majesty's authority of Great Britain. I can hardly believe it, though I know this which I have sent you to be the General Major's hand, and that he should know the truth of business there. Yet the other paper from London the 17th of the last month shows so much also.' This letter illustrates the manner in which Gordon family loyalties overrode political differences, just as did the letter from George Gordon the Elder to Sir Robert at the court of King Charles in 1640. 'We hear nothing yet from the Parliament at Edinburgh. How soon anything comes to my hands, your Lordship shall be advertised. Divers of our Moray men were desired by the Committee of Estates at Aberdeen to lend money to the Estates, for the which they shall have the public faith for repayment. Among others Pluscarty was desired to lend three thousand merks. The surname of Mackenzie (as I hear) were desired to lend about fifty thousand merks.'[3]

Mackay benefited from Sir Robert's information in so far as it was digested into Huntly's advice to him. In December 1646 Huntly told Mackay 'that matters are past all further treaty, therefore look to yourself, and advertise me speedily if I shall [reserve] any arms for you.'[4] On the 23rd the English and Scots made the final arrangements under which the Scottish army would retire from Newcastle on receiving its arrears of £300,000. In the new year it marched north, while Charles

[1] Gordonstoun MS. 570. [2] *S.B.* II: 155-60. [3] Gordonstoun MS. 570.
[4] Reay MS. 206.

was taken by the English to Holmby House.[1] Mackay indeed needed to look to himself as the Earl of Sutherland addressed himself to the tasks of stripping Mackay of his remaining properties, and appropriating the largest possible share of the £300,000 from England.

The Scottish Parliament made a beginning in March 1647 by recommending 'to the general officers not to grant any assurance to the Lord Reay, the Master of Reay, William Mackay of Bighouse, Hugh Mackay of Dilred' (or Strathy, who had succeeded on the death of John of Strathy in 1645), 'Hugh Mackay of Scourie, Neil Mackay *alias* William's son, Hector Munro of Eriboll, Robert Munro of Achness, Hugh Munro of Inveran, son of the said Robert, until first they restore the Earl of Sutherland to the peaceable possession of his lands and goods taken from him.' The 'malignancy of Strathnaver' against the Earl of Sutherland is thus seen to have extended over its entire length from Scourie to the Caithness border, and to have included every man of public position.[2] Parliament did not define the Earl of Sutherland's lands in Strathnaver, but it voted him troops which would enable him to make good his own definition, 'taking in consideration the Earl of Sutherland and his sufferings by the Lord Reay and Master of Reay with their adherants in the rebellion, with the report of the grand committee hereanent, and herewith also considering the good carriage and constant affection of the Earl to the good cause and safety of the country.' The Master of Reay had done nothing beyond extending hospitality to Huntly, so that the inclusion of his name appears to be a precaution of the watchful legislature in case Mackay had made any disposition of his properties to his son. Parliament recommended 'that there may be an commanded party of 500 men to concur with the Earl of Sutherland and his people for safety of him and them from the Lord Reay and Master of Reay and their adherants, their incursions and depredations.' Even this did not suffice, for orders were added 'for raising the adjacent shires for repossessing of him to his lands and goods against the said Lord Reay and his adherants.'[3]

The need for such an armament bears upon the problem of the force which the Colonel and Sheriff of Sutherland was com-

[1] Wedgwood 1958: 566-7. [2] *A.P.S.* VI Part 1: 766.
[3] *A.P.S.* VI Part 1: 817.

missioned to maintain in his sheriffdom, although it had so often failed to materialise in the past. Sutherland now informed Parliament about the regiment that had so often failed to march to serve the Covenant, at the same time as he obtained the loan of other troops. An Act was passed 'concerning John, Earl of Sutherland's supplication anent the compts and bygone arrears of his regiment, and the other great charges and expenses debursed by him upon his regiment and otherways in the public service. They appoint and ordain the sum of £3,000 sterling to be paid to the Earl of Sutherland out of the last £100,000 sterling due to the kingdom of England to this kingdom.'[1]

This Parliament attempted to perform one further service for the Earl of Sutherland. The acquisition of lands in Strathnaver in 1642 had not been completed in time to secure a title of nobility to them by letters patent from the King, but any future agreement with Charles would involve the ratification of all Acts of the Scottish Parliament, as had occurred in the past. One of these now referred explicitly to the Earl and his eldest son as 'John, Earl of Sutherland and Lord Strathnaver', and before 1647 was passed, the King had agreed to ratify it among all the other statutes.[2] Such a procedure could not bestow a valid title of nobility, but it satisfied successive Lyon Kings of Arms, and was only dismissed finally as a fiction by a member of the English College of Heralds.[3]

When the Earl of Sutherland had completed his services to the Scottish nation, he returned north in May 1647 to attend to the responsibilities of local government. Mackay wrote once more to Huntly, the King's Lieutenant, for advice as to whether he should resist or capitulate. 'My Lord,' answered Huntly on the 25th May, 'yesterday I received your Lordship's by the bearer, and all I can say for the present is that I am in a daily hope of some good revolution in the King's business of which you shall be advertised how soon it comes. In the meantime let not the present face of things move you to abstain from prosecuting your other just affairs with any of your neighbours, for you may be confident that his Majesty's affairs will be carried in end to the satisfaction of all his faithful subjects, though now Rebellion doth range at random to the full. My

[1] *A.P.S.* VI Part 1: 802-3. [2] *A.P.S.* VI Part 1: 742.
[3] G.E.C. XII Part 1: 563.

next will be perhaps more particular . . .'[1] This appears to have been the last letter that Mackay ever received from the Marquess of Huntly, and he took the hint that it contained.

'The Earl of Sutherland returned out of Edinburgh in May 1647,' recorded his chronicler. 'The Lord Reay and the Master, hearing of his arrival, and what he had obtained against them, did presently write to him; and in a submissive way they offer him all satisfaction, so far as they were able, or lay in their power. The Earl of Sutherland being loathe to enter in blood with so near cousins, harkened to the mediation of friends. Many meetings they had all the ensuing summer. Sir Robert Gordon takes several journeys thither to reconcile them.'[2] The contemporary evidence provides little support for this vignette of an affectionate family gathering, whose differences were dissipated by the benign presence of Sir Robert.

Of the two principal issues, the first had been defined by the Scottish Parliament as Mackay's 'incursions and depradations.'[3] The Gordon chronicler's explanation was that Mackay had forcibly collected rent in the form of cattle from lands at the southern end of the Naver valley which he had previously sold to Sutherland.[4] The two allegations were an attempt to incriminate both Mackay and his heir in any resistance that may have been made by the Abrach Mackays of that area against dispossession, or against the payment of rent in the form of their cattle to the Earl of Sutherland, since his purchase in 1642. Such resistance is not unlikely to have occurred, and subsequent accusations associated it with Neil, whose father William had been the last Mackay of Achness before its sale to Robert Munro, a transaction completed by September 1637.[5] Neil's brother John Williamson was by this time a burgess of Thurso,[6] although he may have retained possession of his former home at Càrn Achaidh for another three decades.[7]

Mackay wrote to the Earl on the 17th July 1647, disclaiming any personal knowledge of disorders in this area. 'Touching malefactors, it is true I sent for Neil, William's son, and Alexander Clerk, to know what they would answer for themselves. Neil answereth, he never wronged your Lordships' country, save when he was sent by me with a party to spy the

[1] Reay MS. 207. [2] Gordon 1813: 538. [3] *A.P.S.* VI Part 1: 817.
[4] Gordon 1813: 530. [5] Reay MS. 3/6. [6] Reay MS. 3/5.
[7] Reay MS. 21/2b.

Frith the day of *Breacach* before the pacification; and marvelleth why your Lordship craveth him more than the rest who were in that party. Alexander Clerk refuseth not to go to Dunrobin when it pleaseth your Lordship to call him.' It may be assumed that Mackay did not write Frith as Gaelic for a deer forest but in its contemporary spelling for the English word 'firth'.

Mackay's papers disclose that the Mudale valley west of Loch Naver was sold to the Earl in 1637[1]. Mackay continued his letter to the Earl on the 17th July 1647: 'Touching present restitution of Strathnaver, I needed not answer it in my former, since it was mentioned in my first. Nor knew I till now that Loch Naver is his Lordship's, and am glad it should be so, that his Lordship be our vassal.'[2]

Mackay's pleasantry was misplaced. While so many people were preoccupied with the issues of religion and government which have given to the history of the seventeenth century such an abiding interest, the Earl of Sutherland's overriding concern was to add Strathnaver to his stolen earldom and bestow it on his heir as a courtesy title. The head of the disinherited Abrach sept in the Strath, Neil Williamson, was a prime target.

Two days later Sutherland replied: 'concerning Loch Naver, although it were not mine but my countryman's, there can be no honourable or conscientious agreement until these lands be restored fully unto the proper owner.' The sheriff acquainted Mackay with his judicial methods. 'Touching Neil Williamson . . . the contrary will be found when Neil shall be put to trial; and for Alexander Clerk, he shall be delivered as worthy of hanging before ever I send for him.' He enclosed a form of submission for Mackay to sign. 'For the Lord Reay and his friends' submission I have sent the form of one herewith. How soon that is sent hither subscribed, the form of the Lord Reay's own shall be sent back.' The Earl concluded his commands to his vassal: 'this is all I thought meet to answer, neither will I trouble myself with further writing till these things be performed, the equity whereof shall be made clear to all.'[3]

The Earl's ultimatum referred to a complaint by Mackay against Robert Gray,[3] and the chronicler whose task it was to

[1] Reay MS. 6. [2] *S.B.* III: 195-6. [3] *S.B.* III: 197.

make the equity of these proceedings clear to all listed among the subjects of negotiation 'satisfaction of the gentlemen of the name of Gray.'[1] The first of these to appear in a capacity useful to the Earl of Sutherland was Robert Gray of Bellon, who was commissioned by the Scottish Parliament in 1645 to uplift the rents of malignants in the sheriffdom.[2] By the 3rd February 1648 the Master of Reay had bound himself to pay Robert Gray £1,248 Scots.[3] The debt mounted by leaps and bounds, £2,996 Scots to Robert Gray,[4] 2,500 merks to his brother Alexander Gray of Creich.[5] By 1650 the debt was alleged to have grown to £8,026 9s 0d, and Mackay was apprised in favour of the Grays in 1653 of 'the lands and barony of Durness, comprehending the lands and others therein mentioned, the lands and barony of Farr, likewise comprehending the towns and lands therein specified, and also the town and lands of Edderachillis, [   ]naver, Strathy and Strath Halladale.[6] When Gray obtained a charter for these lands from the Earl of Sutherland in 1656, the debt was stated to have mounted to £9,616 19s 4d Scots.[7] The collectors of malignant rents were thus given the final pickings of whatever titles remained in Strathnaver. Like the titles of Farquhar and Munro, they passed into Gordon hands.

When Mackay attended a meeting at Lairg on the 21st August 1647 and negotiated through the remainder of the summer, he appears to have enjoyed a sole and quite accidental asset. The mercenary soldier of the Covenant, General David Leslie, was still refusing, in October, to implement the orders of Parliament by sending his troops in support of the Earl of Sutherland's private enterprises. The Gordon chronicler stated that Leslie wrote 'to the Earl of Sutherland, persuading him to agree with the Lord of Reay, seeing that a friendly agreement betwixt so near kinsmen would prove most profitable; and the bringing in of an army to these countries would not only trouble Sutherland, but also disenable the Lord Reay to give him any satisfaction.' The chronicler chose the explanation that 'David Leslie did this in regard of his obligation to the Lord Reay, under whom he had served in the wars of Germany.'[8] But Leslie was unconnected with the old Scottish nobility, and actually

[1] Gordon 1813: 538. [2] *A.P.S.* VI Part 1: 491. [3] Reay MSS, 6/1, 6/17 fl.
[4] Reay MS. 6/3. [5] Reay MS. 6/5. [6] Reay MS. 6/17 f. 6.
[7] Reay MS. 6/17 f. 7. [8] Gordon 1813: 539.

refused the coveted earldom of Orkney from Charles I less than a year previously.[1] He had been involved twice in a massacre of the Celtic peoples, and his repugnance on both occasions had been particularly remarked upon. While Gordon's explanation may be correct, it may not represent the whole truth of the matter. Cromwell refused his troops for Clotworthy's enterprises in Ireland in rather similar circumstances.

But a month after David Leslie's refusal, Sutherland succeeded in enlisting the help of General Middleton, who ordered a lieutenant-colonel with part of the garrison at Inverness to the Earl's assistance. Thus fortified, Earl John moved fast, to gain the maximum advantage from surprise. He 'assembles his countrymen and takes journey with his army into Strathnaver in October 1647.' It was his first recorded visit, and required an army. 'Being encamped at Rossal, the Lord Reay hastens to him with his son and friends, only Neil Williamson excepted, who feared to come, being guilty in his own conscience. There they ended, and in the presence of the whole army the Lord Reay, his son, and the special men of his friends came in to the Earl of Sutherland, and submitted themselves . . . The Lord Reay and all his friends subscribed a blank bond to the Earl of Sutherland for his and his countrymen's indemnity, to be filled up at the Earl's own pleasure.' Rossal, where Mackay had stayed in the New Year of 1619, 'almost healthless' from drinking healths, remains to this day a memorial to the Gordon victory.[2]

In order to mitigate the severity of what might be written in that blank bond, Mackay travelled to Dunrobin with his son, where Sir Robert Gordon awaited them. Mackay agreed to a money payment to the Earl and to Robert Gray, 'for their losses'. He delivered some 'malefactors' to the Earl 'to be punished at his pleasure', though William's son was not among them. The Chief alienated further fishings, lands and woods in the Naver valley 'which lay convenient for the Earl's lands there'. In return, Earl John gave Mackay a discharge of his claim to Durness and 'whatsoever else he had obtained against him'. He returned the blank bond, 'and he writes to the Estates of Parliament and to the Assembly of the Church that they had given him satisfaction'. The supreme organs of church and state had performed their functions, and were no longer required.[3]

[1] *Montreuil* I: 392. [2] Gordon 1813: 539. *S.B.* II: 40-1. [3] Gordon 1813: 540.

Mackay signed this agreement in January 1648, took ship from Thurso in the spring, and sailed away from his country for the last time.

Neil Williamson was still at large. The Gordon chronicler stated that from November 1648 the Master of Reay 'hounded out and encouraged his cousin Neil (*alias* Williamson), Chieftain of the *Sliochd Iain Abraich*, to molest the Earl's tenants in Strathnaver; and to this purpose the Master had entertained the relics of the Irishes in his country. So Neil, assembling some of his kindred, with these Irishes, invaded the Earl of Sutherland's chamberlain in Strathnaver, who was gathering the Earl's rents there: and setting upon him at unawares (expecting no such villainy) they robbed him and his company of such rents as they had gathered in that country, escaping hardly with their lives: for which the fact the Earl pursued the Master of Reay before the ensuing Parliament.'[1] It sounds improbable that the Master of Reay should have involved himself so pointlessly in further dangers of this kind: but it was necessary to incriminate him since he, as opposed to Neil Williamson, still possessed titles to lose. Neil died violently that winter, as so many other 'Irishes' were doing at this time between County Kerry and Cape Wrath. But Sutherland transferred his alleged guilt to the Master of Reay, accusing him before Parliament of having 'violently taken up the suppliant's rents in Strathnaver.' He was voted £10,900 in compensation out of public moneys; an interesting assessment of the value of the lands he had acquired from Mackay, or of the sums he was attempting to extract from them in rent. The Earl was also invested with the office of Lord Keeper of the Privy Seal.[2]

Charles II was proclaimed King by the Scottish Estates of Parliament almost immediately after the execution of his father in January 1649. Donald, first Lord Reay died a few weeks later, and the place of his death remains uncertain. Some have stated that he died in Bergen.[3] Others have supposed that he died in Copenhagen, from where his last surviving papers are addressed.[4] On the 16th January 1949, Mackay received a warrant for 500 dollars from Frederick III of Denmark, who had succeeded his father in the previous year.[5] This supports

[1] Gordon 1813: 546. [2] *A.P.S.* VI Part 2: 353.
[3] G.E.C. X: 754. Mackay 1885: 252n. [4] Mackay 1906: 141.
[5] Reay MS. 208.

the statement of the Danish Ambassador in London in 1662, that the late Chief of Mackay had been granted a pension by the King of Denmark on his last visit to the country.[1] On the 9th February, Mackay sent from Copenhagen a document which reveals that he planned to raise a regiment for the Swedish service in Germany; although the Thirty Years War had at last ended in the previous year.[2] But there is no reference to the first Lord Reay in the Danish or Norwegian state papers of 1648-9, while the records of Bergen were destroyed in the fire of 1702.

In 1649 the Gordons and the Grays took possession of Tongue house itself, seat of the Mackay Chiefs.

An Englishman observed at this time that the Scots, 'though all of one nation, are subdivided into four several factions'.[3] There was Montrose in exile, against whose 'scandalous carriage, pernicious counsels, and contagious company' other Scots in exile warned Charles II: meaning that he had led the Gaels against the Lowlanders.[3] There was the Earl of Seaforth, whose brother Mackenzie of Pluscarden joined Sir Thomas Urquhart of Cromartie in February 1649 in evicting Argyll's garrison from Inverness.[4] There was the faction of Lowland nobles led by Hamilton and Lauderdale who had signed the Engagement. The fourth and most powerful group consisted of Argyll, the Scottish commissioners of the Covenant, and David Leslie their general. All protested their loyalty to Charles II, and warned him against the others. Sutherland belonged to Argyll's party and warned the Estates of Parliament against the new Chief of Mackay.

On the 16th March he informed Parliament that 'the men of Strathnaver with the remainder of the Irishes that were with James Graham in his rebellion has fallen down upon the county of Caithness, where the country people has killed two of the principal commanders and six of their men, and taken ten prisoners'. The Earl of Sutherland asked for a garrison and his request was approved.[5] He was provided with ampler justification when General Middleton and the heir of the Marquess of Huntly, who had been executed, joined Mackenzie; who invoked the Mackay alliance in May. This was something more sub-

[1] Reay MS. 222. [2] Reay MS. 209. [3] Napier 1856: II, 697.
[4] Fraser 1905: 336-7. [5] *A.P.S.* VI Part 2: 721.

stantial than the phantom of Montrose's army with which Sutherland had sought to frighten Parliament. Mackay marched into Ross-shire 'with three hundred able men, well provided with arms and other necessaries,' according to the Gordon chronicler.[1] The Minister of Kirkhill left a graphic description of this latest Highland army on its march south. 'Lieutenant General Middleton, having made his escape out of Berwick into these parts, the Lord Reay and the Mackenzies mustered and made a body of 1,500; and coming over, some at Kessock, some at Beauly, crossed the bridge at Ness upon the Lord's day in time of Divine service and alarmed the people of Inverness, impeding God's worship in that town. For, instead of bells to ring in to service, I saw and heard no other than the noise of pipes, drums, pots, pans, kettles, and spits in the streets to provide them victuals in every house and in their quarters.'[2]

But within the week Mackay was surprised at daybreak in Balveny castle by the Spey, surrounded by horsemen while his own troop of horse was absent. He was captured with '900 Clan Kenzie, Strathnaver men, and Badenoch men: they killed about four score before they were taken.' Huntly, Middleton, and Mackenzie of Pluscarden were able to make their peace with General David Leslie, who was never vindictive on his own account, and who had shewn himself especially well-disposed to Mackay's father some months before. But he could not now save the son from a predicament of such peculiar concern to the Keeper of the Privy Seal of Scotland. The Gordon chronicler recorded: 'every man returned to their own houses, leaving the Lord Reay to suffer for the rest.'[3] Parliament issued a warrant to the magistrates of Edinburgh on the 23rd May 'for keeping Lord Reay and others in sure prison.' Those who kept him company included Duncan, Robert, Donald and John Mackay, a Macleod and seven Mackenzies.[4]

The first reprisal which the Earl of Sutherland obtained in Parliament against Mackay was a garrison of a hundred men, at a monthly charge of £1,114 13s 4d.[5] But meanwhile James Campbell, Provost of Dunbarton, had already received legislative approval for a strange item of business. In June 1649 he showed to Parliament that Mackenzie of Pluscarden owed him

[1] Gordon 1813: 548. [2] Fraser 1905: 338-9. [3] Gordon 1813: 549.
[4] *A.P.S.* VI Part 2: 380. [5] *A.P.S.* VI Part 2: 506.

money. Since Mackenzie was free, while Mackay 'and others that were in the late rebellion are in the Estates' power', Campbell asked if he might receive their fines instead, and these were allotted to him.[1] A Provost, as well as an Earl, was able to use the Scottish legislature as the instrument of his private business. But on the 4th August Sutherland obtained the sequestration of Mackay's entire estate by an ingenious provision. It was enacted that Mackay should not be set free 'until first he restore to the Earl of Sutherland and Sir Robert Gordon their said lands, goods, and rents so wrongously taken from them.' So long as Mackay was in prison while there was a garrison in Strathnaver, it could not have been in his power to withhold lands or rents (which consisted of cattle and other commodities). So the only effect of this provision would be to keep the Chief in indefinite captivity.[2]

The garrison occupied Mackay's seat at Tongue, where the commissioners for the Earl of Sutherland included Robert Gray and another who signed himself 'J. Gray', three Gordons and two Murrays. On the 15th October these issued a bond of protection on behalf of the Keeper of the Privy Seal and his son 'Lord Strathnaver' in favour of Mackay's clansmen during their good behaviour. In return for this, the commissioners undertook to 'deal earnestly' with the Earl 'to be an instrument to the said Lord Reay's and friends' releasements.' All gentlemen and tenants would be secure in their persons and property 'from the garrison.' The Chief's house at Tongue would not be destroyed, the deer would not be taken, the surrounding woods by the Kyle of Tongue would be spared so far as possible.[3] Such were the circumstances in which Farquhar received the lands and barony of Farr, from Skerray to Kirtomy, under the Great Seal of Scotland in January 1650, while to the west of Tongue Robert Gray was installed in Durness and Edderachillis by a charter from the Earl of Sutherland in March.[4] There followed some property adjustments between Gray and Farquhar in the same month of March 1650.[5]

The Gordon enterprise appeared to be almost completed: yet it contained a fatal flaw. The imprisonment of the Chief and the garrison at Tongue would prevent the Mackays from com-

[1] *A.P.S.* VI Part 2: 443. [2] *A.P.S.* VI Part 2: 526. [3] Reay MS. 210.
[4] *R.G.S.* 1634–51: no. 2168. Reay MS. 6/14. [5] Reay MSS. 13/12, 13/13.

mitting any further treasons, while an English administration was about to take the government of Scotland out of the hands of its feudal nobility, just as John Eldar, Clerk and Redshank had prayed a Tudor King to do over a century earlier.

8

Deliverance

DURING the winter of 1649, Montrose was planning to make a landing on the north coast of Scotland, while Charles II planned to bring a Celtic army from Ireland to subdue his southern kingdom. But the news of Wexford and Drogheda led Charles to abandon his Irish plan in favour of the only English-speaking party which offered him a throne. In January 1650 he invited commissioners of the Scottish Committee of Estates to meet him again at Breda.[1] The consequence was that by the time Montrose sailed from Bergen to Orkney in March 1650, Charles II had given a separate commission to the party in Scotland which immobilised his own Highland supporters, and which had already condemned Montrose to death.

Montrose appears to have been ignorant of the state of affairs in the Mackay country, for he gave orders for the mainland landing in April as follows. 'If you shall find, according to your certain intelligence, that all the country of Caithness are in arms to resist you . . . in that case you are not to hazard to force it, but to set for Strathnaver, and there to attempt your landing as with most safety and conveniency you can. Where if you should also find too much difficulty, as by appearance there cannot, you are to apply a little higher, betwixt that and Kintail, which places are all for the King, and there make your descent.'[2] Montrose meant that they should seek a landing at the mouth of the Naver river or alternatively at Skerray, just over a mile by sea to the west, the next port before the great inlet of the Kyle of Tongue, known as Kintail Mackay. All of

[1] Gardiner 1894: I, 126-48, 203-27. [2] Napier 1856: II, 742-3.

this land had become the property of Robert Farquhar of Mounie a few months previously, while Invernaver itself was the northernmost point of the Earl of Sutherland's new properties in Strathnaver, and Tongue was garrisoned by the Covenanters.

When Montrose crossed the Pentland Firth to Thurso on the 14th April, the lack of reinforcements from Strathnaver was not his only disappointment. Ships containing 1,200 men with twelve brass guns had sailed from Göteborg in Sweden, but they were dispersed by bad weather, and only about 200 men arrived from abroad to reinforce his Orcadian levies. Montrose took the east coast route to the Ord of Caithness. His last hope was to defeat Earl John in Sutherland, penetrate to Ross-shire, and there rally the promised Mackenzies to his standard.[1] But the Earl did not stay to fight him. When the 500 untrained Orcadians looked over the Ord of Caithness into the plains and foothills of Sutherland, their ruler sent his cattle into the hills, garrisoned his castles, and retired across the Dornoch Firth to the safety of General Leslie's camp in Ross-shire.[2]

Montrose followed to his doom: for the Mackenzies were in a predicament similar to the Mackays in a military sense. Their Chief was not a prisoner, but he was abroad, excommunicated by the Church, while his castle of Brahan and his port of Cromarty were occupied by David Leslie's garrisons. As a result, the unfortunate Orcadians were almost alone at the rout of Carbisdale on the 27th April. While Montrose fled west and the Earl of Sutherland returned boldly to Dunrobin, Charles II came to terms with the commissioners of the Covenant. On the 21st May 1650, Montrose was executed by the government recognised by the King, after being handed over by Donald Macleod of Assynt.[3]

The hereditary designation of this branch of the MacLeods was Mac Nèill, and Iain Lom MacDonald the bard addressed him thus. '*Mac Nèill* from dreary Assynt, if I caught you in my net I would give evidence to compass your condemnation and I would not save you from the gallows. If you and I should meet in the bogs of Ben Etive, the dark waters of the quagmire would be disturbed and a club floating on top.'

[1] Napier 1856: II, 741-3. [2] *S.B.* I: 254.
[3] Gardiner 1894: I, 236-54. *S.B.* I: 255-6, 262.

Mhic Nèill a Asaint chianail,
Nan glacainn ann mo lìon thu,
Bhiodh m'fhacal air do bhìnne
'S cha dìobrainn thu o'n chroich.

Nan tachrainn is tu fèin
Ann am boglachan Beinn Eite,
Bhiodh uisge dubh na fèithe
Dol troimh a chèile 's ploc.[1]

But while Iain Lom immortalised MacLeod of Assynt in his most terrible poem, Donald Neilson, as he signed himself,[2] was rewarded by the Scottish Parliament with the command of the Strathnaver garrison at Tongue, on the 5th July 1650.[3]

But the imprisonment of Mackay and the garrisoning of Tongue proved to be the decisive miscalculation of the Earl of Sutherland's career in Strathnaver. Had Mackay been treated like Middleton or Seaforth's brother, he could scarcely have failed to join Montrose, and to have shared his fate at or after Carbisdale. Sutherland travelled to Edinburgh in June, but soon returned north again when Cromwell crossed the Tweed in July. Sutherland purported to be raising troops with which to repel the English invader, but he had sent none by the time the battle of Dunbar was fought in September.[4] The defeat of General Leslie by Cromwell weakened the power of the Covenanting party responsible for Mackay's imprisonment. On the 15th December 1650, in Sutherland's continued absence, the Committee of Estates read and approved a report (since lost) in his favour: which informed Mackay that the affairs of the Keeper of the Privy Seal no longer prospered in Edinburgh.[5] Five days later Parliament made its fresh appointments of Colonels of Horse and Foot, by shires. The Earl of Sutherland was named for his shire, but Strathnaver was detached from it as a separate command under Mackay's brother, or alternatively his wife's father, Hugh Mackay of Scourie.[6] The logical consequence was enacted by 'his Majesty and Parliament' on the 24th December, when they abolished 'the giving maintenance

[1] Mackenzie 1955: 58-9.
[2] Gordonstoun MS. 210. Reay MS. 11/15. [3] *A.P.S.* VI Part 2: 605.
[4] *S.B.* I: 263. [5] *A.P.S.* VI Part 2: 619. [6] *A.P.S.* VI Part 2: 623.

to the garrison in Strathnaver, and grants liberty to the Earl of Sutherland if be thinks fit to garrison the same for his own security upon his own charges.'[1]

When Charles II was crowned at Scone on the first day of the new year, the Keeper of his Privy Seal did not attend. He apologised to the King on the 25th January 1651, saying 'that I was not acquainted by any with the diet, nor had I any certain knowledge thereof till about the midst of this instant': which is not the least surprising of the Earl's assertions.[2] After the coronation there was a bustle of recruitment for a new army to oppose Cromwell, in which General Middleton was allotted responsibility for the northern levies.[3] Still Sutherland remained at home, pleading illness for his failure to attend Parliament in March 1651. 'The indefatigable trouble I have had at all occasions, night and day, to hasten the people, hath casten me into a little distemper of body, which, with the settling of my affairs, doth necessitate my humbly begging your Majesty's pardon.'[4]

The Gordon chronicler recorded for publication in 1813 that 'the Earl of Sutherland sent a regiment of Sutherland and Strathnaver men, well appointed, to Stirling to his Majesty.'[5] There had been a time when the Earl held a commission to maintain such a regiment, but although he had been paid for doing so, its existence was never reported by any independent witness; while a garrison had finally to be supplied for Strathnaver from without. He no longer held a commission for Strathnaver, whose contingent was reported by the Minister of Kirkhill in April, as it passed through Inverness, commanded by one of Hugh Mackay of Scourie's nephews.[6]

In July 1651 Charles II himself wrote sharply to the Earl of Sutherland. 'All is now at stake, religion, the liberty of this ancient kingdom, our honour and person, your own particular fortune, and all that can be dear to a man of honour. We expect at this time that you will bestir yourself, and that you will consider nothing but what may set up the army again.'[7] But there is little evidence that the Earl of Sutherland sent any troops to fight in the battle of Worcester.

[1] *A.P.S.* VI Part 2: 627. [2] *S.B.* 1: 263-4.
[3] Gardiner 1894: I, 389.
[4] *S.B.* I: 265. [5] Gordon 1813: 559. [6] Fraser 1905: 378. [7] *S.B.* I: 267.

It is not known when Mackay was released from the Tolbooth at Edinburgh, but it appears to have been after Charles II's departure from Scotland, and the conquest of the country by General Monck. The highly circumstantial tradition which survived in Strathnaver associated his release with Cromwell's authority; and a kernel of historical accuracy may have been preserved in this particular circumstance.[1]

For paradoxically, Cromwell did not come to Scotland with the feelings towards the Gaels there that had enabled him to commit the atrocities associated with the names of Wexford and Drogheda. The massacres and expropriations of Gaels in Ireland, and the plantations and speculations of English speakers in that country reproduced on a larger scale the policies of the Lowlanders towards the Gaels in Scotland. It was with these Lowlanders that Cromwell's own quarrel lay, since they led the Covenanters who had attempted to use the authority both of Charles I and of Charles II to impose Presbyterian Calvinism on England by force.

This circumstance provided Cromwell with a foundation for sympathy towards the Highland opponents of the Covenant. They were not necessarily Catholics, and unlike Ireland, 'in the interval 1560 to 1653 . . . there was no organised Catholic Church in Scotland, but only individual Catholics.'[2] From the north of Scotland it was reported, indeed, in 1651: 'there is a very precious people who seek the face of God in Sutherland and divers other parts beyond Inverness, which, but that I had it from so good hands, I should have much questioned.'[3]

Another factor affected Cromwell's attitude to the benefit of the Highlanders. He had been forced to break the power of the English Presbyterian gentry, and in so doing he had broken the power of the English Parliament which they controlled. In Scotland the Calvinist divines flourished under the protection of a feudal nobility whose power Cromwell set out to destroy, as the Tudors had destroyed it in England over a century earlier. 'Free the poor commoners, and make as little use as can be either of the great men or clergy,' he was advised, and this was the course which he followed.[4]

[1] Mackay 1829: 349-50.
[2] Anderson 1956: 112. [3] Firth 1895: 31.
[4] Firth 1895: xxxiv-xxxv.

The committee of nobles in Edinburgh that called itself a Parliament was abolished. Union between England and Scotland (the dream of James VI) was proposed in December 1651, and sealed two years later by the Instrument of Government. Under this union, Scotland was to be represented in a legislature at London, but in fact Cromwell's parliamentary experiments did not prosper and Scotland was governed, like England, by a military dictatorship.[1] Under its sword the old jurisdictions were abolished and new courts of justice erected. An Edinburgh news-letter of December 1651 reported: 'this day, according to custom, divers Scottish suiters made their addresses to the honourable committee of officers at Leith, where all just expectations were duly satisfied with quick despatches in point of justice (whereas some suits before had hung sixteen years without any period put to it in their old Judicatories), which doth much cheer up the Scottish people . . . in finding more respect and justice from their supposed enemies than ever they did from their own countrymen.' Nicoll confided to his diary: 'to speak truth, the English were more indulgent and merciful to the Scots nor was the Scots to their own countrymen . . . They also filled up the rooms of justice courts with very honest clerks and members of that judicatory.' An English official declared with pardonable pride: 'a man may ride all Scotland over with a switch in his hand and £100 in his pocket, which he could not have done these five hundred years.' And Bishop Burnet, looking back on those times, gave his judgment: 'at no time the Highlands were kept in better order than during the usurpation.'[2]

The improvement in administration could not be due to racial superiority, the Lowlanders being identical in race to those on the southern side of the former frontier. But the new administrators belonged to a new professional order, such as Scotland had not possessed the same opportunities for evolving under the rule of the feudal magnates. They possessed names such as Fitch, Overton, Deane, Cobbett and Alured: names that never affrighted the air, in either camp, at Agincourt. But they were the kind of men whom Cromwell promoted because 'they made some conscience of what they did'; the sort who appeared in a

[1] Terry 1902: xxi-xxiv.
[2] Firth 1895: xxviii-xxix. Firth 1899: xxxviii.

law court to be 'very honest clerks.'[1] The Gordon chronicler related how this new foreign power moved into the world formerly dominated by his surname. 'At length the English army . . . crossed the Spey in December 1651 and came into Moray, and so to Inverness, where they planted a garrison. Thence they marched through Ross, Sutherland, Caithness and Orkney, putting all these countries under contribution and assessment, planting garrisons where they pleased. Thus with the loss of the liberty of my nation, I end both this year 1651 and my collections, having neither heart nor encouragement to proceed therein.'[2]

In February 1652 the feudal estates were broken up by nothing more ceremonious than a Declaration. Vassals who had followed their lords in the late war 'shall not only be pardoned for all acts past, but be set free from their former dependencies and bondage services; and shall be admitted as tenants, free-holders, and heritors, to farm, hold, inherit and enjoy, from and under this Commonwealth, proportions of the said confiscated and forfeited lands under such easy rents and reasonable conditions as may enable them, their heirs and posterity, to live with a more comfortable subsistence than formerly, and like a free people delivered through God's goodness from their former slaveries, vassalage and oppression.'[3]

In April 1652, 'Mr Robert Gordon, Deputy for the Shire of Sutherland', communicated the assent of this sheriffdom to the proposed union between Scotland and England.[4] Argyll capitulated in August.[5] By the end of 1652 Scotland was apparently pacified, and Colonel Robert Lilburne succeeded as commander-in-chief in December.[6] Lilburne thus became the representative of the new régime, through which the Earl of Sutherland might yet complete the policies in Strathnaver which he had not been able to complete through the authority of Charles I, the Covenant, or Charles II. The Earl of Sutherland began to entertain the English military commander in the spring of 1653, as Lilburne informed Cromwell.

'I was a year ago at his house,' wrote Lilburne on the 11th April 1654, 'and found very much civility and religion in the family, and I hear his sons are both of them much affected to us, and inclined to church fellowship. I have been thinking some-

[1] Hill 1961: 280. [2] Gordon 1813: 561-2. [3] Firth 1895: xxxv-xxxvi.
[4] Terry 1902: 178. [5] Firth 1895: 48-50. [6] Firth 1895: xxxi.

times that if your Highness should call the elder son to London, and some other young gentlemen that are virtuously inclined, whom I could name to your Highness, and afford them your Highness' countenance by receiving some breeding under your Highness and amongst the English, it would in time get us a good interest here.' Lilburne had been fully informed of the other price of this good interest. 'I hear the Lord Reay is very active against us (a most unworthy man), and that the Earl of Sutherland is driven out of his country with his sons, and Middleton hath turned his lady out of doors, and sent her after him, and his land and estate is exceedingly wasted by Middleton and his accomplices . . . I think if it be true that the Lord Reay is so active, if his lands were given to repair the Lord Sutherland it were but just.'[1]

It was indeed true. The Earl of Glencairn had assumed the leadership of a royalist rising in the spring of 1653 and in addition to Highland Chiefs, many Lowland noblemen had flocked to his support with understandable alacrity. General Middleton had arrived from abroad with the King's commission in February 1654, landing at Thurso, where Mackay joined him with 200 men. According to Captain Peter Mews, who accompanied Middleton, Sutherland was not 'driven out of his country' as he complained to Lilburne; 'but leaving his house and retreating to the rebels, gave us some cause to suspect that we were not so safe as that we should trust ourselves to the country unarmed.' The extent of the Earl of Sutherland's cowardice was apparently unknown to them, despite the precedent of Montrose's last campaign.[2]

On the 26th July 1654, at Creich in Sutherland, General Middleton used his delegated powers to strip the Earl of Sutherland of all his titles in Strathnaver, leaving him, however, with his original properties in Sutherland. 'Whereas the Earl of Sutherland, notwithstanding all fair endeavours to invite him to his Majesty's service hath neglected to join with the army under my command: not raised his men or contributed his assistance to bis service, but on the contrary withdrawn himself from the country and resided in the enemy's quarters, to the great prejudice of his Majesty's service . . . I do by these powers sequester all the lands belonging to the Earl of Suther-

[1] Firth 1899: 83. [2] Firth 1899: 118-9.

land within Strathnaver and Lochnaver for his Majesty's use: and in consideration of the affection and forwardness of the Right Honourable John, Lord Reay in his Majesty's service, do authorise and empower him to receive, lift and take all the rents and emoluments and profits from the said lands in any manner whatsoever arising, and to possess and enjoy the same, and to exercise all manner of power and authority within the jurisdiction of the same, in as full and ample a manner as the Earl of Sutherland did . . .'[1]

Middleton was defeated in July, and on the 5th August General Monck reported to Cromwell: 'Middleton is marched into Caithness with the remainder of his forces, which are about two hundred horse and six hundred foot. I have sent Colonel Morgan command to march after him.'[2] By the time Middleton opened negotiations with Monck in December,[3] Tongue house had been destroyed; either by Cromwellian troops, or perhaps by Mackay himself in denying it to the enemy. For Charles II wrote to Mackay in January 1655, saying he had been informed by Middleton and many others of his services, as by burning and destroying his lands to frustrate the rebels. He assured Mackay that he would 'retain the memory thereof till he fix such a mark of favour on him as may both repair what he had suffered for the King and be a record to posterity of his fidelity and loyalty in a time of so general a defection.'[4]

Mackay meanwhile awaited Middleton's further orders. He received a letter from the King's General on the 9th February from Dunvegan,[5] and a second on the 30th March in which he was informed that the Macleods were about to accept conditions, and he would be wise to take similar measures for his own safety.[6] It appears that Mackay then felt free to write to General Monck concerning terms. He received a letter from Monck on the 5th May 1655, acknowledging a letter and enclosing 'such conditions as I shall grant to your Lordship . . . I shall therefore expect your final resolution within the space of five weeks after the date hereof.'[7] Mackay agreed to terms in which 'the said Lord Reay, together with all those of his party included in this capitulation, whether officers, private soldiers or servants under his Lordship, who have not killed

[1] Reay MS. 211. [2] *A.P.S.* VI Part 2: 888-9. [3] Firth 1899: xxviii.
[4] Reay MS. 224. [5] Reay MS. 212. [6] Reay MS. 213. [7] Reay MS. 214.

men in cold blood, shall enjoy their estates, both real and personal, without any trouble or molestation.'[1] Despite the Earl of Sutherland's careful briefing of Lilburne in 1653, and Mackay's convenient revolt in 1654, Sutherland was again cheated of his prize in 1655. He wrote in April to Sir Robert Gordon's heir Sir Ludovick, from Dunrobin, asking him 'to get an pass for me and my convoy to Strathnaver from the Colonel, that I may go about my affairs with the Lord Reay and my tenantry there.' On the back of his letter has been scribbled, in what may be the draft of a reply, 'I hear the General hath refused to subscribe your losses.'[2] On the 22nd January 1656, Sutherland represented to the government in London that he had 'lost £5,336 by his affection to the state,'—presumably he was describing his affection for Cromwell's state—'and £2,000 by taking away of the ward-holding and superiority in Scotland, the Act for which is a benefit to others, but a loss to him. Begs reparation, or liberty to compound for wardships with those that hold of him, and exemption from taxes meanwhile.'[3] Sutherland was still able to obtain the office of the Scottish Privy Seal, but be sued for compensation in vain.

Mackay had received more favourable treatment from an English military dictator against whom he bad risen in rebellion than his father had received from the Stewart sovereign whom he had served with such fidelity. But the exiled Stewart sovereign had promised that on his return to his kingdom he would reward the loyalty both of the father and the son. Meanwhile the Earl of Sutherland's affection was little requited: 'for my Strathnaver rent Captain Campbell hath gotten of it already above 700 merks: so I can hardly expect one hundred pounds from that, considering how evil payers they are . . . There can little be expected out of the parish of Kildonan in regard much of the land there is blasted with the water in the summer spates.'[4] In Glasgow, Robert Baillie observed in 1656: 'our state is in a very silent condition . . . Our nobles, lying in prison and under forfeiture or debts, private or public, are for the most part either broken or breaking.'[5] In the same year Sir Robert Gordon of Gordonstoun died, aged seventy-six.[6]

[1] Mackay 1906: 435. B.M. Add. MS. 33596 f. 35. [2] *S.B.* II: 173–4.
[3] *C.S.P.D.* 1655–6: 127. [4] *S.B.* II: 175. [5] Baillie 1841: III, 317.
[6] *S.B.* I: 203.

9

Restitution

JOHN, Chief of Mackay attended the restored Parliament in Edinburgh in 1661, as the second Lord Reay.[1] He saw his feudal superior give his assent to the annulment of all the legislation of the previous twenty-five years: much of which had been initiated by the Earl of Sutherland against himself. Mackay submitted a report on his own and his father's losses.[2] The Earl of Lauderdale wrote from London to the newly created Earl of Middleton in Edinburgh, to inform him that these losses were to be compensated.[3] But the Earl of Sutherland did not share the fate of Argyll, and Mackay did not receive his compensation.

In February 1664 Charles II wrote to his Lord Commissioner for Scotland, the Earl of Middleton: 'whereas our right trusty and well beloved the Lord Reay and his father ever since the beginning of these troubles hath been most faithful and loyal to Our Father of glorious memory and to Us; and by the same hath suffered much by their several and longsome imprisonments, with the often hazarding of their lives and to the ruin of their estates and fortune: and being willing and desirous that the said Lord Reay may be rewarded and repaired of these great losses; therefore We do heartily recommend him to you and Our Parliament, that such an effectual course may be taken for his subsistence and reparation as may be answerable to our expectation: and further We desire that Robert Gray of Arkboll, being found by his letters to have moved and conducted the enemy to Strathnaver, whereby the Lord Reay was necessitated

[1] *A.P.S.* VII: 4. [2] Reay MS. 220.
[3] *A.P.S.* VII: 266, Appendix 77, Appendix 32.

to burn his houses and destroy his country and friends: therefore Our will is that the said Robert Gray be prosecuted, whereby the Lord Reay may have reparation of his losses and he be made liable to what further punishment you and Our Parliament shall find him . . .' The end of the document is torn.[1] The mediaeval methods of reward and punishment had returned, and a scapegoat for the policies of the Earl of Sutherland had been found in one of his servants.

Robert Gray had been appointed one of Sutherland's 'Commissars' at Tongue in July 1649, while Mackay was imprisoned in Edinburgh. In July 1650 Donald Macleod of Assynt had been appointed commander of the Strathnaver garrison at Tongue, until Parliament abolished it in December. But Mackay was not released until about July 1651, and it is possible that Robert Gray continued as the Earl's representative in the capital of the Mackay country during the entire two years of the Chief's absence in prison. During this period Robert Gray received his infeftment from the Earl of Sutherland, ostensibly in payment of a rocketing debt, of Mackay lands in March 1650.[2] At the same time Robert Farquhar assigned a debt of Mackay to Robert Gray;[3] Farquhar had received his infeftment from the Earl in the barony of Farr in February 1650.[4] It is hard to judge the genuineness of these ever-increasing debts of the first Lord Reay and his son to the men to whom they were least likely to apply for credit.

In the spring of 1653 Glencairn's rebellion against the rule of Cromwell compromised Mackay's position again, for Sutherland instantly reported his disaffection to Lilburne, who reported the matter to Cromwell. Mackay did not regain a position of safety until May 1655, when he capitulated to General Monck. The assignation of Mackay's debt from Farquhar to Gray, begun during the 1649-51 period of Mackay's imprisonment, was completed during the 1653 period of Glencairn's rebellion.[5] In 1653 Mackay was apprised also in the lands and barony of Durness, and also the lands of Edderachillis, while even Strathy and Strath Halladale, which belonged to other members of his family, were apprised.[6] In February 1653, Gray turned upon Hugh Mackay of Scourie, whose detachment

[1] Reay MS. 226. [2] Reay MS. 6/17 f. 5. [3] Reay MS. 13/13.
[4] Reay MS. 9/4. [5] Reay MSS. 13/11, 13/12, 13/13. [6] Reay MS. 6/17 f. 6.

the Minister of Kirkhill noticed as it marched to fight for Charles II at Worcester. He received his assignation for debt on the 2nd May, and by August 1655 he had received his charter to Edderachillis from the Earl of Sutherland.[1] Between Robert Gray's first commission from Parliament in 1645 to uplift the rents of malignants and 1655, he had made a fortune. But by 1664 he had been picked out, in place of his master the Earl of Sutherland, as the culprit.

The King had given as the reason for this that Robert Gray had 'conducted the enemy to Strathnaver.' An undated indictment of Robert Gray among the Reay Papers shows this to refer to Mackay's retreat after Middleton's last defeat, when Tongue house was destroyed. '1. He was an conductor and guider of the usurper's forces into Caithness, being upon the pursuit of his Majesty's forces then standing under the command of his grace the Lord Commissioner. 2. He did act for and with the rebels, and specially by going with an party of the usurper's forces from Scrabster Roads in a man of war to reduce the Lord and his friends (being then in arms for his Majesty) unto the usurper's subjection.' This interesting count in the indictment suggests that a frigate may have negotiated the perilous approaches of the Kyle of Tongue.

'3. He was an member of their councils, and privy adviser in all their actings during their abode in Caithness. 4. He carried constantly sword and pistols, horses at what rates he pleased, sent out parties at his pleasure from any of the usurper's garrisons to plunder and quarter for his pretended debts, to the prejudice and ruin of several of his Majesty's subjects.'[2] If such a charge as the last could be brought against Robert Gray, it was the more applicable to the Earl of Sutherland, who had begun the practice earlier, and who alone could make it fruitful by the issue of charters.

It does not appear that Charles II's plan of February 1664, to reward Mackay at the expense of Robert Gray, achieved any immediate result. On the 4th April, Charles II wrote to Frederick III of Denmark, recommending Mackay to him,[3] as Lauderdale informed Mackay on the 4th May. He also told Mackay that his wife, Hugh Mackay of Scourie's daughter, had been soliciting diligently on his behalf. When she returned from

[1] Reay MSS. 13/16, 13/17, 13/22. [2] Reay MS. 227. [3] Reay MS. 228.

her visit to London that May, she brought with her a letter from the Earl of Bath which assured Mackay: 'your noble lady who brings this hath been very industrious and solicitous in your affairs here.'[1]

The saviour of Mackay's estate was Sir George Munro of Culrain, Commander-in-Chief of the army in Scotland, whose daughter Ann was married to Mackay's heir in 1677. General Munro is shewn to have been superior of Eriboll in 1678, from whom his cousin Hugh Munro of Eriboll held his estate.[2] In that year the General obtained many of the bonds which imperilled the Mackay lands, and in June 1679 he raised an action of reduction against the Grays and Gordons who held charters of apprising for these lands.[3] By this time the original Robert Gray of Bellon was dead, and had been succeeded by his son Robert.[4] John, Earl of Sutherland died in October 1679,[5] but he had already conveyed 'the whole lands and estate of the earldom' to his son, who in 1675 had conveyed them by tack to Sir Robert Gordon of Gordonstoun and another principal for seven years.[6]

The Book of Mackay summarises the ensuing process as follows. 'The principal plea of the prosecution was, that the Grays and others, in 1649, unjustly extorted from John, then Master of Reay' [a curious slip] 'ruinous bonds on pretended spoliation, while he was in prison and lying at their mercy, and that afterwards on the strength of these bonds they got themselves infeft in his lands. The verdict of the Court was, that as Reay committed the acts of spoliation complained of in the capacity of a soldier with the King's commission, and that as a few years thereafter his own lands were spoiled and his house at Tongue burnt while serving his Majesty, the extorted bonds and subsequent charters of apprising were null and void. Further, that as Sir George as assignee of the bond of 1637 the first claim over the estate pertained to him, and that as the heritor raised no objection it was within his right to secure the estate by a charter of apprising. This Sir George did, and then handed the charter over to his grandson George, third Lord Reay.'[7]

[1] Reay MS. 230. [2] Reay MS. 18/8b. [3] Mackay 1906: 160.
[4] Reay MSS. 14/3, 14/4. [5] *S.B.* I: 275. [6] *S.B.* III: 203-13.
[7] Mackay 1906: 160.

Edderachillis exemplifies what occurred, as it concerned Mackay of Scourie. Robert Gray of Bellon obtained a decreet of apprising to these lands on the 27th December 1649.[1] A charter from the Earl of Sutherland followed on the 15th March 1650.[2] In 1655 a second charter to Edderachillis was issued to Robert Gray, now of Skibo,[3] and in 1670 Robert Gray issued a precept in favour of his son Alexander Gray of Creich to the Edderachillis lands,[4] who obtained seisin in 1672.[5] But in 1673 Robert Gray disponed his title in Edderachillis to Sir Ludovick Gordon of Gordonstoun,[6] and in 1677 Sir Ludovick passed it to his son Sir Robert Gordon, younger of Gordonstoun.[7] So when Edderachillis was returned to Colonel Hugh Mackay of Scourie on payment of 8,000 merks in 1680, under General Munro's settlement, the disposition was made by Robert, son of the late Robert Gray of Skibo, with the consent of Sir Robert Gordon.[8] As to the circumstances of the Grays at this time, a John Gray, prisoner in the Cannongate, was released on bail in August 1680.[9] The Privy Council minuted on the 15th May 1682: 'King's advocate to raise a process of treason against Robert Gray, prisoner in the Cannongate.'[10]

It might be expected that the three volumes of *The Sutherland Book*, published by Sir William Fraser in 1892, would throw further light from the muniments at Dunrobin upon a process which demolished the labours of half a century by members of the family of Sutherland in Strathnaver. The fact that it is unmentioned in this compilation is not, however, hard to account for. Under the settlement concluded in 1681, the Chief of Mackay retained Mudale, Gnub Mór, Gnub Beg, Rossal, Syre, Langwell, Skaill, Càrn Achaidh, Invernaver, Skelpick, Rhinnivie, Farr, Kirtomy, Borgie, Torrisdale, Skerray, Island Ron, Island Colm. These townships (with the omission of Achness) comprise the entire strath of Strathnaver, from Mudale beyond Lochnaver to Invernaver at the river-mouth, with the coastal townships to east and west of it in the barony of Farr.[11] As the eldest sons of the Earls of Sutherland continued to use the style 'Lord Strathnaver' without letters patent, it was tactful, even in 1892, to conceal the fact that this pretension

[1] Reay MS. 6/13. [2] Reay MS. 6/14. [3] Reay MS. 13/22. [4] Reay MS. 13/24. [5] Reay MS. 13/25. [6] Reay MS. 13/27. [7] Reay MS. 13/33. [8] Reay MSS. 14/3, 4. [9] *R.P.C.* (3rd S) VI: 534, 571. [10] *R.P.C.* (3rd S) VII: 431. [11] Mackay 1906: 160n.

was stripped of the merest semblance of propriety by ownership within the Naver valley.

Robert Gray had almost succeeded in 1656 in gaining possession of the barony of Durness: here Mackay went to live after the destruction of Tongue house, and here Lord Lovat visited him in 1669, as the minister of Kirkhill related. 'They live now at Durness, whither my Lord came, longed for, and got a most friendly welcome . . . The Lord Reay contrived all manner of sport and recreation to divert his dear Lovat, as he termed him; sometimes out at sea in barges a-fishing, sometimes hawking and hunting, sometimes arching at butts and bow-marks, jumping, wrestling, dancing . . . All the gentlemen of the name of Mackay convened, and so to the deer hunting, for my Lord Reay hath the finest and richest forest in the kingdom for deer and roes, their number and nimbleness . . . My Lord Lovat having stayed a whole month and more in Strathnaver and, we may say, wearied with excess of pleasure, thinks of returning home the beginning of September, loaded with courtesies and obligations. My Lord Reay gifted him a curious, curled, black shelty horse, several excellent firelocks, bows, and a sword that perhaps for goodness and antiquity might be called the none-such, and two deer greyhounds. My Lady gifted him a plaid all of silk, party-coloured, her own work.'[1]

Here, in the extreme north-west of the British mainland, the son of that much-travelled Chief, the first Lord Reay, appears to have re-created the antique pattern of life of the former Lords of the Isles and the lesser Celtic patriarchs. It may not be fanciful to suppose that he had learnt the lesson that Christian IV intended to teach the young nobles of Denmark, when he established the academy at Sorø that young Mackay attended with his brother Angus in 1628. A Catholic had reported in 1638: 'in the Hebrides and Highlands of Scotland there is no city, no town, no school, no civilisation; no one can read except a few who have been educated at a great distance from home.'[2] While the literature and learning of the Mac Mhuirichs alone disprove this statement, it might have been harder to disprove before 1638, and except in an English sense, on the northern mainland. But by 1634 Durness already had its first surviving Gaelic poet in the Rev. Alexander Munro, and in Ruairidh

[1] Fraser 1905: 483. [2] Bellesheim 1887: IV, 71n.

Mackay its piper in the tradition of Donald Mór MacCrimmon.[1] Its Chief was described in 1669 in Durness as the patron of the ancient sports while his wife wove silks in the Tigh Mór. The seeds had been sown in this tiny village near Cape Wrath which were to demonstrate that civilisation, if planted, can flourish anywhere. Mackay's brother Angus left the Danish service, in which he had risen to the rank of Lieutenant Colonel, before 1659 and was settled in Melness.[2] It is to be noticed that his lands included Fresgill on the west side of the Moine, as well as those of Melness on the east side of this great headland.[3] If Angus Mackay chose to reside at Fresgill for fishing from barges or while hunting the deer, he was able to look due west to the home of his brother across the water in surroundings amongst the most beautiful in Europe, to be made famous by one of Scotland's greatest poets. Both of these brothers possessed wives who belonged to the local Gaelic society: the Chief being married to Hugh Mackay of Scourie's daughter, while his brother was married to the daughter of Alexander Gunn of Killearnan.[4]

Mackay also arranged an alliance with the Gordons in 1665, when his daughter Jane was married to Robert, third son of the Earl of Sutherland. As they lived at Langdale in Strathnaver, it appears that this match was a compromise, in which a dynasty formed of a union of the two families was to be founded in the Naver valley.[5] If such it was, it was as ill-fated as that of the Montacute and Capulet families, as the Minister of Kirkhill recorded. In 1671 'a Dutch merchantman of 250 tons, loaded with wines, brandy, spices, iron, salt etc., a very rich cargo, was cast in upon the coast of Strathnaver, where Admiralty is not much regarded. All the country flocked about the shore. The people, not knowing then the strength of brandy or such foreign liquor, drank to excess of it, and I heard it said that this very ship's loading debauched Caithness and Strathnaver to that degree that very many lost their lives by their immoderation. Mr Robert Gordon, the Earl of Sutherland's son, being but newly married to Miss K. [sic] Mackay, Lord Reay's daughter, a high-blooded saguin, fell accidentally with some comrades and took a great latitude, drinking liberally even to excess. At length

[1] Maclean 1953: 283-306. [2] Mackay 1906: 321.
[3] Reay MSS. 27/2b, 27/7. [4] Reay MS. 27/3. [5] Mackay 1906: 157.

he got free of them, escaping with his life to take some rest. Shortly after, these cup-filled villains came into the gentleman's chamber, being in bed with his bride, obliges him to rise and drink so many healths in his shirt standing. The poor, modest, bashful lady had not the confidence (lest critically construed) to challenge them, or call her husband to his bed. With reluctancy they parted. Robin went away, laid him down, but never rose.'[1]

Mackay's overture to his Mackenzie kinsfolk took the form of a bond of friendship which he signed with the Earl of Seaforth in 1672. It referred specifically to the practices that had caused so many of the recent troubles in the north. 'None of us shall buy pleas or debts, nor have we bought any against others.' Sir Donald Macdonald of Sleat was present to witness this document in Assynt, while from Strathnaver there came as signatories Hugh Munro of Eriboll, Hector Munro of Obsdell, Angus Mackay of Melness, Hugh of Bighouse, the Tutor of Scourie, and 'Robert Mackay in Achness.'[2] It is interesting that this nephew of the last William Mackay of Achness should sign himself thus. In 1666 Robert Mackay was resident as a tacksman at Letterloyal, and he was one of the six in whose names the Reay estate was secured in 1673.[3]

An example of the debts that the signatories perhaps had in mind is one of 5,225 merks which Mackay incurred to a Mackenzie in 1624. This had been assigned to Alexander Corbett by 1636.[4] In 1649 it was assigned by Robert Gray of Arkboll (*alias* of Bellon and Skibo) to Robert Gray of Swordale, in whose hands it remained at the time when the bond was signed with Seaforth, and when the final settlement was registered in 1681.[5]

Mackay's heir rebuilt Tongue house, and it was ready for the occupation of his bride Ann Munro in 1678, the year after their marriage. But neither the Master of Reay nor his father lived to see the successful outcome of General Munro's action for the recovery of the Mackay titles in Strathnaver. The Master was killed in 1680 while he was hunting in the Reay forest, and Mackay his father died before the year was out, leaving a two-year-old baby as the third Lord Reay.[6] In the time

[1] Fraser 1905: 493-4. [2] Mackay 1906: 440. [3] Mackay 1906: 248.
[4] Reay MS. 12/1b. [5] Reay MS. 12/8b. [6] Mackay 1906: 161.

and circumstances, this child and his clansmen were extremely fortunate in the Chief's other grandfather, General Sir George Munro of Culrain.

His minority also left the initiative to the senior branch of Scourie to take clan Mackay's phenomenal revenge upon the royal house of Stewart. Little could Mary ,Queen of Scots have suspected, when she made a Mackay Chief vassal to Gordon of Huntly, that his descendant would drive her dynasty from the throne for ever. Little could Charles I have dreamt that men of the clan he had used and ruined would ruin his son. Nor is this to be wondered at, for what occurred is one of the most strange accidents of Britain's history.

For a century and a half after the first Lord Reay raised his regiment in 1626, young men from Strathnaver continued to take service in the armies of Scandinavia and of the Netherlands. Hugh Mackay of Scourie, brother-in-law of the second Lord Reay, found his way into the Dutch service in a curious manner. He was serving as a Captain in the Royal Scots Regiment which Charles II sent to France in 1672, to fight under Louis XIV against the Netherlands.[1] At Bommel he was billeted with a family whose daughter he wished to marry: but her mother forbade the marriage until Hugh Mackay transferred from the French service to that of her own nation.[2] This was rendered easier by the fact that Scottish regiments had fought for decades in the service of the United Provinces, while retaining their British nationality.

But like the Mackay regiment in the Thirty Years War, they had gradually lost their national character. It was the advent of Mackay of Scourie that reversed this trend, and that reopened the flood-gates of recruitment from the Scottish Highlands. Prince William of Orange 'one day asked the brave General Mackay, lately come to his service from France, if he was not surprised and ashamed at the behaviour of his countrymen, the Scots Brigade; and he could not conceive, he said, the cause of their being so much changed and degenerated from what they had formerly been; and made an appearance different from what the Scots Brigade had done in the army of Gustavus Adolphus when commanded by his friend Lord Reay. Mackay . . . told the Prince that he was indeed sorry to observe daily

[1] Mackay 1833: xiii. [2] Ferguson 1899: 470.

the bad behaviour of these troops called the Scots Brigade, but he begged leave to tell his Highness that although they had that name they did not deserve it, for that near one half of the officers and more of the men were not Scots, but were Dutch, French, Germans and of all nations.'[1]

The Brigade was accordingly reorganised, and Colonel Mackay was Commanding Officer of one of its regiments when it was recalled to Britain in 1685 by James VII and II to meet Monmouth's rebellion. King James wrote to his son-in-law William of Orange: 'there cannot be, I am sure, better men than they are,' and he promoted Hugh Mackay Major-General before the Brigade returned to Holland.[2]

Hugh Mackay had come to Britain in 1685 with a Dutch Colonelcy, had returned to Holland with a British rank of Major-General, and took his oath before the President of the States General in 1686 on that commission.[3] His nephew Aeneas Mackay, eldest surviving son of the second Lord Reay, arrived in the Netherlands to take a Captain's commission in November 1684[4] Early in 1688, these officers were suddenly compelled to choose between two princes, James VII and his son-in-law William of Orange, both of whom General Mackay had served, and with both of whom he was personally acquainted. On Hugh Mackay's choice between them depended the future allegiance of the Scots Brigade in Holland, and it has been said that 'the disposal of this disciplined body of troops became a matter of grave moment, if not indeed the determining factor of the whole situation.'[5] Evidently General Mackay did not make his final decision until the last moment, but it is not perfectly clear upon what grounds Britain's King-maker reached his fateful decision.

In January 1688 James VII told William of Orange of his decision to recall the Scots Brigade from Holland: in March he protested to William over the unco-operative response of the States General. It was said that General Mackay at first informed his officers of his intention of obeying the orders of James VII, but that he was influenced by a visit to the Hague to advise them against doing so. Out of 240 officers in the six regiments, only 60 resigned their commissions and returned to Britain. Among these was Captain Aeneas Mackay, who was

[1] Ferguson 1899: 471. [2] Ferguson 1899: 476-7. [3] Ferguson 1899: xxi, n. [4] Ferguson 1899: 516. [5] Ferguson 1899: 477.

arrested on suspicion soon after his arrival, and imprisoned in Edinburgh. General Mackay sailed with William of Orange in October 1688, as commander of the English and Scottish troops who secured his succession as William III.[1]

Hugh Mackay opened his memoirs of the ensuing campaign discreetly: 'All the nobility and gentry of the Scots nation then at London being met together at Whitehall, to consult of the next best measures to be taken (after King James' retreat into France) for the government of that kingdom, agreed to offer the administration thereof to the then Prince of Orange, our present sovereign.'[2]

Aeneas Mackay was released from prison in December 1688 by order of the Scottish Privy Council, and became a Major in the Scots Greys serving under his uncle. General Mackay was also accompanied by his brother Lieutenant-Colonel James Mackay, and by Robert, brother of Aeneas Mackay, who served as a Captain of a Grenadier company.[3] The infant Chief of Mackay thus possessed four uncles as his anti-Jacobite deputies. Among the few Highlanders to join the new Commander-in-Chief in Scotland (the Scottish Estates confirmed General Mackay's appointment in March 1689) were upwards of 200 men led by Captain Hugh Mackay of Borley and Angus Mackay of Ribigill.[4]

General Mackay was extremely anxious to enlist Gaels, for, as he wrote in June 1689: 'the Highlanders are absolutely the best untrained men in Scotland, and can be equalled to our new levies though they were better armed than they are, particularly those Highlanders we have in head.'[5] But when General Mackay met Dundee at Killiecrankie in July, he commanded a predominantly Lowland force against a Highland one.[6]

He was still writing on behalf of widows in September 1689. 'My Lord. This gentlewoman being the widow of one of the Captains of my regiment killed in the late occasion with the rebels, I could not refuse her a recommendation to your Lordship, in case there be any allowance for such persons. Her husband's name was Lamy—his Majesty knows the people—he was a brave man, and had taken himself up lately so well that

[1] Ferguson 1899: 477-9. [2] Mackay 1833: 3.
[3] Ferguson 1899: 516n, 508n, 515n.
[4] Mackay 1833: 20, 31. Mackay 1906: 167, 293.
[5] Mackay 1833: 230. [6] Ferguson 1899: 479.

I was resolved to recommend him for his advancement when occasion should offer. The most part of the officers of my battalion were killed upon the spot: my brother, Lamy and Captain Angus Mackay, who were as brave as any men could be, were shot, and afterwards being abandoned of their men, despatched with broad swords. My nephew Captain Robert Mackay, who was a young man and his first service before an enemy, fought stoutly for his life, and disengaged himself having received four considerable wounds of broad swords in his head and body . . . I pray your Lordship to do your best to get some consideration for this poor widow.'[1]

Mackay of Scourie had seen little of his native country since his youth, and longed to leave it. 'I am extremely weary of this sort of war, and is certainly fit for a man of fewer years and more accustomed with the manner of the country than for me . . . I hope his Majesty will have the goodness to permit me to take my winter quarters in Holland if it please God I live so long.'[1] He advised that use should be made of his predecessor as Commander-in-Chief in Scotland. 'I am of opinion that it would be for his Majesty's service to make Sir George Munro of his Privy Council, and to give him some pension to stay always at Edinburgh; for though he be old and infirm, he is yet of a sound judgment, and his advice both in military and civil affairs would be of great assistance to the Council.'[1] Hugh Mackay was utterly unselfseeking, and thereby earned the right to pillory the rulers of Scotland in his memoirs. He recorded that he found the 'Scotsmen of those times in general as void of zeal for their religion and natural affection, seeing all men hunt after their particular advantages, and none minding sincerely and self-denyedly the common good, which gave him a real distaste of the country and service.'[1]

He spent 1691 fighting the Jacobites in Ireland, then returned to Holland, and was killed in action at Steinkirk in August 1692. It had been reported that he was to be created Earl of Scourie.[1] Sir George Munro of Culrain died shortly afterwards, leaving Aeneas Mackay as the nearest relative of his nephew, the infant Chief of Mackay. Aeneas succeeded as Colonel of Hugh's regiment, and was promoted Brigadier-General in 1695. His

[1] Mackay 1833: 281-2. [2] Mackay 1833: 272. [3] Mackay 1833: 280.
[4] Mackay 1833: 77. [5] Mackay 1906: 172.

brother Colonel Robert Mackay died of wounds received at Killiecrankie, in 1696, while Brigadier Aeneas died of wounds in 1697. Thus the four anti-Jacobite uncles of the young Chief of Mackay perished by the sword, after having played a part that was perhaps decisive in driving the Stewarts from the throne for ever. But Brigadier Aeneas had married Margaretha Puchler in the Netherlands in 1692, whose descendants were ennobled there before they succeeded to the chiefship nearly two centuries later.

It can be seen that General Hugh Mackay's motives were not clear-cut, and that these did not necessarily include an antipathy towards the Stewart King. He was a soldier in the anomalous position of holding military commissions from the heads of two different states with access to far completer briefing from one of them than from the other, when he was forced at short notice to choose between them. In the former of these countries he was married and had his domicile, preferring it (as his letters reveal) to his country of origin. In addition, the Netherlands had long been the champions of Calvinism in Europe, and Bishop Burnet described General Mackay as the most pious soldier he had ever known. William of Orange was a Calvinist, James VII a Catholic. Perhaps it is not necessary to look further for the underlying considerations that may have influenced Hugh Mackay's fateful choice of sovereign. Yet amongst a people with such strong hereditary attachments as the Gaelic people have shewn throughout their history, it is legitimate to look further when such an attachment is snapped at last. It is possible to doubt whether Hugh Mackay and his other relations could have betrayed James VII, had they not been cured of any remaining sense of obligation to the Stewart dynasty through the treatment of the King's predecessors.

If such is the case, it is a tragic paradox that James VII, to whom the Gaels owed more than to any previous Stewart King, should have been the one to pay the final account for the behaviour of his forbears.

With the passing of the Stewarts, the long resistance of the Mackays to the feudal order of which they were the apex appeared to have been won at last. No new dynasty was founded at Scourie, equal in status to the house of Sutherland, to protect their interests. But they were safe throughout the eighteenth century from persecution, either as Jacobites or as religious dissenters. Chiefs of Mackay continued to dwell in the Tigh Mór, or Big House, at Tongue and Durness, that ultimate bastion of Celtic society and culture throughout Gaeldom.

It was not until the nineteenth century that the house of Sutherland succeeded in implementing the policy laid down by Sir Robert Gordon two centuries earlier, to 'purge the country piece and piece of the Irish barbarity.'

References

A.L.C.P.A., *Acts of the Lords of Council in Public Affairs, 1501-54*. Ed. R. K. Hannay, 1932.

A.L.H.T., *Accounts of the Lord High Treasurer of Scotland, 1473-1566*. Ed. Thomas Dickson and J. Balfour Paul, 1877-1916.

ANDERSON, WILLIAM J., 'Narratives of the Scottish Reformation', II. *The Innes Review*, VII: no. 2, 1956.

ANTON, A. E., 'Handfasting in Scotland.' *The Scottish Historical Review*, XXXVII: 89-102, 1958.

A.P.S., *Acts of the Parliament of Scotland, 1124-1707*. Ed. Thomas Thomson and Cosmo Innes, 1814-75.

BAILLIE, ROBERT, *Letters and Journals*. Ed. David Laing. Edinburgh, 1841-2.

BALFOUR, SIR JAMES, *Historical Works*. London, 1825.

BARROW, G. W. S., 'The beginnings of Feudalism in Scotland.' *Bulletin of the Institute of Historical Research* XXIX: 1-27 1956.

—*The Acts of Malcolm IV*. Edinburgh 1960.

—'From Queen Margaret to David I.' *The Innes Review* XI: 22-38 1960 ii.

BELLESHEIM, ALPHONS, *History of the Catholic Church in Scotland*. Ed. D. O. Hunter Blair. Edinburgh, 1887-90.

BENTINCK, CHARLES D., *Dornoch Cathedral and Parish*. Inverness, 1926.

BLACAM, AODH DE, *Gaelic Literature Surveyed*. Dublin, 1929.

B.M., British Museum.

BOECE, HECTOR, *The Chronicles of Scotland*. Trans John Bellenden. Ed. R. W. Chambers and Edith C. Batho. Edinburgh, 1938-41.

BREVE, *Kong Christian dem Fjerdes Egenhaendige Breve*. Copenhagen.

BUCHANAN, GEORGE, *The Tyrannous Reign of Mary Stewart*. Trans. and Ed. W. A. Gatherer. Edinburgh, 1958.

CAMERON, ALEXANDER, *Reliquiae Celticae*. Ed. Alexander MacBain and John Kennedy. Inverness, 1891-4.

CAMPBELL, JOHN F., *Leabhar na Feinne*, 1872.

CAMPBELL, JOHN LORNE and THOMSON DERICK S. *Edward Lhuyd in the Scottish Highlands 1699-1700*. Oxford, 1963.

CONFLICTS, *The History of the Feuds and Conflicts among the Clans . . . from the year 1031 unto 1619*. Glasgow, 1780.

CRAWFORD MS. Box F. 11. Alexander Ross to Sir David Lindsay: Inventory of Scottish Muniments at Haigh, Crawford and Balcarres II.

C.S.P.D. *Calendar of State Papers (Domestic).*

DEAN OF LISMORE, *Scottish Verse from the Book of the Dean of Lismore.* Ed. and Trans. W. J. Watson. Edinburgh, 1937.

DICKINSON, W. CROFT, *Scotland from the Earliest Times to 1603.* Edinburgh, 1961.

DONALDSON, GORDON, *Shetland Life Under Earl Patrick.* Edinburgh 1958.

—*The Scottish Reformation.* Cambridge, 1960.

—'Foundations of Anglo-Scottish Union.' *Essays Presented to Sir John Neale*: 282-314. 1961.

ELDAR, JOHN, *Collectanea de Rebus Albanicis.* Iona Club. Edinburgh, 1847.

FASTI, *Fasti Ecclesiae Scoticae.* Edinburgh, 1916-61.

FERGUSON, JAMES, *Papers Illustrating the History of the Scots Brigade in the Service of the United Netherlands,* I, 1572-1697. Edinburgh, 1899.

FIRTH, C. H., *Scotland and the Commonwealth, 1651-1653.* Edinburgh, 1895.

—*Scotland and the Protectorate, 1654-1659.* Edinburgh, 1899.

FISCHER, THOMAS, *The Scots in Sweden.* Edinburgh, 1907.

FLOWER, ROBIN, 'An Irish-Gaelic Poem on the Montrose Wars.' *Scottish Gaelic Studies,* I: 113-8. 1926.

FRASER, JAMES, *Chronicles of the Frasers.* Ed. W. Mackay. Edinburgh, 1905.

GARDINER, S. R. *History of the Commonwealth and Protectorate,* 1649-1660. London, 1894-1903.

GATHERER, W. A., 'Queen Mary's Journey from Aberdeen to Inverness 1562.' *The Scottish Historical Review,* XXXIII: 19-21. 1954.

GEC, *The Complete Peerage.* Ed. G.E.C. H. A. Doubleday, Geoffrey H. White and Lord Howard de Walden. London.

GORDON, JAMES, *History of Scots Affairs from 1637 to 1641.* Ed. Joseph Robertson and George Grub. Aberdeen, 1841.

GORDON, SIR ROBERT, *A Genealogical History of the Earldom of Sutherland: with a Continuation to the Year 1651.* Edinburgh, 1813.

GORDONSTOUN MSS., Correspondence from the Gordonstoun MSS. deposited in the National Library of Scotland, and quoted by kind permission of Sir William Gordon Cumming, Bart.

GRANT, I. F., *The Macleods: the History of a Clan 1200-1956.* London, 1959.

GRANT, JAMES, *Memoirs and Adventures of Sir John Hepburn.* Edinburgh, 1851.

GREGORY, DONALD, 'Notices Regarding Scotish Archery.' *Archaeologia Scotica,* III: 248-54. 1831.

GRIMBLE, IAN, *The Harington Family.* London, 1957.

—'The Royal Payment of Mackay's Regiment.' *Scottish Gaelic Studies,* IX: 23-38. 1961.

—'Gael and Saxon in Scotland.' *Yale Review,* LII: 118-22, 1962.

HENDERSON, JOHN, *Caithness Family History.* Edinburgh, 1884.

HILL, CHRISTOPHER, *The Century of Revolution.* Edinburgh, 1961.

H.M.C., *Historical Manuscripts Commission.* 2nd Report. Forbes and Dunrobin MSS.

REFERENCES

H.M.C., 6th Report. Gordon Cumming MSS.

—11th Report, Appendix, part 6. Hamilton MSS.

JACKSON, KENNETH, 'The Duan Albanach.' *Scottish Historical Review*, XXXVI: 125-37. 1957.

JAMES, RICHARD, 'Description of Orkney, Shetland and the Highlands of Scotland.' Ed. Evan Mac Gillivray. *Orkney Miscellany*, I: 48-56. 1953.

JOHNSTON, ALFRED and AMY, *Caithness and Sutherland Records*. London, 1928.

KANCELLIETS BREVBØGER, *Kancelliets Brevbøger*. Copenhagen, 1627-9.

McCLINTOCK, H. F., *Old Highland Dress and Tartans*. Dundalk, 1949.

MACINNES, JOHN, *The Evangelical Movement in the Highlands of Scotland 1688-1800*. Aberdeen, 1951.

MACKAY, ANGUS, *The Book of Mackay*. Edinburgh, 1906.

MACKAY, GEORGE, 'Two Unpublished Letters from James Graham . . . to Sir Donald Mackay . . .' *Juridical Review*, LIII: 298-317, 1941.

MACKAY, HUGH, *Memoirs of the War Carried on in Scotland and Ireland 1689-1691*. Ed. James M. Hog, Patrick F. Tytler, and Adam Urquhart. Edinburgh, 1833.

MACKAY, JOHN, 'Mackay's Regiment.' *Trans. Gaelic Society of Inverness*, VIII: 128-89. 1879.

—*An Old Scots Brigade*. Edinburgh, 1885.

MACKAY, ROBERT, *The House and Clan of Mackay*. Edinburgh, 1829.

MACKENZIE, ALEXANDER, 'Old Ecclesiastical Records of Badenach.' *Trans. Gaelic Society of Inverness*, XII: 415-29. 1886.

MACKENZIE, ANNIE M., *The Poems of Ian Lom*. Aberdeen University Thesis. 1955.

MACKENZIE, W. C., *History of the Outer Hebrides*. Paisley, 1903.

MACKEPRANG, M., 'Christian IV's Ridderakademi og Skolen.' *Sorø*. Skraevet af Gamle Soranere Udgivet af Soransk Samfund. I: 374-502. 1923.

MACKIE, R. L., *King James IV of Scotland*. Edinburgh, 1958.

MACKINNON, DONALD, *A Descriptive Catalogue of Gaelic Manuscripts*. Edinburgh. 1912.

MACLEAN, JOHN, 'Am Piobaire Dall.' *Trans. Gaelic Society of Inverness*. XLI: 283-306. 1953.

MACNICOL, D. C., *Robert Bruce, Minister in the Kirk of Edinburgh*. 1961.

MACRAE, DUNCAN, *A Handful of Lays written by Duncan Macrae*, 1688. Ed. Malcolm MacFarlane. Dundee, 1923.

MARWICK, HUGH, *Ancient Monuments in Orkney*. Edinburgh, 1952.

MARY OF LORRAINE, *The Scottish Correspondence of Mary of Lorraine*. Ed. Annie I. Cameron. Edinburgh, 1927.

MATHESON, ANGUS, 'The Trial of Sir James Macdonald of Islay.' *Trans. Gaelic Society of Glasgow*, V: 207-22. 1958.

MICHELL, THOMAS, *History of the Scottish Expedition to Norway in 1612*. London, 1886.

MONTREUIL, JEAN DE, *The Diplomatic Correspondence of . . . 1645-48*. Ed. J. G. Fotheringham. Edinburgh, 1898.

REFERENCES

MUNRO, ROBERT, *Monro His Expedition with the Worthy Scots Regiment (Called Mac-Keyes Regiment)*. London, 1637.

NAPIER, MARK, *Memoirs of the Marquis of Montrose*. Edinburgh, 1856.

NICOLSON, ALEXANDER, *History of Skye*. Glasgow, 1930.

NUGAE, ANTIQUAE, Harington Family MSS. Ed. Thomas Park. London, 1804.

Ó CLERIGH, LUGHAIDH, *Beatha Aodha Ruaidh Uí Dhomhnaill*. Dublin, 1948.

PITSCOTTIE, ROBERT LINDSAY OF, *Chronicles of Scotland*. Edinburgh, 1814.

POYNTZ, SYDNAM, *The Relation of Sydnam Poyntz 1624–1638*. Ed. A. T. S. Goodrick. London, 1908.

PRESBYTERY RECORDS OF INVERNESS, *Records of the Presbyteries of Inverness and Dingwall 1643-1688*. Ed. William Mackay. Edinburgh, 1896.

RAMSAY, JOHN, *Scotland and Scotsmen in the Eighteenth Century*. Ed. A. Allardyce. II vols. Edinburgh, 1888.

REAY MSS., Papers of the Chiefs of Mackay, Register House, Edinburgh, calendered by Dr C. T. McInnes.

R.G.S., *Register of the Great Seal of Scotland*, 1306-1688.

ROBERTS, MICHAEL, *Gustavus Adolphus*. Volume II, 1958.

R.P.C., *Register of the Privy Council of Scotland*, 1545-1625. New Series 1626-1660. Third Series 1661-1689.

R.P.S., *Register of the Privy Seal of Scotland*, 1488-1574.

RUSHWORTH, JOHN, *Historical Collections of Private Passages of State . . . 1618-1644*. London, 1659-92.

RYSTAD, GORÄN, *Kriegsnachrichten und Propaganda*. Lund, 1960.

SAGE, DONALD, *Memorabilia Domestica*, Wick, 1899.

S.B., *The Sutherland Book*. Ed. Sir William Fraser. Edinburgh, 1892.

SCHULTZ, *Schultz Danmarkshistorie*, I. Copenhagen, 1941.

SCOTICHRONICON, *Joannis de Fordun Scotichronicon*. Edinburgh, 1759.

SINCLAIR, THOMAS, *Caithness Events*. Wick, 1899.

SKENE, WILLIAM F., *The Highlanders of Scotland*. Stirling, 1902.

SPALDING, JOHN, *Memorialls of the Trubles in Scotland and in England 1624–1645*. Ed. John Stuart. Aberdeen, 1850-1.

S.R., Swedish Military Rolls. Krigsarkivet, Stockholm.

STATE TRIALS, *A Complete Collection of State-trials* . . . London, 1730-5.

SVERIGES KRIG, *Sveriges Krig*. III-VI. Stockholm, 1936-9

SWEDISH DISCIPLINE, *The Swedish Discipline*. London, 1632.

SWEDISH INTELLIGENCER, *The Swedish Intelligencer*. London, 1634.

TERRY, C. S., *Life and Campaigns of Alexander Leslie, first Earl of Leven*. London, 1899.

—*The Cromwellian Union 1651-2*. Edinburgh, 1902.

VITA S. MARGARETAE, *Vita S. Margaretae*. Ed. J. Hodgson Hinde. 1867.

WEDGWOOD, C. V., *The King's Peace*. London, 1955.

—*The Thirty Years War*. (Penguin Edition) London, 1957.

—*The King's War*. London, 1958.

—*Truth and Opinion*. London, 1960.

Index